SODIUM BALLS

A Reverend's Journey

by

Rev. Robert P. Mitchell, M.Div.

Dotty
Many blessings and happy
reading

Bob Mitchell

RoseDog Books
PITTSBURGH, PENNSYLVANIA 15238

RoseDog Books
585 Alpha Drive
Pittsburgh, PA 15238
Visit our website at *www.rosedogbookstore.com*

ISBN: 978-1-4809-7281-0
eISBN: 978-1-4809-7304-6

Prologue

Faith?

Who in blazes does he think he is? How dare he judge my faith?

The burn reached my cheeks, now the searing red of embers. Struggling to keep a grip on my temper, I didn't answer Harry, but later my mind kept revisiting this conversation, and agonized about whether or not he was right.

One time I said to him, "You know, Harry, Joan and I sing in church every Sunday. Our choir director, a guy by the name of Rob Davis, a devout Christian, prays at every rehearsal, and reminds us every Sunday morning that our singing must glorify Christ. Joan and I pray regularly at home, and we teach Sunday school. I'm on the Board of Trustees, the Education Committee, and several others, and we go to our Bible study covenant group faithfully every week. Isn't that enough?" I wanted to say, "For you," but thought better of it.

Harry looked at me thoughtfully, then replied rather pedantically, "Bob, that's all well and good, but do you know the Lord Jesus Christ? Do you have a personal relationship with him?"

I felt a familiar singe of anger rising in my throat. "Yes, of course I do. My brother, Johnnie, you know him—the missionary in France you support."

Harry nodded affirmatively.

"Well, he led me to the Lord twenty-two years ago."

"That may be," Harry replied nonplussed, "but your life doesn't show the fruits of the Spirit. I'm concerned about your spiritual health—you seem to devote yourself more to music than to the Lord. I think you need to find the Lord again."

. . . . .

It was a bad day in November of 1978, blustery, wet, cold, and I was feeling miserable. A gust of wind had blown my hat away as I tried to make my way across Scholastic's vast parking lot. The cursed wind had turned my umbrella inside out with nowhere to trash it. I hated getting wet when dressed in a suit and tie, especially in a storm like this. I felt as if I were wandering around in one of those blue-colored sci-fi movies with the world disintegrating all around me. Rain trickled down my neck and annoyed the snorts out of me. Again I wondered if Harry was right. I didn't feel particularly Christian just then.

Harry was a small, compact guy with dark, chiseled features. Quite handsome, actually, but always serious. He didn't smile much, and I can't remember a broad grin. I used to kid him about looking more Italian than Irish, but he took it in stride. Clearly his sense of humor hid behind a bush somewhere.

We first met at the T J Lipton Company in Englewood Cliffs, New Jersey, in the late sixties. I was in Personnel; he worked in Benefits. From the get-go, I was Number One on his must-convert list. The fact that he didn't accept me as a true Christian both annoyed and perplexed me, because Johnnie had already told me when I was still in high school that I had to know Christ. He showed me in the Bible how I needed the Lord. Then he made me get down on my knees and pray with him—the Sinner's Prayer. At first I was very uncomfortable, but I have to say, my "born-again" experience was quite real.

Admittedly, I drifted away from the church when I went to college, especially when I went to New York City to study voice and opera at the Mannes College of Music in 1960. I quickly became totally absorbed in music, singing, and the cultural milieu that swept me off my feet. I could feel the stage dust teasing me, and oh, those sweet onstage kisses transported me to another world. Puccini's soaring music lifted me out of myself, and all those colorful sets and costumes! Cheez! A whole new life for me! Yes, an imaginary one, but I was hooked on opera.

For us singing students, church became a means to pay the bills. In those days, opera majors could get paid to sing in church choirs. In fact, Central

Presbyterian, where I sang for my four years while at Mannes, had an all-professional choir.

After college, I blush to admit that church still was not a big part of my life. By 1967, I had been married five years to Joan, was working full time, and singing professionally in other churches and synagogues. By this time I was also performing leading tenor roles with the small opera companies that were all over the place in the New York metro area. I had more important things on my mind than religion, or so I thought. I believed my operatic singing career was about to take off, so I spent most of my time and energy on that—when I wasn't working, of course. I always had a full-time job.

Harry didn't approve of opera. He thought it was sinful. I shook my head. That was Harry. Even though his persistence annoyed me, he was, and remained my best friend largely because of his connection with my brother Johnnie. And he lived close to us. Plus, he handled our life insurance—I never knew a more trustworthy person than Harry, so I sucked up my annoyance. But he never gave up trying to convert me.

I must admit, singing opera exposed me to a number of sins. One was self-indulgence. To sing the classical music I was being trained to perform, most of which was in foreign languages, I spent most of my waking hours thinking about singing techniques and learning my music. When did I have time for Christ?

The second temptation became onstage love-making with beautiful singing partners. When an actor says, "T'amo," or "Je t'aime,"[1] he has to feel it sincerely, so that it's believable to the audience. My mantra was, "Acting is Believing," which came from a book I had read with that title.

More than that, we players touch each other, we kiss, we embrace. The warmth of friendship can easily turn into passion. It often did for me. The trouble came when we carried our stage love offstage. Was seeing your colleague for lunch committing adultery? What about my hidden thoughts for my stage partner? What about those exchanged glances, or the soft touch of hands, or a stolen kiss or two? Does that constitute adultery? (See Matthew 5:28)

Anyway, how could Harry know anything of this? I never shared these thoughts with him. Could there have been something in my behavior that betrayed me?

---

[1] "I love you," in Italian and French, respectively.

• • • • •

One sultry summer night Joan and I sat at our kitchen table opposite Harry, while he explained a new insurance policy he thought we needed. Even with sweat trickling down his face, he was all business—no kidding around with Harry. He picked up his iced tea with the cubes clunking around in his glass, and took a sip.

I couldn't help wondering if he actually tasted the orange juice that Joan had added to the lemonade in the tea, a recipe of her mother's. *I doubt it*, I thought to myself.

I decided to have a little fun. With my winningest smile, I asked him, "Harry, have you ever stopped to think that since we Christians are going to Heaven anyway, why do we need insurance?"

He slowly set the drink down and looked up from his papers, his eyes serious. "You're joking, right, Bob?"

I picked up my glass. It felt good—to my hand, at least.

"Well, yes and no," I began, sweat beading on my forehead. I flicked some of it away with my fingers. "Actually, I'm sort of serious. I can see the irony in prayer, and sometimes I wonder about certain scriptural promises."

"What do you mean?" he said, his face clouded over as he dabbed his forehead with his napkin. Harry couldn't tolerate anyone questioning the Bible. His body tightened like a leopard ready to pounce. His eyes bored a hole in me as if saying, *How dare you challenge Scripture?*

I took a sip of my tea, enjoying the new flavor, and its cooling effect. Setting my glass down, I continued, "If we truly believe we are in God's hands, why do we need insurance? Amish folks, for example, refuse to buy insurance. Why shouldn't we too reject it—on the same grounds they do—that God takes care of us?"

Looking a bit harried, Harry said, "Bob, I often get that from *un*believers." *Was this a snipe at me?*

"Yes," he went on, "we're in God's hands, but we need protection from accidents and other unexpected calamities. Bad stuff happens, you know, and we need to have money to pay for damages, sickness, and the like."

"But don't we pray all the time for God to protect us from bad stuff? Why doesn't He do it?"

I reached up to unbutton my shirt, only to discover it was already unbuttoned. It didn't feel like it. Oh, for central air conditioning!

He said, "If I could answer that question, I wouldn't need to sell insurance." Harry picked up the policy he wanted us to purchase, and was about to proceed.

Wait a minute, I thought. *Was Harry actually making a joke?*

Joan and I looked at each other and we laughed out loud.

I slapped the table in glee.

Joan and I were cut from the same cloth: Joan has a great sense of humor, and we both love classical music, opera, and singing. She was a very fine soprano and we loved singing together. She also had a gift for languages, and helped me immeasurably with my song and opera texts in European tongues.

While she grew up a Christian Scientist, together we have explored the Bible and church beliefs, and have come to agree on most points. Though she immediately picked up on my teasing Harry about the Bible, she usually never spoke until spoken to.

Harry looked up at the two of us, his face a mask, trying to hide his uneasiness. He continued, a bit churlishly, "We simply can't know the mind of God. It's up to Him to run the universe, not us." He looked down at his papers, trying to redirect our attention back to the business at hand. "So we need to be prepared for whatever comes our way," he said, hands waving in the air. He pulled a sheet out of the pile and slid it across the table to us.

In past discussions with him, I usually backed off about this time. But now I decided to press him harder. I sat back and looked up at the ceiling, deliberately ignoring his paper. "I agree we can't know the mind of God—except for what He tells us in the Bible. Would you agree with that?" I rocked back to the table and looked him in the eye.

He looked down, avoiding my gaze, and mumbled, "Yes."

I think he suspected I was baiting him, because he then took all the other papers in front of him and pompously jogged them on the table.

I leaned forward, pointing a finger at him. "So then, how do you explain John 14:14?" I asked. "Jesus says, 'If you ask *anything* in my name, I will do it.'"

Harry laid the papers down, but they stuck to his fingers. He shook them off, letting them scatter as he leaned his head back, and said dismissively. "Oh, Bob, this question's as old as the hills. The key is, 'in my name.'"

Joan watched me intently, wondering how I would answer his gambit.

I shook my head. "Harry, we *always* end prayers with the Lord's name. We say, 'In Jesus' name, or something like that. Doesn't that count?"

While avoiding eye contact, he said, "Only if it's sincere."

"Only if it's sincere?" I raised my voice. "So, who's to judge that?"

"God, of course. That's the point. He decides." Harry looked down with a smirk, and gathered his papers again as if this conversation were over.

Not dissuaded, I went on, anger rising in my tone, I said, emphasizing each phrase with gestures, "So if I ask God to protect my house, and I implore Him with tears, and ask His protection for my family with all the conviction I can muster, and it burns down anyway, *you're* saying my prayer was *insincere?*" I reached for my drink again, hoping the ice would cool my temper a bit.

Holding his papers still for a moment, he replied smugly, "That's the only conclusion I can come to."

I pursed my lips, shaking my head at the rigidity of his thinking. Then I looked at Joan imploringly, my brow furrowed.

She shrugged her shoulders.

I looked away as I emptied my glass. I was really peeved.

Harry peeked at us under his eyebrows as his lips curved ever so slightly into a smirk of victory. He began to shuffle through the pages again and, finding the one he wanted, he pulled it out, and set it down before us as if this Bible conversation had never taken place.

I could feel my armpits soaking my shirt as my temper was about to explode. I wanted to shout, "Where's God's mercy in your thinking? There are other conclusions a thoughtful person might suggest. For example, perhaps God had a plan for that person, allowing an illness that would in the end heal a relationship, or…" I stopped and thought, *What's the use? He's incapable of thinking outside his tiny box.* I stood up and stomped into the kitchen, glass in hand.

• • • • •

Harry always had a simplistic answer for anything biblical. That irked me, not that he had an answer, but that it was always such a simple-minded one. Besides, the Bible doesn't require answers of us, and often doesn't even offer its own explanations. We are to follow, trust, and obey, yet I believe God wants us to explore questions and those apparent contradictions, such as I pointed out. The Bible was penned by people, and often not written by the person we think it was. Jesus never wrote a word of it. Language itself is a human invention, not God's. Anyone who has studied other languages knows how fallible language can be, and the great difficulty with translations. Few laypeople read the Bible in its original languages.

In addition, I believe a *question* is more important than an *answer*, because there is often more than one viable answer to any question. Some well-meaning Christians know only one "answer" to a given text, and refuse to entertain any other point of view. I call this "*either-or*-thinking." "*And*-thinking" permits other viewpoints. With "and-thinking," everyone wins, because "and" is inclusive. "Either-or-thinking" separates us by demanding a choice. When we are forced to make a choice, someone has to lose. This is why the world is so divided, and scared to make choices—because we're all afraid of losing. Fear leads to anger. Anger leads to fights (and wars). "And-thinking" brings people together.

As I came back into the room, Joan's eyes met mine once again. We signaled each other to drop the argument. It was too hot for such a discussion anyway.

·   ·   ·   ·   ·

Years ago, a college professor led a Bible class Joan and I attended. She (the professor) made this extraordinary remark, "When we enter a church, God doesn't expect us to leave our brains at the door."

Having said all that I said that night, I sometimes wondered if Harry's unyielding faith was really the correct way to believe. Heart and soul. Give no quarter. After all, doesn't Jesus speak about child-like, unquestioning faith? Yet when I encounter passages such as John 14:14, "If in my name you ask for anything, I will do it,"[2] I have often wondered about such extravagant promises.

I've met people, especially those who have lost loved ones, or perhaps those who suffer from a debilitating disease, who complain that God doesn't answer prayer. When I raised such questions in Bible classes I led, I found that others struggled with these texts just as I did.

[2] New Revised Standard Version.

But Harry never questioned anything in the Bible, even stories like those in Genesis 1 to 3, and in the Book of Jonah. Genesis 1 speaks of creating the world—or the cosmos for that matter—in seven days. Well, obviously, that doesn't make any logical, historical, or scientific sense. Clearly this text cannot be regarded as historical or scientific. Genesis 3 speaks of a talking serpent, an extraordinary fruit tree, and two people's struggle about whether or not to eat the fruit. And Jonah is a folk tale about a man running from God who encounters many supernatural occurrences. Are we to take these stories at face value? Well, it depends upon what you mean by "face value." If you mean that we are to believe exactly what we read, then my answer is a resounding no.

People who read these stories as *fact*, don't understand the nature of literature. Stories are designed to send us moral messages, not historical accounts of events. The trick is to discern the difference.

Harry accepted everything in the Bible as literal, historical fact, insisting that modern science and history are wrong. Sad to say, he was not alone in that misguided opinion—not by a long shot. Far too many people believe as Harry did; they say that science is not only wrong about widely-held theories like the Big Bang Theory, or more recently, global warming, but also that such teaching is "of the Devil."

Such arguments for me simply make no sense. When they invade the political realm, I really get upset. I hate it when people dispute established scientific or historical facts using religion to do so. That irks me.

Jesus always taught in story. We call them "Parables." They're often fantastic, and most Christians I know, including Harry, have no trouble looking for the message, rather than waste time arguing about whether or not a camel can go through the eye of a needle, or whether or not Jesus walked on water. Rather, we need to ask, what's the lesson to be learned?

Because I am an "and-thinker," I don't have to choose between science and the Bible. That's "either-or-thinking," and everybody loses.

You see, Harry, my friend, I'm sure your mother read fantasy stories to you when you were a child, and you probably enjoyed them. Take *Jack and the Beanstalk* for example. No one (except children) believes that any beanstalk on earth can grow like that. It not only mocks science, but it simply defies common sense. So why do we read such literature?

To stretch our imaginations and learn how to live together in peace.

We look for the message in the story, not the events that took place in the story.

Truth lies in the life's lessons. So, why should we strain our credulity to believe that a serpent can speak to humans, as in the Genesis story? Why not simply ask ourselves, what is this story trying to tell us?

I've long since decided that the truth of Adam and Eve is simply that God *did it*. God created it all. God was here before the Big Bang, and God made it all happen, and continues to do so. By so believing, God, history, and science come together in '*and*-thinking."

. . . . .

As it happened, I never chanced to say all that to Harry, who died at far too young an age.

. . . . .

Harry had been after me for some time to come to the Wednesday night Bible studies he hosted in his home in the south part of Bergenfield, only eight minutes away.

I said, "Gosh, Harry, right now I have too many rehearsals, opera, and concert gigs. This year I'm involved with six different opera productions. Wednesdays I have voice lessons in the city, and I'm exhausted by the time I get home. Besides, Rob is already four years old. I'd like to spend *some* time at home."

Harry said, "There are some people I want you to meet. They can answer your questions."

What questions? You mean that I don't accept the Genesis story as scientific fact?

On a Wednesday I happened to have free, I went to his Bible meeting, where I had occasion to talk to one of his elders about what he thought of the Creation Story vis-a-vis science. His demeanor reminded me of a college professor, one who carried himself with great humility. He smiled, and unlike many other Evangelicals who loved to trash evolutionary science, this man was different. He said, "You know, the truth of our faith does not rest on Old Testament stories. None of them can diminish what Christ did for us on the cross. That's what's important."

Amen to that, I thought.

Later that evening, Proverbs 3:5 came up: "Trust in the Lord with all your heart, and lean not on your own understanding...." Harry took me aside and suggested that I leaned too much on my own understanding, on my brain and my intellect, rather than the Word of God. I needed to let go, to let Christ in—to trust Him with *all* my heart, not my brain. Then we found a corner somewhere and prayed the Sinners' Prayer together, much as Johnnie and I had done all those years ago.

Being overly tired that evening and still uncomfortable with Harry's narrow way of thinking, I really wanted to go home, but something held me there. I thought of Johnnie, who was now in France, I longed to talk to him because he had a way of guiding me with probing questions that dug deep into the soul.

At this point I excused myself from Harry and went into the bathroom. My heart cried out to God, *What am I doing wrong? Why is my soul so disquieted, Lord?*

That night on the way home, and later in bed, I lay awake arguing with God about whether or not I truly was a Christian. *Could Harry be right, God?*

The following morning, I got up earlier than usual and left for work before anyone else was up. Dragging my feet to the car, I suddenly stopped and looked up at the quiet pre-dawn sky and felt somehow revived. What a sparkling day lay before me! The sun was not quite over the horizon yet, but its red-orange glow glistened in the tree tops. A new day was dawning; a new world was on its way. I took a deep breath—my lungs rejoiced.

Yes, God creates a fresh cosmos with each new day, one that can lift us up and fill us with hope—if we let it. *Thank you, Lord, for waking me to your glorious creative power....*

As I drove through Tenafly, and up the hill toward Englewood Cliffs, I happened to catch the red light at Engle Street. I huffed in frustration. I hated having to stop for this particular intersection. It always seemed interminable, and on *this* morning, it truly dowsed my spirits. I fought to hold them, but my sleep deprivation joined my grumbly side—when suddenly...

A dazzling, blinding light hit me in the face. It flooded the car. I was scared, maybe the way Peter, James, and John were on the Mount of Transfiguration. True, my light came from the sun, yet I sensed from crown to toes that it was more than the sun's light. It embraced me, it filled me with a glow and warmth that I knew had to be *Shekinah*, the very *Presence of God*.

Tears rolled down my cheeks. The turmoil that had kept me awake all night and bedeviled me for years melted away. I felt peace and joy as I never had before. My whole body felt as if a warm breeze with a scent of laurel wafted over and through me. Never before had I felt so light and airy, as if I were being lifted into the sky by some unseen power. I always wanted to soar like a bird—now my soul looked down from the clouds, gleefully laughing, swept across the hills and trees spread out before me as I floated along.

Then, back at the wheel, someone somehow got in the car and sat beside me in the passenger seat. I turned to see who it was, but there was no one there. I thought I saw a shimmering shape beginning to take form. A person? I couldn't tell if it was a man or a woman. As I watched, a person with a hood began to take shape. Whoever it was, he or she faced forward.

"Is that you, Lord?" I whispered, as my now awake senses tried to figure out who it was. Although I couldn't actually *see*, I *felt*—I *knew* the Presence had to be Christ. Then He slowly turned towards me, eyes gleaming. Was I hallucinating? His quivering face began to take form, and glowed with a radiance that ebbed and flowed from light to dark. I felt refreshingly warm.

But those eyes! Their color morphed from light to dark, dark to light, with changing expressions as they glistened with every word and movement. The iridescent hood flowed over His entire body. Sometimes I thought I could see right through Him and out the window. His voice was strong, neither bass nor tenor. Could this be a woman?

"Where are you headed?" Christ asked in a striking, gender-unidentifiable tone.

"I wish I knew," I murmured, shaking my head in bewilderment, trying to lighten this intense moment, and to make sense of it. Embarrassed, as I realized something cosmic was happening, I meekly looked down at my lap. My voice probably shook faster than my hands. I felt totally bowled over.

"Do you know what road you're on?"

"Clinton Avenue," I said, not thinking that Christ probably had a different "road" in mind.

"Are you sure of that?" He said, looking forward again.

"Right now I'm not sure of anything," I murmured.

"I know, Robert. That's why I'm here." Christ pointed straight ahead.

My eyes followed His finger.

"Let's take a different road," He said. "I want to show you something."

"But, Lord, ah, Sir—Madam…I'm sorry…." I said, embarrassed. "I'm running late…please, I have to get to work, ASAP."

His gaze remained forward. I turned too, to see if the stop light had changed.

Much to my astonishment, the traffic light, the intersection, and all the cars and houses had disappeared. There was a small wagon trail in front of us with two worn wheel tracks, and a patch of green grass running up the middle. Trees towered above the path like two lines of telephone poles on either side, the top branches forming an archway high above the narrow cow path. I felt as though I were about to enter a magnificent cathedral. The leaves glowed from green to bright orange. Another light from above the trees made it seem like midday.

Without any help from me, the car began to move slowly forward along this pathway. As we came to a rise, I thought I could see a light ahead. It glistened white at first, but the more I looked at it, it seemed to take the shape of an altar, with a majestic reredos[3] behind it. The trees came alive in a kaleidoscope of colors. The archway dazzled me like Christmas lights in a vast Sistine Chapel-like dome.

"Is this the entrance to Heaven?" I asked in a trembling voice.

Christ smiled in a fatherly way, but didn't answer. As we moved forward, the road itself changed direction, right and left. Then we started up a hill, and down again, then to the right and to the left, making me dizzy. I couldn't see the wall for a while, then it reappeared, its lights growing brighter as we approached. We came to another hill, rather long, and the reredos was completely out of sight. The surrounding lights became dimmer. *Why?* I wondered.

Fear suddenly gripped my heart; I turned to Christ for reassurance. His face remained looking straight ahead. I was scared.

Without moving, He said reassuringly, "Robert, I'm here," then slowly turned to me.

---

[3] A reredos is the wall behind the altar of a church. In large churches it is typically dazzlingly ornamental.

Again, He called me, "Robert," I thought. Only my family calls me that. Ah, I get it! "Robert" is my proper Christian name. "I don't mean to be rude, Sir, but I have to get to work. I'm already late…."

Christ said, "Robert, can you trust me to get you to where you're supposed to be?"

Where's that? Wait a minute, is He talking about Heaven? Is that where we're going? Have I died? What about my life here and now? My family, my career?

I looked out the car window again. The trees sighed as if to calm my raging thoughts. They reminded me of Rev. Beam's encouraging words to follow God's will. I had forgotten them.

Then the scene with my father refusing to sign the college loan flashed into my head. I looked up to the trees. "What's going on here?" I felt like shouting, *Which way am I to turn? Where does this road lead, Lord?*

I turned back to Him. "Please, Lord, with all due respect, I don't get what's going on here." My face was a mask of fear. I pleaded to Him with praying hands, "Please, help me understand what's going on here. All I can think about right now is that I have this important meeting at 8:15. It's already…."

I looked at my watch. The various hands were turning in a slow dance on the clock face. The fixed numbers were partnering with the hands in an intricate minuet. I thought I was going crazy.

"Am I having a nightmare?" I asked aloud.

"No." Christ's voice rang with authority, yet was pleasing to the ear. He turned slowly to me with sad eyes.

"Then why do I feel so afraid?" My eyes met His.

He smiled tenderly. "Only you can answer that."

"Being with you I shouldn't, I guess."

"That's right, my son. So then, why are you afraid?"

A warm hand rested on my shoulder.

I looked but couldn't focus my eyes on it. Yet this strange hand filled me with confidence, and comforted me. "I don't know," I said absently.

"Apart from me you can do nothing," He said, lifting the hand from my shoulder.

"John 15:5," I murmured, as if to prove I knew my Bible.

Christ nodded. "Yes, that's the last part of the verse. What comes just before that?"

"I don't remember." I felt downcast.

God nodded, and His voice again began to sound like a woman's, a strong mezzo-soprano, melodious, almost singing, "I am the vine and you are the branches. Those who abide in me, and I in them, bear much fruit because…"

"…apart from me you can do nothing." I finished his sentence. "Or should I say, *I* can do nothing."

He paused and looked at me with comforting eyes, and put an arm around my shoulders—right through the seat. "Robert, you're too hard on yourself. You don't need to carry your childhood miseries around with you."

I looked at Him, puzzled, just as new light began to shine through the windshield.

Christ answered my unspoken question with another question. "Do you remember how your father told you you'd never amount to a tinker's damn?"

The memory of my dad's cruel words stung me to the quick. I wanted to jump out of the car and run away, but I felt glued to my seat. Tears erupted. I looked away from Him, angry and hurt that he brought these dreaded words back to me.

"You continue to believe what your father said, don't you?"

"No, I *don't*, not anymore," I shouted, scowling at him, defiant. "Dad was wrong. Why did you bring up this old ghost?"

Christ's voice changed to a lower, firmer pitch, and said, "Robert, if you've driven this curse out of your consciousness, why do you continue to castigate yourself about it? Why do you continue to think of yourself as a failure? Why do you continue to think you can't do anything right?"

Anxiety hit me. Ghosts of my father, and other feared authority figures from my past shook me to my very core.

God turned to me, eyes now a soft sky-blue, and in a subdued, yet clear voice, said,

"Robert, your father was wrong, and he may not speak for me. No one can. I decide what you'll amount to. Your job is to trust that. To trust me. And to do that, you must follow me day by day, not just when the mood suits you. This is what Harry has been trying to tell you all these years."

I bowed my head in remorse. God began to hum softly as a mother calms a baby. I reached for a tissue to blow my nose, but couldn't find one.

Then I looked up, I couldn't see out the windshield. I reached for the steering wheel to try to take back control of the car, but it wasn't there. Instead, I found myself standing in front of a mirror in the Scholastic men's room near my office. In place of the steering wheel, I had my hand on the soap dispenser. I quickly looked to my right. Christ was no longer there. I spun around to search the room. No Christ.

I looked at my watch: 8:12.

Oh, dear Lord, Rudy'll be looking for me. (Rudy was my boss.) I quickly splashed water on my face, and dried it and my hands. Hurriedly, I stepped out of the room and rushed down the hall to my office. My assistant, Dolly, wasn't there, so I picked up the meeting folder from my desk and dashed off to the conference room.

As I entered, Rudy smiled and pointed to a seat.

The clock on the wall showed exactly 8:15.

This morning's experience with Christ had lifted me out of my doldrums. Yes, I had always thought of myself as a failure for not making a career in opera, but God now proved to me that my life belongs to Him, not my father, not even to me. That made my day. In fact, it gave me new *life*.

As I approached my seat at the conference table, Rudy's face was buried in his notes. I found an empty chair and sat down.

My thoughts were still with Christ. *Okay, Lord, you win. I'll follow you. And I'll even sing Gospel music—if you want me to.* I wondered if God knew how much I hated Gospel music.

Christ, still in my head, smiled down at me, and I laughed out loud. *Of course God knows. He's part of the Trinity. Each ones knows what the others know.*

"What's so funny, Mitch?" Rudy asked, as he looked up, a frown of concentration covering his face, papers still in hand.

"Oh, just that I got here on the dot," I chimed cheerfully.

Rudy looked at his watch. "Okay Mitch, you're on time for a change. So what's so funny?" He laid the papers down in front of him and stared at me.

"Oh, nothing. I'll tell you later, Rudy, okay?" As I sat down, I grinned and winked at him.

His serious face suddenly lifted into a broad, Rudy beam. I opened my file with a smile and a new lease on life. Yes, God is good!

Chapter One

Growing Up; McVeytown, Pennsylvania

Mom hovered over my crib at bedtime and sang softly and sweetly:

"Now I lay me down to sleep,

I pray the Lord my soul to keep,

God bless Mommy, Daddy, too.

And make all God's children

Honest and true."

It was a hot, stuffy night, as I fidgeted and fussed against the sweltering twilight. Her voice soothed me—but she had stopped singing. Angrily I resumed my squirmy battle against the sticky sheet and heavy-laden air in the room. I felt like screaming.

Sweat beading on her brow, Mom cooed seductively, "There, there, Robert, go to sleep."

I felt a cool hand on my head. I stopped squirming. If I could have spoken, I'd have said, "Do it some more, do it some more." That gentle touch made all the difference between sleep and squall.

What her five-foot two stature may have lacked in command, she compensated with energy, verve, and laughter. Fun flowed from her as easily as singing. Her persona was packaged in her nickname, "Cricket," a name she adored. No one knew where it came from, but it embodied her spirit. Light brown hair tumbled no lower than her neck—usually tucked under a cleaning bonnet. She trimmed it herself—I don't think she ever saw the inside of a

1

beauty shop. She never fussed about how she looked. Besides, Dad would've trounced such a frivolous expense.

She always wore "specs," she called them, and later in life, she lost the sight in one eye from glaucoma. At first she moped around the house, especially when it rained and she couldn't hang the wet laundry outside. She had Dad construct a maze of ropes around the kitchen and dining rooms. With eight people in the house, including Grandma and Aunt Carrie, the washing machine rumbled incessantly in the kitchen. It felt damp downstairs when she did the laundry, and it smelled like a large professional laundry.

Every now and again you'd hear a disguised swear word, like "Darn!" when Mom tripped over something she didn't see. "Who put that chair there?" she'd yell at no one in particular.

Little by little she emerged from the dark place glaucoma had consigned her to, and found her childlike spirit again, especially when she discovered she could still drive. She got so excited about that, that she bragged to others, "I'm blind in one eye and can't see out of the other."

"How can you drive with only one eye?" somebody would ask.

"I don't know, but that never stopped me. I *have* to drive, or we'd never have food on the table." Such was her indomitable spirit.

When I was born in McVeytown, PA on July 15, 1939, it was also on a very hot, sticky day, Mom told me years later. "I was so uncomfortable carrying you that summer," she said, "I thought you'd never get here. When you were born it was a good thing Aunt Flo was there. I don't know what I'd have done without her."

"Why was she there?" I asked years later.

"To get you born. She was like a midwife for me."

"What's a midwife?"

"Old Doc Steele was busy that day and couldn't come to the house. When babies are born, you can't do it by yourself. Women who helped at birthings were called midwives. Don't ask me why."

"I was born at home?"

"Of course. There wasn't a hospital for miles around. All babies were born at home in those days."

"What did Aunt Flo do?"

"Well, she helped deliver you, and then cleaned you up, and all the mess…"

"Cleaned me up? Why?"

"Gettin' born is messy. Took a lot of towels," she chuckled at the remembrance. "You were a good baby, though. Aunt Flo adored you."

Of course, I have no direct memories of this time, only the stories. And some of those became family legends. For instance…

I had yet to reach my first birthday. It was a pleasant summer day that following June when Dad and Mom drove Johnnie and me to Aunt Carrie's general store for some groceries. Johnnie sat right against Dad. I was stuffed in between Johnnie and Mom. All of us were cramped into the front seat of that little Willys, which had no back seat.

On arrival, Dad parked the car in front of the store entrance with the driver's side next to the curb. Dad looked at three-year old Johnnie and commanded, "Now you sit still here. We'll only be a minute. You take good care of Robert, y'hear?"

Mom got out on the passenger side, and joined Dad as together they went into the store.

In those days the streets had high middles for drainage purposes, so the car leaned toward the curb. Mom easily let her door shut itself because it stuck up in the air when she opened it. For some reason, Dad left his door open. Perhaps he thought he had closed it, or that there was no need to close it since they'd be right back. But since his door faced down, it swung out 'til it caught itself in the grass on the other side of the curb. So, it was almost wide open.

"As soon as Dad left," Johnnie told me recently—these are his words: "I, an almost three-year-old, scooted over to get behind the wheel. I sat there for a bit, then wiggled up to the front edge of the seat, so I could grab the steering wheel and 'drive' the car. I was so intent on my play that I didn't see you tumble over behind me and begin to slide along the seat towards the open door.

"The seat was rather wide, with ample room for you to pass behind me unnoticed. In fact, I didn't realize that you had slid by till I heard you hit the curb and start crying. I got scared and started to cry, too.

"Mom and Dad came running, and rushed us to the doc's. Then Dad took me home and went back for you and Mom.

3

"I ran into the living room and hid behind the big easy chair. I crouched down as far as I could, fearing the storm that was to come when they got home. As far as I can remember, they let me off rather easy, because they took my part in this debacle as something that shouldn't have happened, since a toddler is not the kind of guardian one should have for a little baby.

"However, this episode comes back to my mind rather frequently, and I shudder when I think what could have happened, but didn't. I praise our Lord that it all came out well in the end."

Yes, I could have been killed, or maybe broken my neck, but I must suppose God had other plans for me. In most situations like this, Dad would have come down on Johnnie like a tornado in a chicken coop, but he didn't.

Mom had a different version of the story, which she told me when I was an adult:

She came running out of the store as soon as she heard Johnnie wailing. She rushed to the car to see what the matter was, and almost stepped on me, lying unconscious in the gutter next to the curb. With an "Oh my God, Robert!" she reached down and picked me up. Blood was beginning to cake in my hair, while still running down my face and clothes, and now on hers as well. "Robert, wake up!" Turning to Johnnie, who was still wailing, she asked him desperately, "What happened?"

"Wa-a-a-a!" he replied boisterously.

She reached into the car, around Johnnie, and grabbed a cloth diaper from her baby bag. She began wiping some of the blood away to see the wound better, then applied pressure to stem the bleeding, all the while speaking loudly to try to wake me up.

By this time, Dad had arrived at the car.

"Oh my God, Ja—!" Mom cried again. "I think Robert's dead."

Dad replied, "He's bleeding, so I doubt he's dead."

He bundled us all into the car and rushed to Old Doc Steele's office. He dropped Mom off and took Johnnie home. Mom, still a bit dazed, rushed into the office and frantically announced, "My baby's hurt. He may be dead for all I know. He won't wake up. Please, may I see Doc Steele right away?" Looking down at me, she continued, "Maybe he's lost too much blood… he's so little…."

The nurse leapt to her feet and rushed to knock on an examining room where Doctor Steele was with a patient. She hurriedly entered without waiting for a response. A few seconds later, the good doctor stepped into the reception area. Seeing Mom so upset, and as an old friend of the family, he said, "Cricket, what happened?"

Handing me to him she blurted, "Robert fell and hit his head. Please tell me he's not dead."

Doctor Steele took me in his arms and immediately rushed to a second, empty examination room. There he applied a bandage, asking the nurse to hold it in place, took his stethoscope, and listened for my pulse. "He's alive all right," he announced to my mother, nodding his head confidently. His smile broadcasted his relief. "Just unconscious," he added, almost flippantly, in an effort to calm Mom. "His pulse is strong, and I don't think he's lost too much blood."

His smile reassured her. She took a deep breath.

"Nasty gash," he continued. "It'll need stitching. Otherwise he seems to be all right. Babies are resilient, as you of all people should know. How many is this, four?"

Mom looked at him, not knowing whether to yell at him for reminding her of all her carnal activity, or to hug him for declaring me out of danger. For his part, the good doctor saw that Mom had returned from her panic state, and kept smiling to reassure her.

She had birthed five children, all under his care. Her first child, a son, had died, but Dr. Steele said "four" deliberately so as not to remind her. Mom later always referred to him as "Old Doc Steele," reflecting her affection for and trust in him. She often said that there was no other doctor like him.

My wound required only three stitches. No big deal as it turned out, no transfusion necessary, and I've lived long enough to tell the tale. The resulting scar became a sort of battle trophy throughout my childhood. Little by little, it seemed to move higher on my forehead, closer and closer to my hairline. There was a time when my hair covered it. Later in life, as my hair began to recede, it seemed to follow my hairline upwards. By my mid-thirties it had disappeared altogether.

· · · · ·

By today's standards, my parents were clearly responsible for this incident, especially Dad for leaving the door open. In those days, parents usually found ways of blaming the kids for such accidents. No one would have complained to the authorities as they do today. There were few laws to protect children, and there was an ethos that whatever happened in the family stayed in the family.

• • • • •

When Johnnie and I outgrew the crib, she put us in a small bed together, and sang the same "Now I Lay Me down to Sleep" ditty to us. Soon, after hearing our two older sisters, Joan and Margaret ("Cissie"), singing it across the hall, Johnnie and I soon joined the budding family choir.

Joan, the eldest, sturdy and solid, was the tomboy of the family, who later morphed into a boy-crazy beauty, never lacking a Phys Ed beau. She loved sports—and guys, and could always be counted on to light up a room with fun and laughter. Cis, on the other hand, must have been stuck in a closet when cheerfulness was handed out. She was always bookish and skinny, often cranky and even belligerent at times. I guess she took more after Dad, while Joan clearly was cut from Mom's bouncy cloth. Johnnie and I probably fell out of a Tinkertoy box. We had sticks for limbs and were always on the go. I was always regarded as the brainy kid of the family, a biological aberration of some sort, I can only surmise.

• • • • •

Middletown

A year after I was born, we moved to Middletown, Pennsylvania, near Harrisburg, where Dad got a job as a draftsman at the Middletown Army Air Force base. He remained there through most of World War II. This period remains shadowy in my memory, yet there is one story I can share, again with Johnnie's help, that has spiritual reverberations.

Apparently while we were playing together, Johnnie somehow tricked me into saying a naughty swear word: *damn*. In the forties, this word was as odious as the f-word is today. Children did not say such words without getting their mouths washed out with soap. (For corroboration, see Jean Shepherd's, *A Christmas Story*.)

Of course, Dad could say whatever came into his head. And such words were never far from his lips with his short fuse. After Johnnie "made" me say *damn*, he immediately threatened to "tell on me." Incensed at his deceit, I flew into a rage not unlike Dad's. Johnnie walked away laughing, making me all the madder.

According to my three-year-old logic, the only appropriate action to take was to make him say it as well, thus making us equally naughty. He wouldn't tell on me because he knew I would tell on him. I followed him outside, and when he bent down to play with a toy, I grabbed a brick and stood over him with the missile aimed at the top of his head, and yelled, "Say *damn*, Johnnie, say *damn*!"

He refused, so I dropped the brick on his head. I don't remember what happened next, but according to Johnnie, his head bled profusely, much as mine had in McVeytown. He says he ran into the house, crying loudly—more likely screaming. Dad was there and bandaged his wound. He told Johnnie that his dressing was just like the hats that sailors wore.

"I was so proud of that 'hat' that I didn't want to take it off," Johnnie said to me as he related this story.

Neither he nor I remembers what repercussions came my way.

For Mom, my ordering him to say "damn" *was* the story. She told it so often that it became a family catch-phrase: "Say *damn*, Johnnie, say *damn*!" She would giggle like a naughty schoolgirl every time she repeated the word *damn*, relishing repeating the forbidden, sinful word. She delighted in the naughty in whatever guise, but she also washed our mouths out with soap a couple of times when she caught us using dreaded swear words.

"Big folks can swear, but not kids," she declared.

"Why?" we asked.

"Because I said so."

End of discussion.

$\bullet \quad \bullet \quad \bullet \quad \bullet \quad \bullet$

Chapter Two

Heir Apparent; Lock Haven, Pennsylvania

We lived in Middletown through most of World War II. Then Dad's skill as a draftsman landed him a similar drafting job at Piper Aircraft Corporation in Lock Haven, Pennsylvania over a hundred miles northwest of Middletown, where we moved in 1944. I don't know exactly what he "drafted," but from what he little said about it, I suspect he created formal plans for building airplanes from rough drafts the designers sent to him.

I remember well that we kids attended Sunday school faithfully at Trinity Methodist Church on Main Street. We learned Bible stories and the rudiments of behaving as Christians should, or Mom's version of it, which was, "Behave yourselves, and stay out of trouble." Sometimes she added, "Whatever you do, don't get caught."

· · · · ·

Looking back on it, I've often wondered what Mom's sense of morality had to do with Christianity. Today I'd say, not much. Maybe superficially, but it didn't come close to what I learned later in life. But when growing up, all I knew was that we had to go to church, and that we were supposed to behave, to be good boys and girls. Sunday school for me, both as a child and as a teaching adult, however well-intentioned, missed the mark. The following story is a typical example.

• • • • •

One morning in fifth grade Sunday school class, the lesson mentioned the word *circumcision*, from the story in Luke 2:21 of the rite performed on Jesus. Having no idea what it meant, I raised my hand. Our teacher, Dr. Ulmer, a professor at the local college, looked up from his teacher's pamphlet, unaccustomed to being interrupted by a question. He was a tall man with light, well-kept hair, fair skin, and light brown eyes. He was every inch a dignified college professor, from his brown tweed jacket with suede elbow patches to his brown, soft leather shoes. He had a kind face, but he always kept a distance from us boys, as if he were afraid of possible discipline problems he wasn't used to since he began teaching at the college level many years ago.

He shifted his glasses to try to see better who asked the question. Removing them as if they were too dirty to see across the room, he scanned us boys seated all around the table, trying to find who asked the question. Finally, his eyes landed on me because all the boys were looking at me, aghast at my brazenness. No one asked questions. It was an unwritten, unspoken rule among the boys.

"You have a question, Robert?" said Dr. Ulmer, also taken aback.

"Ah, yes sir. What does that word, 'circum-' or whatever-it-was, mean?"

"*Circumcision*, you mean?" Dr. Ulmer blinked, replacing his light-rimmed, bifocal glasses back on his nose. He then looked up toward the ceiling as if that were a necessary part of framing his answer.

After a pause, he looked down at us to begin his discourse on the subject. He made it sound like a scientific inquiry, but to boys our age, any mention of genitalia, penis in this case, sparked the word *sex* in our pre-adolescent imaginations.

The class consisted of twelve-year-old boys—no girls—at the predawn of sexual awareness. To me, *circumcision* was just a big word. Some of the boys knew what it meant—or *thought* they knew. Some blushed while others snickered as they elbowed the boys next to them.

We were not supposed to know about *sex*, a mysterious, alluring word, never uttered in polite society. You weren't supposed to ask, nor were you supposed to read about it, so how *could* you learn about it? The only literature on sex that seemed to be around was considered smutty by adults, and thus, by us too, so if you were caught with it, you'd be in trouble.

In reality, we boys learned from one another. And since none of us knew much about it, it became a game to bluster others into thinking *you* knew and they didn't, sort of like the shyster that sidles up to you and opens his coat. Every kid knew to run like the wind from a guy like that, and so it is with the facts of life: you're to run like the dickens—unless you're the shyster, and only those gifted with a great deal of bravado could get away with being one.

As Dr. Ulmer droned on, we became more and more restless. By the time he finished his recitation, I realized I had listened to more about circum-what-ever-it-was than I thought I would ever want to—or need to know. *Okay, so I think this word has something to do with a boy's thingamajig and being born? Right?*

What popped into my head just then was the word *chop*, because I vaguely remembered Mom had used that term in connection with newborn boys getting "chopped." At that time, I had pictured a small, specially designed hatchet, used in conjunction with a toy-like chopping block. I guessed that doctors must use such a contrivance for the job.

Ouch! That must have smarted. No wonder babies squalled when they were born…what if the doctor missed?

It never occurred to me to question why girl babies also cried when they were born.

When I asked Mom if I had been circumcised, she blushed and looked away. "I don't know what Old Doc Steele did, exactly," she began, very embarrassed. "All I know is he said he didn't believe in it. What difference does it make to you?" and she walked quickly out of the room.

Mom's frequent admonitions to not *get caught* puzzled me. In a way, I felt *caught* by asking this naïve question that was a very intimate, private subject in the 1950s. I had no idea that it would unleash such a backlash from my friends. The boys made me feel *caught* by asking it, since they teased me mercilessly about it afterward.

Was there a Christian message in this?

• • • • •

11

Singing and God sprang from the same source in our house with songs like, "Jesus Loves Me," "I Would be True," "Away in a Manger," "Silent Night," and the host of holiday and Gospel hymns Mom hummed and whistled around the house. Often in the evenings she'd sit at the piano and plunk her way through her favorite hymns, those that she could manage at the keyboard, always urging us to join her. In later years, after I had studied piano, she insisted that I play.

On holidays like Thanksgiving, Christmas, and Easter, the house was suffused with the to-die-for aromas of roasted turkey, cookies, and other desserts, all of which made us obnoxiously impatient for dinner to begin. Over the top of clanking lids and clinking utensils, we'd beg, "Mom, can I have a slice of turkey?" Or, "Mom, please, please, can I have one of those cookies?" pointing longingly at the plate. Our mouths watered 'til they dripped.

"Wash your hands and go sit down," came the imperious reply.

After we had feasted until we boys had to loosen our belts, Mom would wash some of the dishes, then hang the washcloth over the sink, and announce quickly before any of us could skedaddle, "C'mon everybody, time to sing."

Since only one year separated each of us, except Johnnie and me—we were almost two years apart—she had little trouble managing this small troupe. She'd gather us around the piano like a hen with her chicks and begin singing familiar festive hymns.

Sometimes she'd yell out to Dad, who had disappeared into his shop in the next room, "Ja—!" (She never pronounced the -ck.) "Come on. Get your violin and join us."

Dad, five-foot-eight, sported black hair combed straight back in tight waves. Not a single hair ever turned grey, nor did he lose any. Every once in a while he grew a Clark Gable moustache, but only if a new Gable movie appeared in a local movie theater. He maintained it for a while, then suddenly it would disappear.

Unfortunately, Johnnie and I inherited our hair from Mom's side of the family. Her brothers had brown hair, too. Brown and bald, later, grey and bald.

Dad would rather use his hands than his voice. Scratching out "Carolina Moon" on his dime-store violin, or punching the keys on the piano with his index finger summed up his instrumental accomplishments. Sometimes he joined the family choir, mostly not. It all depended upon whether he had a rush job with a looming deadline—and his mood, of course.

• • • • •

Dad puzzled me. When we were small, he loved to play games with us. At Christmastime, he'd set up the electric trains around the tree. Johnnie and I would stand around and watch, hankering to help him, but he insisted upon doing everything himself, including running the trains. "Too dangerous for you kids," he'd mutter by way of explanation. Johnnie and I would look at each other and shrug. We wanted ever so much to get down on our hands and knees and join in. I loved the sounds of the cars clicking along the tracks and the hum of the engines. We'd squeal every time the crossing gates clanged down as the trains rushed by.

"Please, Daddy, can we run the train?"

Once in a while, Dad would relent and let us take a hand at the transformer which controlled the trains, but he always hovered over us like a mother hawk over her chicks. Soon we just ignored him. Sometimes we'd sneak back into the living room when he was working, and run them ourselves. We took turns operating the transformer while the other one would take care of derailings, of which there were quite a few.

The aroma of the Christmas tree mingled with the 3-in-1 oil and artificial smoke from the engine, all of which tingled our nostrils. Pine needles, providing another savory fragrance, were a constant source of train wrecks. Sometimes we delighted in those mishaps; other times we got into scraps over whose fault it was: "You knocked those needles on the tracks, you clumsy ox!" All grist for our memory mills.

For Easter Sunday Dad made the most scrumptious and sweet-smelling chocolate Easter eggs you could imagine. Each one weighed several pounds. I never knew how he managed to get peanut butter into the middle of them, but he made them from scratch. We were never allowed to see what he did—he made them in the middle of the night.

But after we found them in our baskets on Easter morning, he took them back and had Mom parcel them out to us so that we wouldn't "eat them all at once. They'll make you sick."

13

Everything he did for us during the holidays was supposed to be a surprise, and when we were small, they were. He loved our expressions of delight when we found his goodies.

In summer, he delighted in taking us for rides in the car out in the country. I loved the wind whipping through the windows, with the fragrance of fresh-cut fields wafting into the back seat. Even a barnyard odor had a certain richness that soon became familiar. Cows mooing, birds squawking, tractors rumbling along the road or cutting a swath in a field all added to our excitement. Johnnie and I loved those rides. I can't speak for our two sisters.[4]

Dad loved to cook hamburgers in the backyard. The smoke from the grill wafted the mouth-watering aroma of hamburgers and hot dogs all the way into the house. *Golly-gee, did they hit the old taste buds just right!* After a pleasant day's swimming in the river, what more could you ask? As the sun slowly settled behind the trees and over the hills in back of the old homestead, Mom would get us all singing around the campfire. Yes, as corny as it sounds, it was home, sweet home. I miss it.

•　•　•　•　•

Dad operated a printing business out of our home on Susquehanna Avenue. In an age when the printing industry began to modernize with all manner of robotic machinery, Dad was a throw-back to the eighteenth century, when printing was done on manual machines. He owned two noisy vertical impression printing presses, one of which required the operator to pump a foot pedal.

Later Dad got an electric motor to replace the foot operation, but the basic technology hadn't changed—though it was easier for the operator not having to pump. He owned two large cases of type, that is, individual pieces of lead about an inch and a half in length with a letter, numeral, punctuation, or other symbol stamped on its end. A type setter earned his title because he "set type" by hand. Each letter was placed in a hand-held tray, wedged to fit tightly into the press frame that held the type. After finishing one line, the type setter would take it to the table that held the press frame and transfer the completed line to the frame. Yes, it was a slow, tedious process, fraught with

---

[4] Nor can they speak for themselves, both having passed away within a couple of months in 2012.

the ever present possibility of spilling the type while transferring it from the hand-held tray to the press frame. More than once, I can tell you, the pieces of type slipped out of my hands and scattered all over the floor. When that happened, you'd have to throw out every piece of type and set it all over again in case a type face had been damaged in the fall. Visual inspection of the typefaces didn't reveal a slight dent that could only be seen on the finished product. You could never take the chance that no piece had been dented. So you always had to set that line over again. It felt like going back to square one of the entire job.

At least that work didn't add to the din in this noisy machine room—except for a spill, which made its own special clattering noise, not to mention the cursing and shouting that followed in its wake.

All this technology predated electricity, much less today's techno gadgetry. One thing missing from today's computer-driven gizmos: the strong odor of motor oil and grease necessary to keep the presses running. You could smell Dad's shop twenty paces away. Further on hot days.

Later Dad purchased a "modern" flatbed press that was a marvel by comparison with the older vertical ones. Its name, "flatbed," indicates the advantage of having the press frame already in the press, so that the step was eliminated of having to place the type in the frame on a table and then transfer the frame to the vertical press. But it had more moving parts clacking back and forth than the older ones, raising the decibel level. Instead of feeding the paper by hand into the press, it had metal "fingers" that did the job. This press was Dad's pride and joy, and the loudest of all. It was one of those fingers that caught my hand—that story below.

He eked out a living with these machines. In the early fifties his major customer was a large paper mill that ordered labels for their shipping boxes. Local funeral directors bought programs, much like greeting cards, for funeral services. An ice cream manufacturer ordered its various flavor labels printed directly on the ice cream containers. Dad had figured out how to fit these containers into one of the printers.

He also had a photography business in which he both photographed people, and processed film and picture prints. One of his biggest lines of work was to make enlargements of pictures. Dad originally had all this equipment in McVeytown.

· · · · ·

In the early fifties, Dad had converted the dining room into his print shop, crowded it with two presses, two set-up tables, an electric circular saw table, and a large chest of type[5] drawers. Because of the space limitation, he could only have one of us working with him at a time. Dad trained each of us how to set type, the job I spoke about before.

My eldest sister Joan was the first heir apparent to take over Dad's business, and then Cissie was for a brief stint. Johnnie, the next in line, worked for him after I had moved away. The official job title for a printer's helper was "printer's devil."

Dad was an exacting taskmaster, and everything had to be done his way. Suggestions were pooh-poohed. Doing it your own way was not tolerated. Sometimes he'd get so mad at us that he "fired" us. Then he'd complain to Mom, and cajole her to get us back. She was always the go-between, a job she never cared for, but for which she seemed to be born. I can still hear her placating voice, "Now, Ja—, you know you want _____ to help you. Why can't you two just work things out…?"

In between Cissie and Johnnie, I became the next heir apparent. However, my duties began with cleaning and oiling the printing presses at the crack of dawn each morning. What a yucky job that was! Black, dirty oil all over the presses and in trays underneath them, and soon on your hands, face, and clothes. At first it smelled sort of pleasant, but after a few weeks of it getting into your fingernails, hair, and places you couldn't believe it got into, you began to resent that odor. I also hated the slimy, sticky feeling on my hands, especially when I sat down at the piano. A musician with dirty black oil under his fingernails? Did I have a conflict of interest, or what?

After that introduction, Dad instructed me in type setting, described above, indeed an intricate and very tedious task. We all hated it. As I became more familiar with the equipment and procedures, Dad "promoted" me to operate the presses, increasing my pay from zero to zero. Although I didn't realize it at the time, it was a very dangerous job, and today, it's illegal for children to

---

[5] "Type" refers to the small metal blocks with individual letters used in old-fashioned printing presses. For more information, Google, Spread of European movable type printing.

operate any of the presses he had, including even the ancient foot-pumped one in the cellar.

As I already mentioned, the scar on my left hand remains a permanent legacy from my stint as a printer's devil. I was twelve or thirteen when that incident occurred:

I was in the process of installing a fresh paper seal around the main press drum of the flatbed press. This was part of the set-up procedure—you always changed the paper seal on the drum before you did anything else.

Having locked the one end into its clamps, I was holding it taut with my left hand to be sure in was flat and didn't wrinkle. I was then to slowly spin the drum around so that I could attach the other end of the seal to its other anchors on the drum, making sure it was tight and smooth. It was difficult to turn the drum by hand (for a host of reasons), so Dad had showed me how to jog the motor button to let the machine turn it slowly.

I reached down the side of the press with my right hand to find the "on" button. If you tapped it lightly, it would immediately disengage, moving the drum a few inches. You had to repeat this process until you got the drum where you wanted it so you could fasten the other end of the seal.

There was a risk: holding the button down started the machine. It flew. Getting it stopped again required another push of the button. Ordinarily, by that time, the drum would have rotated around several times. With the seal not attached to both ends, it would be torn to shreds in seconds, and perhaps cause serious damage to the press. Tapping the button lightly would start it in little jerks, and stop immediately. It took a series of taps to get the drum into position so you could attach the other end. Dad did this all the time, and he showed me how to do it. This was not the first time I had done this.

On this occasion I must have tapped it too hard, and instead of it starting and stopping, it kept on going. I should have let go of the paper seal and immediately pulled my hand out, away from the flying "fingers" that were designed to snatch the stationery off the drum after the piece was printed, and deliver it to the other side, dropping it on a receiving shelf. But in one panicky instant I feared Dad would go ballistic if I let go and ruined the seal—as if I could have saved it in any case. No way! Very stupid decision, Robert. As quickly as I could, I jammed the button again to stop it, but it was too late. In that second, one of the "fingers" caught my hand and jammed it into the drum. Other fingers caught my shirt sleeve, tearing it to shreds.

Somehow the machine stopped just prior to amputating my left ring finger and pinky. Across the back of my left hand, crossing above the two fingers diagonally, the sharp steel finger had neatly sliced the skin so the muscles underneath were exposed. A surgeon could not have done a better job. But my hand was now pinned tightly against the drum so that I couldn't move it. It happened so quickly I didn't feel any pain—yet—and now, because the machine had pulled me away from the wheel that turned the drum, I could only touch it with my right-hand fingers. I couldn't budge it. I was truly stuck.

Dad was out of the room at the time. I yelled, "Dad!" as loud as I could, which might not have been very loud at all because of my pain and disorientation.

While waiting for him, with persistence I managed to nudge the wheel backwards a bit. But my fingers were now slippery from sweat. I needed a full hand grip to turn the wheel. My left hand remained a prisoner of the press finger, which remained under my skin where it had sliced its way in. From my sight angle, I couldn't see how to get my hand free. How it didn't damage the muscles…only God knows.

By this time Dad came back in the room. When he saw me struggling, he rushed over, yelling, "For Christ's sake, Robert, what the hell happened?" he started to shout, "I step out of the room and…." By this time he was close enough to see my trapped hand and he stopped yelling. He immediately reached in to help me extricate it from the press.

"Ouch!" I yelled.

He reached down and backed the wheel so that my hand was no longer jammed against the drum, but each move was excruciating. He managed to slip my hand off the press finger. Already noting my white-as-a-sheet face and blurry eyes, he had his other arm around my chest for support.

I leaned back in his arms and drew my hand closer to inspect it. He took a step back holding me tightly. The first thing I noticed was that there wasn't much blood. I looked closer. A flap of it was neatly folded under the adjoining skin like a tucked-in bed sheet, with the muscle tissue underneath fully exposed. When I saw those muscles, I fainted.

Dad gently lowered me to the floor and yelled, "Cricket, get in here, quick!

I was semi-conscious and could hear her voice screaming, "Ja—, what happened? What's Robert doing on the floor?" but it was like a faraway dream.

"Take it easy," Dad said, "he's just fainted. He's going to be all right."

"Fainted? Why? What happened? Is he hurt?"

"He got his hand caught in the press…"

"What? His hand? What happened to it? Will he be able to play the piano again? Why haven't you called the doctor?"

And on it went, but the exchange became a mishmash in my swirling head.

Dad suddenly took charge. "Cricket, get me a towel to wrap his hand in. We have to stop the bleeding." (Apparently, it began bleeding profusely.) He sat me up, and said, "Robert, can you hear me?"

I nodded.

"Look, I'm going to have to take you to the doctor. You need stitches. It doesn't look bad—your hand is still intact. It's just a cut across the back. Seems to have missed a major vein or artery. I don't think anything is seriously wrong, but it's gotta be attended to right away. Don't worry. Can you get up now?"

I nodded weakly, and with his help I got up.

Mom came back with a large cloth and hovered around me like an animal mother licking newborn babies. She gasped when she saw the wound, but didn't say a word.

Silently we all went out to the car, Dad holding me up and guiding me along.

It was a quiet, but tense ride to the doctor's office.

She kept asking, "Robert, are you all right?"

I would nod slowly, afraid my head might fall off. I thought I had lost the use of my left hand forever. I was sure I would never play the piano again, nor would I be able to press the strings of a violin with my left hand ever again. I leaned my head on the window in despair and looked out, tears rolling down my cheeks. At first, everything appeared white. My body shivered and I felt nauseous despite the pleasantly mild day. With my right hand I rolled the window down an inch to let in some fresh air, bracing the towel around the wound against my knee so it wouldn't fall off. My hand began to throb in earnest. I was afraid to look at it—maybe it was bleeding harder, or maybe my ring finger and pinky would fall off right here in the car. What a mess that would be.

That's how it felt, anyway.

Red blotches began to appear on the towel.

The sun seemed to get brighter, and the trees looked a little strange. I squinted at them. They looked pale and pastel, just the way I felt. Were they crying for me, praying that I would be able to play the piano, and maybe even the violin again? Tears flooded my eyes.

Their concern touched me. Thank you, Lord Jesus.

It took seven stiches to close the cut. It healed just fine. Ever after, every time I happened to notice the scar, this story flashed through my mind. Soon after the incident, I was gingerly playing the piano again, thank God. It hurt, but the doc said, "Do it. It'll be good for it."

The violin came later. That scar, unlike the one on my forehead, has remained....

• • • • •

Did I love my dad? I think all of us had a love-hate relationship with him. We loved him just for being husband and dad, but we were all scared of him. His favorite maxim for raising children was "Spare the rod and spoil the child. Doesn't it say so in the Bible?" (See Prov. 13:24)

Mom was our bulwark; we turned to her for comfort. If we wanted something from Dad, we asked her first—so she could pave the way, or grease the pan, whatever. When he raged at us, we sought her for comfort.

I don't ever remember getting genuine comfort from him.

Yet, his good qualities included a sterling work ethic, a good model for us. He had artistic talent, carving his own plates for printing, not an easy job. He was also quite adroit at adding tints to photos for his photography customers, turning black and white prints into color prints, which were very costly in the 1950s, even though Kodacolor had been around since 1944.

How his labor was cheaper than the price of color film, I cannot fathom. Yet, his results were quite impressive. How quaint all this was when compared with today's technology.

He loved to show us how to do whatever he was working on at any given moment, but we couldn't ask too many questions. Talking was *his* domain. With a treasure trove of stories on all manner of subjects, he'd share them with anyone who'd listen, including us kids, of course.

Sometimes he held forth on serious subjects, such as religion and politics. Dad had his own understanding of God and Jesus. No one in the world could follow his logic on religion. At least, that's my observation. The only thing that was clear was that his ideas were the only ones that mattered. He'd become quite frustrated when no one listened to him, and he often would storm out of the room if that happened. He even railed at the television when anyone didn't see things the way he saw them.

Some of his stories were funny. He loved bathroom humor, Mom called them, "off-color jokes." Poop was always a favorite subject, but I'm eternally grateful that I cannot remember any of those. He'd wait for us to laugh. We'd look at each other, embarrassed, then we'd turn crimson and giggle ourselves silly. Then he'd join in.

I remember him teaching me how to clean his hunting rifle. He said it was a "30-awt-6," (I now know this means 30 06). Even though I don't remember what he taught me, I remember it as a positive one-on-one experience.

On another occasion, he took Johnnie and me out to fire an old nineteenth century muzzle-loader, a prized possession of his. But before we left, he showed us how to load it. He poured gunpowder into the muzzle from a horn. I don't remember how he measured it, but I'm sure he was exacting. Next, you tamp it down with the rod from under the gun barrel. This musket had firing caps, a small copper thimble-like thingamajig that you placed over the firing nozzle, which the firing hammer ignited when you pulled the trigger. First make sure the gunpowder was tamped into the rifle so that it touched the firing cap, otherwise it wouldn't fire.

When it was my turn out in the field, I pulled the trigger, and the kick almost knocked me on my fanny. Everybody laughed, including me. You could almost feel the ball rolling out of the barrel. Gunpowder smoke wafted into our nostrils and made us sneeze.

The rifle was so heavy it was very awkward to hold straight, especially for a kid. Many a grown man could not have held it still enough to fire straight.

21

Anyway, as we all watched the ball spiraling though the air, nowhere near the target, it eventually bounced off a tree. We all burst out laughing, none more than Dad.

By the time I reached my teens, Dad had run out of options for an heir to the business. I was it. I think it was because of this, he spent so much time cajoling me to join him. I finally did, because I thought I could turn Dad's business into something quite grand once it was in my hands.

He invested all his efforts into grooming me to take it over. After learning the fundamentals of the shop, he started taking me along on sales calls to customers. On the way, he would lecture me about how to close a deal. But when we got to our destinations, I was embarrassed by his shyness and inability to do what he had instructed me to do. His own mantra was, "Practice what you preach," but somehow he couldn't follow his own advice. That disappointed me, and at the time, really ticked me off. How could he presume to teach me what he couldn't do himself? The reason I was so angry was that I feared for the business I would inherit. Would it be in shambles?

A typical impromptu sales call went something like this:

We'd enter an office or showroom where our prospect was. Dad typically wore casual brown khaki trousers, or even his work pants. At least he took the trouble to change into a clean blue sport shirt. I too had on a freshly laundered sports shirt with my usual dungarees and sneakers, de rigueur dress for teenagers of the day.

"Oh, hello, Mr. Schaeffer. How are you today?" Dad asked without smiling or taking Mr. Schaeffer's proffered hand. Mr. Schaeffer smoothly placed both hands on his hips. He was dressed in a dark blue business suit with a conservative, light blue and yellow patterned tie. White shirt—a must in those days. He appeared to be well-coiffed and manicured. I also spotted a large diamond ring on his right hand; a solid gold wedding band on the left. When we got closer, I noticed his Fabergé fragrance.

This clearing house showcased a wide variety of products, from clothes to household appliances. Sales people were busily talking to clients or checking the shelves for who knows what. The hum of activity suggested a lucrative and well-run enterprise. I was impressed.

"Jack, how nice to see you. Is this your son?" he asked, nodding to me. "He looks like you."

Suddenly Dad appeared stage-struck. He didn't speak for a moment, apparently unable to make up his mind what to do next. He looked toward me, held out a hand toward me, and said, "Ah, well, yes, this is my son, Robert. Ah, Mr. Schaeffer, do you need any printing today?"

"Printing? So sudden, Jack? Can't you lead into it a little more…gently?" said Mr. Schaeffer, with a jovial air of confidence. He pointed to a round table in a corner of the large area, surrounded by chairs, presumably for guests. He moved toward the table signaling us to follow. Dad just stood there, watching him. I stepped in behind him, motioning Dad to follow with me. He scowled, but slowly complied.

As we stepped toward the room, I began to notice more details: pictures and posters of their products on the walls, and stacks of shelves with goods for retailers to examine. There were also cubicles scattered around the entire floor with clerks and other sales folks scurrying back and forth, some talking on telephones, others with customers. Large appliances stood in lines.

"Hey, c'mon in and sit down a spell." Looking at Dad sympathetically, he said, "You look tired, Jack." He scanned Dad as one would a small child, and with a grand smile, chimed, "Hey, how about a *good* cup of coffee, umm?" Mr. Schaeffer laughed, more to lighten the scene than anything else, I thought. "You must try our latest variety of Folger's."

Dad loved coffee, but he just stood there, looking rather morose, goodness knows why. "Ah, no, Mr. Schaeffer, we, uh, are on a tight schedule today…. Is there anything I can get for you? Business cards? Order forms? Stationery?"

"My goodness, Jack, you're all business, aren't you?" Mr. Schaeffer whirled around to locate a lovely middle-aged woman on the other side of the room, signaled her to bring us coffee. He turned to us, "Can't I have Grace get you a cup of coffee, Jack? Com'on, sit down. Please." He stepped over to me and offered his hand, which I took enthusiastically, a wide grin flashed across my face. "How about you, son. What was your name?"

"Just call me Bob. It's easier than Robert," I smiled and shrugged my shoulders.

Mr. Schaeffer chuckled and affectionately clapped me on the shoulder. Dad scowled.

Was he jealous? I couldn't figure out what Dad's problem was. I was doing what he had told me to do. What's this behavior all about?

"Bob it is," Mr. Schaeffer said, and robustly shook my hand. Again he grandly motioned us both to sit at the table so we could talk. I started for the table, smiling at Mr. Schaeffer to acknowledge his hospitality.

Dad caught my arm before I could sit, and said hastily, "We have to go. We've got a lot o' stops to make. C'mon Robert." He turned and started for the door.

My eyes followed Dad for a second, then I turned to Mr. Schaeffer. I opened my palms and grimaced with an expression that said, *What can I do?*

Mr. Schaeffer looked totally bewildered, his eyes following Dad. He turned to me, his ruffled eyebrows saying, *What's going on?*

I looked at him sympathetically and returned his questioning gestures. I glanced back at Dad, who by this time was already pushing his way through the front door. Fearing he might leave me behind to walk home—to teach me a lesson, I turned back to Mr. Schaeffer and said softly, "I'm very sorry, sir." I sadly shrugged again, and turned to jog after Dad, waving a hand back at the befuddled salesman as I went through the door.

This story is a composite of several sales calls Dad and I went on. One can readily see why Dad was not a successful businessman. Fortunately, enough people knew Dad through the church and through other contexts that he managed to make a living. For example, he did a lot of printing for Johnny Yost, an undertaker, a good friend of the family. People like Johnny understood Dad as an excellent artisan in his field, so they overlooked his inhospitable manner and became solid customers whom Dad served for many years.

But when it came to selling to new, potential customers, Dad seemed incapable of following his own advice. I was totally unschooled in how to sell anything, but I instinctively knew that Dad was a total bust at this. You simply can't treat people this way. I wanted to help Dad understand this, but he could *never* hear suggestions from me. In his own words, he'd "cloud up and rain all over me."

My future was not with the J. B. Mitchell Printing Co.

• • • • •

Looking back on my childhood and early religious training as I see it today, a major shortcoming—in my not-as-humble-as-it-should-be opinion—was that we learned *about* the Bible, rather than study the Bible itself. Oh yes, we learned many stories, but from approved Sunday school pamphlets and workbooks, as well as through toys and games, but we rarely opened a Bible. When we did, it was typically to learn the names of the books or some such mechanical exercise. Now and again we memorized some verses, but I don't recall ever looking them up in the Bible, nor reading the stories from the Bible itself.

My thesis is that Bibles are to be read and studied so that students become familiar with its structure and contents. The Bible is difficult reading, no question, but today there are many translations designed for young people. Growing up on them guides the young reader towards reading the "real thing."

Perhaps my discomfort about the way we educate kids foreshadowed my seminary understanding of God's Word. One of the greatest lessons I learned was that the Bible is more than a book. As one sage[6] said, the Bible is the only document ever written that asks the reader to answer yes or no to its content. A "yes" leads to eternal life; a "no" does not. There's no *maybe*, or *I'll think about it*. You simply cannot walk away from the Bible without making that choice. Nor can you claim that the Bible is "just literature," as many claim, comparing it to Shakespeare and other great bards. To take such a position is tantamount to saying "no" to it, according to Professor Weber (see footnote).

This is why it's so vital to teach children the Bible itself, and to encourage them to read it. For me, to approach the Bible spiritually and contemplatively is to touch God, and to be touched by God. John 1:1, for example, refers to God as *The Word*, also a word for Christ later in scripture. Reading God's Word evokes the same tactile experience we have with the Communal bread and wine—His body, the bread—His blood, the wine, as well as the baptismal waters that have cleansed our souls. This awareness deeply moves me.

---

[6] Professor Otto Weber, a twentieth century German theologian. See his Foundations of Dogmatics, Volume I, Wm. B. Eerdmans Publishing Co., Grand Rapids, MI., reprinted 1988. Translated by Darrell L. Guder, p. 247. The original German text was first published in 1955 in Neukirchen, Deutschland.

Children need to learn that kind of reverence for the Bible, to absorb it into their beings, and to live it. Such a feeling would replace the childhood attitude of thinking of the Bible as a talisman. As a child I was terrified to let a Bible touch the floor, much less drop it. Now I see how irrelevant such a fear is.

• • • • •

Chapter Three

Music of the Spheres

By the time I was in the sixth grade, a new boy named David Wolfe showed up at both Trinity Methodist Church and Roosevelt Elementary School. He and his widowed mother had moved to Lock Haven from Renovo, several miles up the Susquehanna River. She had remarried—her name was now Mrs. Watkins.

I had always looked forward to being in Mrs. Nye's sixth grade class because I had heard great things about her from older students now in Junior High School. I had also seen her in school assemblies, and scurrying around the halls, always with a smile and a friendly greeting to students and teachers alike. She even stopped to talk to me once, "Oh, Bob, I'm so looking forward to having you in my class next fall." How did she know my name? No one had ever greeted me like that before, so naturally, I was thrilled.

We all arrived at school on a muggy September morning, the heavy air full of dampness and gloom, smelling a bit like an old shoe pulled out of a creek. Despite our clingy clothes and dank skin, there was a certain excitement, a whiff of expectation in the air for what the sixth grade and Mrs. Nye might have in store for us.

Dave stood out because he was new, tall, and thin with rather thick glasses. He also was wearing a sweater, totally not needed, so it drew the attention of the class bully, Tom, as I recall his name. I didn't notice Dave arrive because I was busy loading school supplies into my desk. Tom was also in his seat, about three desks to my right, but always quick off the mark, started making cracks about David as soon as he walked in. "Another skinny-looking brain. That's all we need. Cheez!" and "Where'd he come from, Mars?" His buddies laughed.

Anybody new for a jerk like Tom clicks on his diabolical side. When Dave took off his sweater and hung it on the coatrack, his thin, sheet-colored arms seemed to shine. Tom pointed at him, encouraging his buddies to join him, and giggled, "What a skinflint!" They laughed maliciously. But the buzz and commotion in the room all but drowned out this pathetic sideshow.

Dave acted as if he hadn't heard, but you could see in his eyes he had, and it stung. He recovered quickly with a knowing smile. He seemed to be logging his attacker into his mental computer bank. As he located his seat in the back of the room, one of Tom's henchmen sitting on the end of a row stuck out a foot to trip Dave, but his long legs stepped over it. He sat down in the last row, next to the end seat, from which he surveyed the entire room.

Tom, from his seat toward the middle of the room, began making faces at him.

When Dave looked up and saw him, he burst out laughing as a child would at a circus clown. He pointed at Tom. Other kids looked at Tom to see what had triggered Dave's sudden mirth.

Tom abruptly stopped with so many eyes on him. His light complexion reddened, drawing attention to his tawny hair and freckles. He quickly swung around facing front mumbling something like, "I'll git you for this."

At this point Mrs. Nye, who had been occupied with a pile of papers on her desk, suddenly stood up. Had she seen the interchange between David and Tom? Who knows? She announced in a commanding voice, "Good morning Sixth Grade! I'm delighted to see so many bright faces this morning. You know why? Because we're going to have fun this year." Her sparkling blue eyes swept around the room with a dazzling smile, causing most of us to smile in return.

Tom still had a puss on.

Mrs. Nye's gaze stopped on him. "Tom? What's the matter?" (Actually, she *had* seen what had transpired between Dave and him. She knew a bully when she saw one.)

"Nuthin," muttered Tom.

"Oh? That's not what I saw just now—when a new student came into the room."

Tom fidgeted, trying to make his body language say, "So what?"

Dave's cheeks turned a little pink.

"Do you two know each other?"

Both boys shook their heads.

"Well then, both of you stand up and face each other." A pause. "Come on, do it," she said more firmly.

Both boys rose.

"Face each other."

Tom slowly turned back to face David.

"Tom, meet David. David, meet Tom," she chimed with a beaming face.

At this point, David stepped away from his desk and quickly took giant steps to Tom's desk, extending his hand to him with a broad grin. "Glad to meet you, Tom," as he took Tom's reluctant and somewhat limp hand in his. Noting Tom's hesitation, he added with a grin, "I mean it—I'm really glad to meet you."

Tom sat down, looked up at him, and as they shook hands, he smiled without speaking, but his eyes said, *Hey, maybe you're an okay guy after all*.

Mrs. Nye beamed. A potential conflict had just been averted.

Or had it?

In warm weather Dave wore colorful patterned short-sleeved shirts. In winter, he came to school bundled in a parka with a matching fabric hat, his glasses steamed over. His long fingers might suggest that he played the piano. He did, actually.

Because David didn't react as the class bullies expected him to, they soon left him alone.

As the weeks went by, we all—including Mrs. Nye—noticed how bright David was. He liked science, math, music, history, and English, and quickly led the class in all academic areas. He was conscientious about his studies, as I was, and we soon gravitated to each other.

His awesome knowledge of so many subjects impressed me. He could also articulate what he read, as well as explain complex ideas in simple language. I felt inferior to him in the beginning, and braced for the razzing that I expected to receive from other students, as well as my father, brothers, and sisters,

"David's smarter than you-u-u!"

But David didn't flaunt his knowledge; he shared it. If I didn't know or understand something, he explained it in such a way that I was eager to let him do so. He never rubbed my nose in my ignorance. I rose to the challenge and began to express my ideas and knowledge of the science projects we were working on, to which he would respond, "Yes, but…" or "That's interesting," or "Well, if that's true, how do you explain such-and-so?"

• • • • •

Growing up in homes where saying grace at meals and praying at bedtime were mandatory, along with going to church on Sundays, David and I were oblivious to the current religious and political battles that deeply divided science and religion. Science for us was simply a way to better understand God's creation, and indeed, to provide a window into the mind of God, hazy as it may be. We were concerned more with the question of *how* God created the universe, rather than the question of *why* God created it. We also did not ask if God actually existed. For us, God just *was*.

• • • • •

Through his influence I began to read more, and discovered the joy of reading encyclopedias, science books, and journals. I would ask him, "How do you explain what I read in so-and-so…?" That triggered a dialogue that enriched both of us.

One day we were walking to his apartment after school, he having invited me to supper, after which we had planned to work on a school science project. I said something that elicited the response, "But Bob, that's a *non sequitur*."

"A non-*what*?" I looked at him quizzically.

"Oh!" he said, realizing I didn't understand those words. "That's a philosophical term that means, 'it doesn't follow.' It's Latin. Philosophy, like math and science, must obey certain rules. *Non sequitur* is one such rule. Are you familiar with syllogistic logic?"

"No," I said, shaking my head. The November breeze felt good in my face. The leaves had already turned brown and were floating down like a gentle snowfall. I caught one in the air.

"Well, you may have seen that if $a = b$, and $b = c$, therefore, a must also = c." David absently brushed away a leaf that had stuck to his heavy sweater.

"I never heard that, but it sounds logical." I examined my leaf closely.

"Okay. So, if someone insists that a does *not have* to equal c, then we'd say that's a *non sequitur*, because it's been proven mathematically that a does indeed equal c. Understand?"

"Yes," I said, as my finger traced the veins of the leaf. "But does this only work for math?"

"No, this principle applies to any kind of logic. Say, for instance, that someone says it's going to be sunny outside. You ask, 'How do you know?' They say, 'Because I just won the lottery.' The logical question is, 'How can the lottery affect the weather?' Logically and practically it cannot. Scientifically speaking, we need more reliable indicators that predict the weather. Actually, this person is telling us how he feels. It's more a poetic statement than a logical or scientific one. Do you follow what I'm saying?" He turned to me.

"Sure." I stopped walking and held my leaf up to the light to see how the veins looked. The leaf, from a maple tree, had turned brown around the edges, but still had reddish-orange colors arrayed in the center. David stopped to watch what I was doing. I offered it to him with a smile. "Here's a thank you for your friendship and guidance. I want you to know how much I value both. Sorry about the brown edges."

David beamed and chuckled as he delicately grasped the stem with two fingers. I thought he would simply cast it away as we walked on, but he stopped, reached into his pocket, and pulled out a handkerchief. He carefully placed the leaf in it and wrapped it as though it were a precious pocket watch, making sure it remained flat. As he carefully slid it into a large side pocket of his sweater, he smiled at me and said, "Thank you. How about some hot soup?"

We enjoyed many such walks and talks. My *true* education began with his friendship, for he taught me that education is not about facts, but how you arrive at facts, and the methodology for solving problems. Einstein once said when someone asked him for his phone number, "I don't know. I never clutter my mind with facts that can be looked up. I use my mind for thinking." Education ideally is the process of learning how to think logically and reflectively. Computers only store and provide information.

Mrs. Nye began to see David and me as a team. She encouraged us in every way, and singled us out as "leaders," her word. I was surprised to be included, imagining my father's cynicism, "You have to be a follower first, before you can become a leader," he'd say with emphasis on the first *you* and the word *leader*. She assigned us science projects for the class because she knew we had already formed our own science study partnership, operating out of David's apartment in downtown Lock Haven.

Mrs. Nye enthusiastically endorsed a project we undertook that grew out of our excitement over the 1950 Oscar-winning film, *Destination Moon*. This movie set us on our own course of space exploration. "Why don't you boys prepare several projects on rocket design, fuel options, and flight trajectories, and landing on the moon? The class would love it."

"Wow!" we said almost in unison. We looked and each other. Broad grins bounced back and forth. "Sure, we can do that. C'mon, let's get busy."

We centered our attention on how to get to the moon. Exploring it would come later, although in fact, we never got that far. Getting there was our challenge.

David's bedroom shelves were crammed with advanced texts. Today he'd probably be accepted into special college programs for kids. No such opportunities existed then. I felt like Dr. Watson to his Sherlock Holmes, running to keep up with him. Sometimes I felt quite stupid, and certainly ignorant, but he never made me feel that way. Rather, he always treated me as an equal.

Our first challenge was to draw up plans for a rocket. We discussed at great length Werner von Braun's V-2 rocket design used in *Destination Moon*. I said, "you know, Dave, I've always thought the V-2 rather inefficient because of its egg-shaped middle. Seems to me it should be nail-shaped, so the wind would not be forced away from the controlling fins in the back. That way they could be much smaller, reducing drag. I know everyone these days favors the V-2 shape."

Indeed, decades later, the Apollo rockets would bear out my thinking. We, of course, had only paper, pencils, and our eleven-year-old imaginations to test our theories. Along with David's books, of course.

One Saturday, as we sat conferring in David's room, his laboratory, he asked,

"Why take off straight up in the air?" He shot a hand straight up. "Imagine the energy that consumes, pushing directly against gravity, not to mention atmospheric drag. More energy requires more fuel. Liquid fuel is heavy, making the entire load exponentially heavier. What if we could use gravity in combination with the rocket's own inertia?" He leaned back in his chair, smiling at his new idea.

"How?" I asked, looking him straight in the eye. I could not conceive what he was proposing. Rockets always took off straight up. What other choice was there? I leaned toward him expectantly. I knew he'd thought this idea through, "So tell me what you have in mind."

David stood up, facing me. He held out his right arm with his elbow bent, palm down in front of him, pretending his arm was the rocket. He swept it down and then back up in a continuous motion, at the end of which his hand and arm were pointing up to the sky.

With his hands leading the way, he said, "I propose we lay the rocket on a dolly mounted on a track of some sort, and get it moving horizontally, then down a steep incline. The middle section of the track would curve back up a hill so that the last section of track points straight up toward the sky. That way, we could take advantage of the rocket's own weight, its inertia plus gravity, to help power the liftoff. Also, the rocket would be leaving the ground at a significant speed instead of a standstill. Its inertia would help overcome gravity faster and more efficiently." He stopped to look at me for my reaction.

I jumped to my feet and paced the room, imagining his scenario. "Yes, I see what you mean," I said. Also using my hands to demonstrate, I went on, "So, you mean, like, if we found two mountains separated by a valley…like joining two ski slopes across a smooth valley floor from one another."

"Yes…" David beamed in agreement.

I was on a roll. "We could place the rocket on the top of one mountain, run it down the slope, and back up the side of the other mountain with enough speed for a smooth lift off. That's brilliant, David."

We stood facing each other for a moment, eyes bright with excitement. Spontaneously, each of us clasped the other's hand and shook it vigorously, laughing like the schoolboys we were.

Of course, we didn't have the resources to test our theories and designs, but David got right to work on both the math and the physics of these ideas. We also discussed them at length that day and at future meetings.

The following year, 1951, we jumped up and down in jubilation when another space movie came out, *When Worlds Collide*, which had a take-off system much like the one we had dreamed up the year before. We felt vindicated and saluted each other with another fervent handshake. Not bad for a couple of twelve-year-olds!

A week or so later, David said, "Bob, I came up with another idea since last time. If we were to use solid fuel instead of liquid fuel, it would be much safer and more efficient. We need to do more research, but I think it's considerably lighter than liquid fuel, and certainly much easier and safer to store than liquid fuel, not to mention loading it into the rocket itself. Surely it would be less costly overall."

His idea was supported many years later in the solid rocket components used in the Space Shuttle Program.

One afternoon, we were working on getting the right chemical mixture for the solid fuel, using David's chemistry set, when we mixed a small portion of magnesium with potassium nitrate on a test dish. He smiled proudly as he set a match to it, "Here goes!"

The resulting explosion knocked us both to the floor.

I yelled, "Holy sh—!" catching my unwanted cussing. I began to cough. "Let's get out of here." The smoke stifled me. My eyes began to tear. Yet in my panic I froze to the spot.

"Open some windows," David shouted.

I shook myself into action and ran to the nearest one and threw it open as Dave scurried out of the room. I headed for the bathroom to try to get the smoke out of my throat. I spit into the toilet, then grabbed the tumbler to gargle and swallow some cold water. I bolted out to look for him.

He was opening windows in the living room. "Quick, Bob, go into the kitchen and open that window. Maybe the cross breeze will drive the smoke out of my room."

I flew into action. Then I heard the clatter of bucket and mop. Dave arrived in the kitchen and headed for the sink. "I think we'll need these," he commented wryly. "See if you can find some old towels in the closet over there," he said, pointing. He ran some water into the bucket.

"Will these do?"

"I guess so. Let's see what the room looks like."

Much to our dismay, the explosion had left a telltale black smudge from the wall to the ceiling, filling the entire apartment with smoke. Our hearts pounded with a combination of exultation and foreboding. At first we looked at each other without speaking, *We did it!*

Then, almost instantly, *Omigosh, what have we done?*

We knew that the power released had "solved" the solid fuel problem, but we faced a more immediate predicament. If there had been smoke detectors at that time, we would have been standing before an angry fire official trying to explain what we had been up to.

David abruptly left the room and came back with a portable fan. We set it up hoping to drive away the lingering smoke before Dave's mother came home. Then we set to work scrubbing and wiping as if we could hear Mrs. Watkins climbing the steps to the apartment.

A week or so after the experiment, Mrs. Watkins invited me to have lunch with them. From her voice on the phone, I figured she didn't suspect a thing. However, during our meal she alluded to indoor experiments that could be dangerous. David and I exchanged surreptitious glances that said, "She knows!" But why was she being so understanding about it?

· · · · ·

Recently, I got in touch with David to ask him if he remembered what happened.

"Oh, yes indeed," he said.

"What did your mother say?" I asked, hardly able to keep my excitement in check, both for reaching Dave by phone, but also to be speaking with my friend with whom I had lost touch for nearly forty-five years.

"I don't remember exactly," he began cautiously, "but she was surprisingly subdued about it. I was more concerned about what my stepfather would have done." Dave felt his mother's soft-pedaled approach had protected us from his stepfather's wrath.

"But *how* did she know?" I could hardly contain my curiosity.

"Twelve-year-olds don't clean as well as we thought we did."

•　•　•　•　•

Another interest David and I shared was music. For me, music is God's own special gift to us. Neither Dave nor I had any thoughts about becoming musicians, or even pastors back then, but we lost ourselves in music when we weren't occupied with science projects. It was Dave who introduced me to classical music, which was just a word to me at that time. I had no idea of the treasures to be found in it. We spent many hours together listening to classical LP recordings on Sunday afternoons in his grandparents' apartment.

He introduced me to composers I didn't know, such as Debussy and Ravel, and performers of whom I had never heard, such as pianist Walter Gieseking, a Debussy master, and numerous symphony orchestras and conductors. Interestingly, no singers—Dave was not into opera or singing, other than choral music. My fascination for that came later. To this day, I have the LP recording of Debussy favorites played by Gieseking that David gave me one year for Christmas. I measure all other pianists who play Debussy by this recording.

Another favorite was Tchaikovsky. We listened to his symphonies and orchestral pieces, such as *Capriccio Italien*. Also Rimsky-Korsakov's *Capriccio Espagnol*. Then there were the impressionists: *Daphnis et Chloé* of Ravel, *La Mer*, *Nocturnes*, and *Prélude à l'après-midi d'un faune* by Debussy, and others.

Before David, I didn't know what a piano concerto was. Rachmaninoff's famous Second Piano Concerto became my all-time favorite—when played sensitively, it always moves me to tears, especially the second movement.

Then there were Schumann, Chopin, and Grieg.

What a musical incubator those afternoons were for me! I loved them.

Listening to music like that, either alone or with a friend, always draws me closer to God. Music transports me to another realm, sometimes sacred, sometimes romantic, sometimes introspective, and sometimes festive.

Music shaped my understanding of everything, including God.

• • • • •

In my high school years, I had a job in a drugstore in downtown Lock Haven, and I earned the money to buy my first hi-fi phonograph. But first I wanted to understand more about the new technology of "high fidelity." Uncle Vin and Aunt Kay, who lived in New York City, were coming to visit next Christmas, and I couldn't wait to ask Uncle Vin about it. He was my mother's baby brother, the favorite of all her siblings. After serving in the Army, Uncle Vin used his radio training to become a radio technician for the Radio Corporation of America in New York. There he fell in love with a stunningly beautiful Jewish woman, who became my Aunt Kay. Some of our extended family shunned her because she was Jewish. She was always my favorite aunt because of her liveliness, intelligence, great sense of humor, and exceptional kindness. Both of them made me feel important, and worthy of respect. I treasure their memory.

New York City was the City of Oz to us Mitchells in Pennsylvania, as none of us had ever been there. So when the Trautmans came to town, it was an *event*. They dressed in fancy clothes and drove the latest model car. My dad's cars were typically ten years old.

When Mom told Johnnie and me they were coming for Christmas, we whooped and hollered for joy.

"Now, listen, you guys, I don't want you picking on your cousin, Paul, y'-hear?" Mom warned.

Paul was younger than both of us, and we considered him to be fat. We teased him mercilessly about it—I don't know why. Maybe it was because we were skinny, being poor. We thought he lived an uppity life because they were rich. *I mean you have to be rich to live in New York City, don't you?* Paul always had anything he wanted. We considered him spoiled—so we picked on him, just because we could, I guess.

Actually, we were stupid to treat him that way, because hurting his feelings didn't make us feel any better. I suppose we *believed* we felt better, but we knew deep down inside, it wasn't so. Nevertheless, we justified ourselves by looking at him as one bad rich kid vs. all us poor relations, you know, the proud-to-be-poor syndrome.

That December had been a rough one—for grown-ups anyway, Jack Frost piling snow upon snow on us. We loved it—sled-riding, snowball battles, hiking in the woods. By Christmas, the weather had brightened, but the heavy snow was still piled up next to the driveway the day the Trautmans came to visit. We listened for tires crunching as if waiting for Santa Claus himself to arrive.

"Wow, they're here!" Johnnie and I ran to the back door to greet them. They pulled into a space in the backyard where Dad had cleared snow for their car.

Cousin Paul got out first, and we stared awkwardly at each other.

"Hi, Paul. How are you?" We took turns shaking his hand.

"Tired after that trip. It's a long way here," he grumbled. Casting his eyes around disdainfully, he continued, "You have snow. A *lot* of snow...." His voice trailed off as he gazed around at the trees and buildings festooned with the white stuff.

"Yeah.... Hey, you wanna go sleddin'?" Johnnie asked excitedly. He and I nodded in agreement and ran to the porch for the sleds.

"I'm not dressed for that," Paul said, standing his ground. "Besides, in New York, it's always cleared away for us. Our streets are clean. We don't have it all piled up all over the place like here," he said, pointing around the yard and out to Chestnut Street. "If *we* want to go sledding, there are plenty of places to go...."

Always the jibes. By this time he had lost our attention. He loved to look down on us country rubes because New York was the greatest city in the world. Lock Haven was just a small dump, as far as he was concerned. We always imagined he lived in a grand house on a grand street, much as we saw in old movies, and Paul knew he could impress us with all the great happenings in New York. Everything was better there than here. He kept that image alive.

Then Aunt Kay stepped out of the car, strikingly lovely, decked out in a long, furry black coat with a matching hat, looking to me like a goddess from heaven. Her lips were bright red, enhancing the sparkling blue eyes with long lashes, a touch of makeup. She looked as if she had just stepped out of a fashion magazine. I was riveted, catching her radiant smile that melted me right into the snow.

"Rob-et," she called me in her New York accent, "look how big you've gotten!"

She walked right up, eying me up and down. I didn't know whether to shake her hand or hug her. We're not a hugging family, and Mom had told me a lady should offer her hand first. She didn't, but her rare beauty and smile mesmerized me. I wanted more than anything to embrace her, kiss her as in the movies, but, as a gangly adolescent, looking up at a woman so glamorous and taller than I, well, I just stood there, tongue-tied and blushing.

Just then, Uncle Vin got out of the car and sauntered over to us, grinning from ear to ear. He was about Aunt Kay's height, but wider than her slim frame. A warm, brown Cossack hat gave him a few more inches. His long over-coat matched the color of his hat and his twinkling eyes as he stepped forward to greet Johnnie and me.

He shook hands with both of us. By this time, Joan and Cissie appeared. Uncle Vin and Aunt Kay greeted them both warmly. When Mom came out on the porch, Uncle Vin looked up and called to his sister, "Hi, Cricket!" waving both arms energetically in the air. Aunt Kay also looked up and waved at her, and said, "Oh, Cricket, it's so good to see you again!"

By now, Dad joined the entire Mitchell clan to welcome our visitors, with greetings and kisses and "so-good-to-see-you" all around. My two sisters were never shy about hugging. That gave me the opportunity to get my hug from Aunt Kay.

"Come on in, you guys, it's too cold to be standing out here," Mom shouted as she returned to the porch. With a welcoming smile, she turned and waved an arm for all to come in.

And the presents they brought! That year I got my first and only-ever pair of rabbit-skin, fur-lined gloves. I still have them—they haven't fit me for years, but I could never bear to part with them.

•   •   •   •   •

The temperature had dropped the day after Christmas as I was sitting with Uncle Vin at the kitchen table. Everyone else had scattered by then. The windows' frosting glazed a silhouette of fanciful trees and sparkles that caught my imagination. We had just eaten lunch, and the hot cocoa still simmering on the stove smelled so good. The steaming mug warmed my hands as did its contents my insides.

Uncle Vin, sitting opposite me, had the Trautman family face, with a prominent nose and brown eyes. Every hair in place, slicked across the top of his head. His brown-rimmed glasses made him look professorial. He smiled at me and said, "So, Robert, what did you want to talk to me about?"

"What should I look for in a hi-fi record player? I've saved up enough money for one, but I don't know what to look for—or listen for. Can you help me?"

He got up from his place and came around to my side of the table, bringing a chair with him. "Is there some paper I can write on?"

I quickly ran into the shop and lifted a piece of stationery. I set it in front of Uncle Vin.

"This will do fine," he said, taking a mechanical pencil from his pocket. "You see, Robert, the latest sound technology is called, 'infinite baffle.'" He then skillfully drew diagrams to illustrate his explanation.

This was a moment of adult caring I rarely experienced in my life. He made me feel important as a person by treating me as an equal. To this day, I recall the warm bond that developed between us from this time together, a moment I'll never forget.

His lesson was clear enough for me to buy myself a hi-fi phonograph.

Unfortunately, my memory of the rest of the visit has long since faded, or melded into others. I do remember that we all had a good time, eating special Christmas meals, going for walks and sledding in the deep snow in the woods, singing around the piano, Paul playing his guitar and singing for us, having snowball battles, and skating on the river or ponds, whichever was the safest. I'm filled with good feelings about that time whenever I think of it.

After the holidays, the Trautmans returned to New York, also glad they had come.

Armed with Uncle Vin's diagrams and explanations, I set out for downtown Lock Haven to purchase my first LP record player, or phonograph. The sales person quickly corrected me, saying it was a "High Fidelity Phonograph." David had already contributed to my store of knowledge by suggesting a Zenith, but I decided on a Philco because I liked its sound better.

With my purchase, I was the envy of everyone in my family. I broke it in with the Gieseking LP from David.

* * * * *

Christmastide always invokes music to me. I don't mean the radio's endless repetitions of Gene Autry and Berl Ives singing secular Christmas hits, but rather, the music that touches the soul, reminding us of the Birth of the Savior and what that means to Christian believers. I wrote the following ode to music and science out of a deep thanksgiving for all of God's creative activity, both present and past:

Music and science are gifts from God to help us to appreciate God's creation. Music of the spheres speaks to the depth of the soul, bringing us into God's presence. Science helps us to understand and appreciate God's Creation. Both bless and enrich us.

When I hear the jangling, clanging, pounding, rhythmical music that draws most people to it, I feel the physical, earthy excitement to which they respond, but I lament the loss of contemplation and beauty that classical music offers. Sometimes in the car, I can't find a classical music station, and I sorely miss the soaring melody of a violin, the plaintive answer of an oboe, and the sparkling power of a brass instrument. I also long for the harmonies and multi-faceted structures of classical music, and the ability of a choir to touch our innermost selves. Pounding rock rhythms force me into a place I don't want to go, so I promptly turn the radio off.

I love jazz and "oldies" like Frank Sinatra, Tony Bennett, and Ella Fitzgerald, as well as modern singers like Josh Groban and Audra McDonald because they sing rich melodies and draw us into the song's story and our innermost feelings. They have pleasant voices, smooth melodic lines, and they sing so that I understand every word. That's important to me.

It's Christmas time as I write these words, and bitterly cold outside. The hymn, "In the Bleak Midwinter" comes to mind. The words were written by the nineteenth century poet, Christina Rossetti. In the early twentieth century, composer Gustav Holst, set Rossetti's words to music, and it became a standard in Christian hymnals. In the 1980s, British composer, John Rutter, created a touching choral arrangement of the hymn, which can be heard on his 1987 CD release, *Christmas Night.*

"In the Bleak Midwinter" lifts me to another time and place. Listen to the exquisite words of her third verse:

What can I give him, poor as I am?
If I were a shepherd I would bring a lamb;
If I were a wise man I would do my part;
Yet what I can I give him?—give my heart.

The immediacy of the words paints a picture that draws us in by the use of the first person. The word *poor* evokes the street urchins and lower class so well depicted in *A Christmas Carol* by Charles Dickens, who was Rossetti's contemporary.

Or it can remind us of ourselves in its spiritual sense.

Rossetti weaves the Christmas symbols *shepherd*, *lamb*, and *wise man* into her compact text, again with the use of the first person. The last line invites us to do our part to serve others, while giving our heart to Him who is mentioned but once in the entire poem. What can we give Him, but ourselves?

What music in her words!

These immortal words joined with Holst's setting melt even the hardest of hearts. Mr. Rutter's arrangement renders the last line with long, sustained notes that die away, bringing tears to my eyes.

What poetry in this music!

Music of the spheres has formed and shaped who I am, and I live humbly in awe of this precious, powerful gift. It inspires me, soothes me, and lifts me into His very presence.

It saddens me that so many people have never discovered these riches. The Apostle Paul says that he becomes a noisy gong and a clanging cymbal without God's love (1 Cor. 13). If music is only about rhythm, we lose the total gift. God surely must weep.

• • • • •

On sunny summer afternoons, David and I often took hikes in the woods. He seemed to know every plant and bush, and particularly whether or not it was edible. Given that most of them were inedible, we always had little packets of peanut butter crackers for munching. I generally carried a backpack with outdoor paraphernalia and a canteen of water.

As we strolled through the cool woods and sun-stifling fields, we discussed a wide range of subjects.

By this time, David had left Trinity Methodist because Mrs. Watkins felt that David needed more Bible-centered nourishment. Not knowing how his new church differed from ours, I asked him about it as I trailed along behind him down a narrow path.

"Oh, yes," he began, stepping carefully over a nasty root across the trail. Pointing to it for my benefit, he continued, "We now attend First Baptist Church over on Church Street. My mother felt it was closer, but more importantly, it's Bible-centered."

"What does that mean?" I asked, shooing away a cloud of mosquitoes.

"Well, it's very different from Trinity Methodist. You know that what we learned in Trinity's Sunday school were mostly *stories*. Where were the Bibles? Everything was in workbooks and other types of materials. We have study materials, too, but most of what we do comes directly from the Bible. And we have to memorize a lot of Bible verses."

"Why?" I asked. Just then we came out of the woods into a large meadow, stretching out before us. The grass was waist-high, the flying bugs a nuisance. As I swatted at them, we paused, considering which way to go. I noticed that David ignored them. They didn't seemed to bother him at all. Maybe it was me and my fussiness about getting stung that made me overreact. The grassy fragrance wafting off the field helped me to forget about them. I took off my cap to wipe my brow. At the bottom of the field I spotted a gate and pointed to it. "Do you know where we are?" I asked.

David looked in the direction of my finger, and spotting the gate, he said, "One of the reasons we memorize verses is to know where we *are* in the Bible— just like we want to know where we are right now. Actually, I don't know, but that gate, sometimes like a pertinent Bible verse, can point to the path we should take. Let's see where it leads." And he started plowing through the tall grass in that direction. I followed, again batting at the bugs while trying to stifle my annoyance.

He continued, "Learning verses is mostly to train the mind—a good mental discipline. Plus, many people feel knowing Bible verses helps in times of trouble. Or when you're lost."

"Are we lost?" I said with a phony fright in my voice, because I had just realized where we were, but I didn't know if David knew. I thought I'd keep it to myself for a while to see if he'd figure it out.

"The important point is that without studying the Bible directly, we can never truly understand what it means to be a Christian," he said.

"How so?"

This began a spiritual dialogue between us that took us to the gate, and has lasted for decades. When he realized the field we crossed led back to the road we just had been on, which led back home, Dave said, "Oh."

"Know where you are now?" I asked with an excessive smile.

"Of course," he said, turning away from me, and stomping away towards home so that I wouldn't see how red his face was.

•   •   •   •   •

David later said that while he could not have *certainty* about his faith, he did have *certitude*, based upon his limited understanding of the Bible and the universe. He explained the difference between the two words: *certainty* connotes scientific absolutes, while *certitude* indicates a conviction about something. For example, he had *certitude* about his salvation, even though he could not have *certainty* about it, i.e., prove it scientifically. At the time I didn't connect with what he was saying.

After our college years, we lost touch and our dialogue died. But I suspect David would be pleased that I never forgot his teaching. I carried his arguments to many an unbeliever. Like C. S. Lewis, I came to believe that our faith stands the test of reason. Science cannot speak to life essentials like hope, love, trust, joy, peace, etc. These things are not susceptible to physics, math, test tubes, and laboratory crucibles. Still, they have their own truth and their own existence. I'm pleased to note that in recent years many scientists have come to accept supernatural data as real and persuasive.

•   •   •   •   •

Back in junior high school, David and I went through various phases. One such was a fascination with hypnotism and telepathy. Another was experimenting with crystal radios. Remember those?

When we got to high school, David and I weren't in the same classes as in the past. Also, we began to gravitate toward different social groups. David remained in the band, while I joined singing groups. I became preoccupied with my job at the drugstore, forcing me to drop band. I had had my epiphany[7] about singing opera, so I joined whatever vocal groups I could. Our paths rarely crossed anymore.

I began spending much more time with Jim Hickey, a classmate who lived on my way to school. He had a workshop in his backyard, which attracted me because I was eager to learn more about cars, mostly because I wanted to impress the girls. Hickey (we called each other by our surnames) was totally absorbed with his motorcycle, a boat he was building, and other mechanical devices. He didn't seem to care much about girls, and had his own disparaging version of "religion." His rebellious nature tickled my fancy, and I enjoyed his company.

Hickey and I saw each other in classes we shared—when he showed up, that is. We loved to talk about all sorts of things. I wanted to learn more about cars and other machines, and he wanted to learn more about intellectual pursuits. He liked to say that religion didn't interest him, but he often brought it up. Unlike David, his arguments lacked knowledge and discipline, but he was a clever debater. He could see to the heart of an argument, and could quickly challenge it.

On the other hand, he refused to enter my spiritual world, so I couldn't help him understand my faith. For him, my language about God was incomprehensible. And he had no patience for things he didn't understand.

In the end, I got into more than I bargained for with Hickey.

---

[7] See the Prologue of, Tales of a Tenacious Tenor, ASJ Publishing, 2014, available on Amazon, et al.

Chapter Four

Fire, Fireworks, and Motorcycles

1956

On a cool November day, in Mr. Hauke's stuffy senior trigonometry class, Barbara Underwood passed a note to me: *I smell smoke! Can you? There's a fire out there somewhere and he just keeps talking on and on.*

None of us knew that a catastrophic fire had just begun that Friday when we were itching to go home. It seems the "Chair Factory," just a few blocks up the street from the school had caught fire.

Once school was out, we all had trouble getting home with all the streets in the neighborhood closed off, fire trucks roaring back and forth, police desperately trying to control traffic. I had to get to work that day to a downtown drugstore. The streets were abuzz with, "Did you see the fire up on Church Street?" "No, the streets are all blocked off—you can't get near the place." "Wouldn't want to. Can you imagine the heat?" "The smoke is awful, don't you think?" "When will they get it under control?" "The smoke covers the whole town. It's killing me." "All the firetrucks…" "I tried, but they won't let you near it." "Yeah, you're right. Not worth the effort." "Geez, I hope it doesn't spread." "Oh my God! All those houses right across the street." "If sparks fly, the whole street'll go up in flames."

That last comment made me think of Hickey. *O my God, their house sits right across Church Street. They're in harm's way.* I resolved to stop by on the way home—if I could get near the place.

When I left work for home that evening, I went up Water Street by the Susquehanna River. Even through the thick clouds of smoke one could see flames tickling the evening sky. I didn't go directly to the Hickeys because the wind had shifted. Black debris, still hot, fell from the sky all around me. The stench curdled my nostrils. Sometimes I held my jacket over my head for protection. I could hear fire trucks, police cars, and all kinds of emergency equipment roaring back and forth on the next block. Hickey was on the block beyond that, where the fire raged. I figured between the traffic and the water that flooded those streets, I had to stay away. *They wouldn't have let me through anyway.*

From home, I watched the smoke billowing into the evening sky, wondering if I could reach Hickey's house. Right after supper I ran down to see how the Hickeys were faring. By now, I had become a regular visitor to Jim's workshop that stood next to the alley right behind his house. I always used the alley to get to his shop, and this time I hoped to avoid police barricades and emergency vehicles by going that way. I encountered a fire barricade at the alley entrance a block above his house, but it was unattended, so I hopped over it and ran unseen down to his shop.

Hickey, a tall, lean guy with slightly stooped shoulders, dressed as usual in well-worn jeans and a solid-colored T-shirt, had blazing blue eyes that twinkled in contrast to his otherwise sloppy appearance. His broad smile could melt any feminine heart. One time he told me he wanted to be a dentist and that's why he always kept his teeth in sparkling order. He had a charming dimple in his right cheek—it always made me smile. Almost as if to strike against fashion, Hickey's hands were always stained black, with fingernails full of ink-colored grease.

When I arrived, I found his parents, brother and sister running around, splashing water on the house with buckets and pans of water to protect it from the intense heat. The hose might reach the upper floors, but already the front of the house was blistering. You couldn't stay out there very long.

Hickey, usually unflappable in any situation, was panicked. He always teased me about my "religion," as he called it, but now he furiously demanded, "Mitchell, what the hell is God up to, goddammit. Where is He when ya need 'im? Here, take this hose…."

Without warning, the water from the hose became a trickle. Hickey held it up to his face, much as a child might. But Hickey wasn't laughing; he was beside himself. He shouted, "OH SHIT! THE WATER'S RUN OUT!" Then he turned toward the street and yelled into the din of fire equipment and raucous voices across the street, "Goddamn you fire trucks! You've drained all our water out. SHIT-DAMN. What are *we* supposed to do?"

Knowing they couldn't hear him, he dropped the hose to his side, looking forlorn. He turned to me. "Damn it, Mitchell, now what are we gonna do?" spreading his arms in supplication. Then he slammed the hose into the muddy yard, glaring at me as if I were the enemy, pointed up to the sky and shouted, "Shit-damn, Mitchell! Where the hell is this God of yours anyway?" Abruptly turning, he stomped off into the house for who knows what.

I stood there, speechless, looking at the anemic trickle of water from the hose. I bent down and picked it up. Suddenly Hickey came storming back out of the house with an empty bucket in hand, soaked from head to toe. He stopped in front of me.

I smiled at him; he glared back.

"Give me the damn bucket," I ordered, now pissed at him for blaming God and me.

"What the hell for, damn it? There's no water."

I grabbed the bucket out of his hand, and headed for the back door of the house, determined to find water somewhere inside. I knew my way around the house from frequent visits. As I came to the back door, Hickey's sister, Kay, was just coming out. I stopped short to let her pass, but we both came to an abrupt halt as our eyes met.

The world around me suddenly stopped. For the first time, I noticed how exquisitely blue her eyes were. When she smiled at me every fiber of my being burst into song. My eyes moved down her radiant, flushed face to her soft lips, and then down to her skimpy halter. It was soaked through, and her nipples proudly declared, "Look at us, you handsome guy!" Watching me admire her bountiful gifts, she smiled coyly and slid past, brushing her bosom across my chest as if to thank me for my admiration. Or was she just a tease? How old was she?

My eyes followed her, enjoying the back of her as much as the front. *How could I have failed to notice Kay before?* Her sexuality riveted me to the spot. As I tried to collect myself, I thought about when I had last seen her. She was just a kid. How did she turn into this gorgeous, sexy woman all of a sudden? Where the heck have I been? She couldn't be more than thirteen. With a body like that? No way. How old is she? I was seventeen.

I can't date somebody that young.

I looked out the door after her. The tight short-shorts and that halter—or more to the point, what's in it, made me wonder. Her snow-white skin told me she avoided the summer sun. But those eyes, that body, the rich, dark, shoulder-length auburn hair. Where did it all come from?

For some reason, I had never given Kay a second glance. Had she been away at a Catholic school? Otherwise, where had she been? Anyway, on this night, her dazzling, sensual beauty froze my brain, stifled my breath, and excited the rest of me.

Hickey came up behind me and clamped a heavy hand on my shoulder, spinning me around to face him. "What the hell are ya doin', Mitchell, ogling my sister? I'll punch your goddamn lights out. Here, get to work." He picked up the bucket I had dropped and shoved it toward me. "We need all the hands we can get."

Somehow, the water began to flow again. After filling the bucket from inside the house, which took a while, giving me space to cool my jets a bit, I went back outside, only to encounter Kay again.

She's been waiting for me. I'm sure of it.

Kay smiled that same you-really-*like*-me-don't-you smile, and bent down to pick up a pan, making sure I couldn't miss how her halter top almost dumped her bosoms right out in front of me. She glanced up and caught me peeking as she casually adjusted her top, letting it bounce seductively. Her entrancing eyes glowed as my face looked like the red sky above us. I turned away to throw my bucket of water on the house.

Throughout the night, Kay and I kept getting in each other's way, deliberately splashing each other, giggling and running back into the house for more water. Hickey yelled, "Cut it out, you guys, and get back to work, dammit all!" He was sending another message, well aware that the wetter her scanty clothes became, the more naked she appeared.

Kay simply ignored Jim, and acted as though he didn't exist. When he went back into the house, Kay and I bumped and brushed each other so that at one point, I threw my arm around her waist from behind and pulled her against me so I could whisper in her ear to ask for a date. She tried to look surprised, but then playfully pulled away saying, "Okay." She purposely butted my swelling groin as she did so, quite aware of my arousal. I felt both embarrassed and thrilled, but also confused by her sexuality. *She's so young*, I thought, *how does she know so much about boys?* I longed for her to show me what she knew, to teach me. But my religious guilt immediately screamed inside my head, "Stop it! Don't even think it." Think what, I wondered? I hadn't a clue how to make love to a woman.

Hickey came out of the house at that moment with an overflowing bucket and threw it on the two of us. We all laughed, shaking ourselves like dogs. Talk about chilling out! By this time we were all freezing and exhausted. The fire continued to rage across the street, and the danger to the house remained. Nevertheless, Hickey decided, "Well, if the house hasn't caught fire by this time, it probably won't. The damn fire can't get any worse. I think it'll burn itself out anyway. Let's get to bed. Thanks for coming down, Mitch."

The night air in back of Hickey's house seemed at least thirty degrees cooler than in front. Kay had disappeared into the house without a word, and when she didn't come out again, I figured she must have gone to bed. Hickey himself went inside, but I waited to see if she might come out again—alone. Maybe she wanted them to think she was going to bed…I waited a few minutes, shivering all the while.

Soon I shook my head in disappointment and began my trek home, freezing all the way.

The fire burned savagely for days, but eventually the firefighters brought it under control, at least to the extent that it was no longer a danger to the neighborhood. The fire officials decided to let it burn itself out. That took nearly a week, and it smoldered for a couple of weeks after that.

Sometime later, after getting parental permission—well, at least *Mrs.* Hickey's consent—I took Kay to a movie, after which I kissed her goodnight on her

51

front doorstep. Our mutual attraction from the wet backyard fizzled before it could catch fire. The more we got to know each other that night, the less we had in common. My attraction to her was purely physical. That scared me, because she was so much younger than I, and I didn't know much more about sex then than I did back in Dr. Ulmer's Sunday school class. The thought of "making out" with a girl sent my blood rushing through my veins, but that in itself embarrassed me—I didn't know what to do with all those pumped up hormones. I clammed up at the thought of asking anyone about it. Sex was taboo, you just didn't talk about it, according to dear old Mom.

Kay was bored with me, that much was clear, so I never called her again, and she never made any effort to contact me. No notes, no messages from friends. Hickey was happy I was no longer "messin' around" with his sister. I had mixed feelings about it. On the one hand, I was relieved, but on the other, I felt I had missed out on something, a vital life experience. Even worse was not knowing what that experience was.

As my friendship with Hickey grew, I visited him in his shop as often as I could. There I learned about motorcycles and cars, as he and his mechanic friend, Rick, spent all their leisure time working on machines and other projects, such as a boat he constructed, and the occasional car repair for a friend.

Hickey's rage that night of the fire wasn't like him. Most of the time he was upbeat. If he couldn't get something to work, he'd jess put it aside and work on something else. Subjects he didn't like he tossed off like a worn out pencil. His interests were limited to science and math in school. Even then, he skipped classes when he had "something better to do."

Some stories about Hickey became high school legends. One of them occurred in our senior year physics class. On the morning of a final exam, he came in very late, to which Mr. Eisemann said, "Nice of you to join us, Mr. Hickey."

Mr. Eisemann's lecture desk stood in the middle of the room, and Hickey had to pass behind him on the way to his seat. The classroom was large, with seats ascending to the back of the room, four or five rows. Hickey sat in the last row, and I, just in front of him to his right.

As he passed behind Mr. Eisemann, he made a face at him that made us all laugh. Mr. Eisemann turned to see what Hickey had done, but by that time

Hickey was in the process of bounding up the stairs on the other side of the room to my right. He looked back at Mr. Eisemann with a generous, toothy grin, and quickly took his seat, mumbling how he would rather be in bed.

Later that morning, we had the exam. Hickey finished his lickety-split. I noticed out of the corner of my eye that he had repeatedly lifted up the front of his shirt during the exam. That puzzled me. I didn't want to be obvious by turning around to look. Afterward I asked him what the shirt thing was all about. He proudly lifted it up, and there, written upside-down on his belly, were all the formulas we were supposed to have memorized. In response to my critical expression, he quipped, "Well, of course they're upside down—to you. How could I write them right side up? Besides, I'd never be able to read them the other way."

Hickey had his own sense of humor—and his own warped sense of justice. He lived by his own rules.

· · · · ·

Hickey had long since pulled me away from David Wolfe's spiritual influence and musical guidance. Hickey was a rebel, to be sure, one with a formidable intellect along with penetrating insight, especially in mechanical and scientific matters. He loved history, but poetry, books in general, and religion smacked of sentimentality to him. His family was Irish Catholic, but not church goers. He claimed not to believe in God, yet he loved to discuss religion and philosophy, with his own homespun version of things, often using his gifts to discredit religion. Fantasy literature, books about love, and the inner workings of the heart just didn't light his fire. As for music, he would discuss the mechanics, but little else. It amused him that I sang and aspired to be a professional singer.

"Mitch, whaddaya want to sing opera for?" he asked as he tightened a bolt on his motorcycle.

"Oh, that's hard to explain. I don't think you'd understand."

"Try me."

"Well, for me opera is the culmination of all the arts. Remember how I told you about how David Wolfe and I used to listen to music?"

He nodded.

"Well, classical music does something for me…I can't put into words…."

He was about to interrupt, but I kept talking.

"Opera—for me, anyway—sits on top of all the arts. You have music—vocal, solo, chorus, and then instrumental in the orchestra, you have dance in the ballets, but you also have art, in the sets and costumes, you have literature in the words, you have drama in the story, you have history, language, religion, social commentary, romance, murder, crime, human behavior—just about anything you can think of in opera. Where else can you find all these elements together in any other discipline?

"Geez," he said, shaking his head. "You're really hooked on this stuff." He picked up a different wrench.

I shrugged. "You asked."

"Yeah, I did," he replied, chuckling and he shook his head. He went on, "So how the hell do you get *into* the opera? It's a pretty elite field, isn't' it? Takes a lot of money, doesn't it?"

My turn to shake my head. "Yeah," I sighed. "I don't know how, but I jess gotta try. Mrs. Graves told me to forget about it."

"Mrs. Graves? You mean the choral teacher?"

"Uh-huh. She said there are too many starving artists out there already. 'Try teaching,' she said. Sounds like my parents."

He smiled knowingly.

Hickey loved to take me for rides on his motorcycle, a pre-war vintage Indian, with a clutch foot pedal on the left, like a car's, and with a gearshift on the right. That was before bikes had toe shifts and handlebar clutches. I begged Hickey to let me drive it, but he was afraid I'd get hurt. It wasn't until one day we were riding on a small county road with no traffic that he finally relented. He stopped, got off, and went over the gears and controls with me.

I mounted the driver's seat and Hickey climbed aboard behind me. There were no safety helmets, nor bars to keep passengers from sliding off the back of the only seat on the beast. I got us going in fine fashion, with Hickey constantly yelling instructions in my ear against the din of the old machine. (It needed a muffler.) As I gained confidence, I cranked up the speed.

All of a sudden, we came to a dip in the road, which ended with a sharp curve to the right. I couldn't find the brake pedal soon enough, and as we plummeted down this short hill, all I could do to prevent us from going through a wire fence was to follow the road sharply to the right. In doing so, I leaned the bike over so that the footpad scraped the road, but we made it around the bend.

"Mitchell, stop this machine, goddammit! Pull it over. Now!" he screamed in my ear. I did. He jumped off the back and ran around to the front, grabbing the handle bar to face me.

"Shit-damn, Mitchell, you almost got us killed. Get the hell off—right now!"

"Hey, I made it around the turn, didn't I? We could've ended up either going through that fence, or even skidding out—but we didn't! I *made* it! Were you hurt? I wasn't, so what the hell is the big deal?" raising my voice as I spoke.

"You were damned lucky, that's all. Now get off. I've a good mind to let you walk home."

He checked the footpad and swore, then began to examine other bike parts, muttering as he did so. "That's the last time you'll ride *this* machine." He always called the motorcycle his *machine*.

That's the first time, I thought. *I hope it's not the last.*

I soon realized he was more concerned for his precious *machine* than for our safety. Whatever the case, he kept his angry promise. I never drove that—or any—motorcycle again.

• • • • •

Hickey's shop buddy, Rick, was a short, wiry guy, with unruly blond hair and grease-soaked hands, who owned a Vincent Black Shadow. Today a vintage bike like his in good condition could fetch $60,000 or more. Rick worked for Lycoming Motors in Williamsport, a company that supplied Piper Aircraft its airplane engines. He helped build them, so he knew engines inside out. In fact, Hickey told me that his own knowledge of engines came from Rick.

The Vincent had a compression ratio of about four or five to one, normal for engines of the period. It made the Vincent very fast, but Rick wanted to make it even faster, so he honed the cylinder heads down to a compression ratio of *nine* to one. When he finished, he realized that fuel was going to be a problem. Ordinary car fuel would not fire this new engine. It required aircraft fuel or the equivalent octane.

He decided there were only two ways to get it. In the fifties, Sunoco gas stations had pumps that blended low octane with high octane gas into various levels which they made available to the public. The high octane was essentially airplane fuel, but illegal to sell. So-o, Rick resorted to "midnight requisitions" to siphon it from the high octane tank.

His second option was to go to the Piper airport and siphon it from planes parked on the field away from the tarmac where nobody could see him. I never went with him, so I'm simply reporting what he told me.

Several months later one night, Rick did invite me for a ride on the Vincent with its new, rebuilt engine. We went south on PA Route 150 through Dunnstown. As we approached the village of Avis, on a straight stretch in the road, he gunned the throttle. Fortunately I had a four-finger-lock grip around his waist, so I was not thrown off the back. It was a small, two-lane road, hard to see ahead, but he began passing cars anyway.

At one point, while we were still out in the oncoming lane with about three cars still to pass, I saw headlights coming from the other direction. Rick opened the throttle all the way. As I tried to see around him, the wind was so strong it pulled my left cheek back as if a large finger had grabbed the left corner of my lip and yanked it back toward my ear. I quickly pulled my head in and hid behind him. Even so, I could see the headlights on the trees coming straight at us as horns started to blare.

Just as he swung back into our lane, cutting off the lead car, those oncoming lights flashed by us like a laser show, horns madly trumpeting from all directions. I peeped over his right shoulder to read the speedometer. It was coming down, but read 115 MPH. I can rightly say that that was the fastest I have ever traveled on land—and on only two wheels at that.

•   •   •   •   •

Nearly twenty years ago, in response to a phone call from our son, Rob, I wrote my first short story. It was about Hickey, a Halloween prank during our senior year, 1956. It won first prize in The Writers' Workshop Memoir Contest of 2014.

The Sordid Story of the Halloween Sodium Balls
Hickey stopped me in the hall on the way to Senior English class. "Hey, Mitchell! Whaddaya doin' for Halloween this year?"

"Nothin', really," I said. "We're too old for trick-or-treatin'."

"I got a great idea. Stop by the shop tonight and I'll tell y' about it." Off he went in the other direction. I started to say, "English is this way," and waved a futile hand at his back.

His shop used to be his father's garage, large enough for one car. Hickey must have cajoled "the old man" into letting him take it over to work on his motorcycle and other projects. The small, shabby building was on the way home for me, so that day I stopped by.

From the open door, I could smell the oil and grease, and when my eyes adjusted to the lesser light, I saw oil stains and smudges that ran from Hickey's fingertips to his elbows. His face, hair and clothes weren't immune either. He sat cross-legged on the ground, wrench in hand, removing some part of his old pre-war Indian motorcycle.

"Come on in, Mitch," he said, flashing his toothy grin.

"Whacha doin'?" I asked.

"Oh, this damn clutch is forever givin' me grief. Ya know, it's a bitch getting parts for an old machine like this."

I shrugged. "Yeah…. Now, what's this Halloween business all about?"

He got up, wiped his hands, and showed me a half-gallon glass jug full of what looked like mothballs, except they were greyer. I looked from him to the jar and back again, puzzled.

He laughed. "Don't worry! I'll show you what to do on Halloween night." He smiled mischievously. "You'll see," his eyes twinkled.

So, late in the afternoon on Halloween day, I went to his shop to find out what he had in mind. He opened a cabinet door, picked up the jar of balls, crossed the room, set them on his workbench, and announced proudly that they were *sodium* balls.

"*Sodium* balls? Where the heck did you get those?" I asked incredulously.

"From the high school chemistry lab, of course. Where else?" His eyes beamed at his little coup. "They're heavy, Mitch, and the glass'll get slippery if it gets wet. So, you gotta be careful with it."

"Whaddaya mean? Wait a minute. How did you get them…? Oh, never mind. You mean *I* have to carry them? On the motorcycle?"

"Who else? There's just the two of us—and I gotta drive." He clapped me on the back with a generous smile. "You can do it, Mitch. Stop worryin'."

"Just a second," I said, pointing to the jar. "What are you planning to *do* with these things? They're pretty unstable, aren't they?"

"Yep. And that's just what we want. We're gonna use that instability to create some funny havoc out there." He noticed my furrowed brow. "Stop worryin', Mitch. We'll have a great time. You'll see."

As he cranked up the Indian, I picked up the jar from the table. It was heavier than I expected, plus it was glass, which I knew would get slippery—especially with sweaty hands. On the back of a motorcycle? *Ye gads!* Already I'm fretting.

Hickey motioned me to get on the seat behind him. I put my left arm around his waist, and held the jar with my right arm as tightly as I could, pressing it against my body. With the throaty roar of the engine leading the way, off we went to the houses of people we didn't like, starting with my next-door neighbor, Mrs. Messerschmidt, a childhood antagonist.

She always yelled at the neighborhood kids for any slight infringement of her property. She'd even built a wrought iron fence between our two yards to keep us out. It wasn't a high fence, maybe three and a half feet or so, made of black iron poles, inches apart, with fancy arrowhead-shaped pointed tops. Just under those spikes, the vertical poles were connected by a decorative bar running the length of the fence—which ran the length of the yard. After her husband died, she reinforced the entire fence with chicken wire. Looked like the dickens. And if we hit a ball accidentally over the fence into her yard, she'd come out of nowhere to confiscate it. She never gave a single one back.

We had a number of apple trees in our backyard, the remains of a long-ago orchard. Our tree nearest her fence still produced a good many apples. My mother loved to make pies and dumplings with them. Part of the tree hung over her fence and deposited apples in *her* yard. Mrs. Messerschmidt picked the good ones for herself and threw the rotting ones back into our yard. It was my job to clean up the apple mess, separating good from bad, often getting stung by bees in the process. I really resented her making my work harder. That's why I didn't object to doing her a bit of mischief.

Hickey parked the motorcycle across the street where Mrs. Messerschmidt couldn't see it, and immediately shut it down. We crouched behind some bushes to wait and see if the noise of the motorcycle gave us away. We also wanted to see that she was home.

As twilight pushed the day aside, a cool breeze wafted across us. Hickey looked at me. Shivering, I clasped the cool glass next to my body. "Don't be a wimp," he hissed. He looked up at Mrs. Messerschmidt's house, which was quite dark. As the sky slowly dissolved into night, he nudged me and pointed to her house. "There's a light in the front room," he whispered. "She's home, and probably waiting for trick-or-treaters."

When Hickey decided the coast was clear, we furtively crossed the street and crawled up her front terrace. He took a small, tin tray out of the bag he carried, and motioned me to follow him. We crawled across her front lawn, using her bushes for cover, and nimbly climbed the three steps to her front porch on our hands and knees.

Carefully Hickey placed the tray under her front doorstep, poured some water in it from a small bottle. He indicated with sign language for me to hand him a sodium ball, which he carefully set on the small lip in front of the outside storm door, placed so that when the door opened outward, the sodium ball would fall into the pan of water directly underneath. I had no idea what was to come, but Hickey did, and he knew I'd be just as surprised as Mrs. Messerschmidt would be.

We worked quickly and quietly. When everything was in place, I rang the bell and we both ran to hide behind the nearest bush.

She came to the door, but didn't open it at first. We could see her pressing her glasses against the small window in the main door to see who might be out there. She knew full well it was Halloween, and expected trick-or-treaters. When she didn't see anybody, she pulled that door open, and then pushed the storm door open for a better look to see who rang her bell.

"*Whoo-oosh!*"

A jet flame shot up in front of her, causing her to jump back, dislodging her glasses. She shrieked as we expected. We snickered from behind the bush, and took her moment of confusion to make our escape.

After three such visits, it was not surprising that we heard police sirens from downtown screaming their way towards Susquehanna Avenue. Hickey hissed, "Let's get the hell out of here!"

He jumped on the motorcycle and cranked the engine into full roar. I jumped on behind him, and we headed down Susquehanna Avenue, lickety-split. I gripped the jar of sodium balls in my right arm with my left arm around Hickey's waist, holding on for dear life as best I could. The jar was heavy and now a bit slippery. My hands were sweaty from the effort, plus the cool of the evening had caused a bit of condensation, which made the dratted jar a nightmare to hold on to. There must have been twenty-five or thirty, maybe more, sodium balls left.

"Where we goin'?" I shouted over the howl of the Indian.

"We have to get rid of these things," he hollered back. "If we get caught with 'em, we're dead meat."

"Where we gonna do that?"

"The Susquehanna."

"Can't we put 'em back?" I pleaded. "What's Mr. K gonna do for lab experiments?"

"Forget it! You wanna get caught for breakin' and enterin', too?"

End of discussion.

We rushed straight for the Lockport Bridge without passing a squad car, lucky for us. They must have come up a different street when we went down. A wonder they didn't hear us, the Indian was so noisy. The jar almost slipped out of my grip a couple of times, especially when we bounced over the railroad tracks. Taking curves at high speed had challenges of their own. I nearly lost my grip on Hickey as he laid the motorcycle almost to the ground turning left onto the bridge. His footrest scraped the pavement, reminding me of my little motorcycle gig. I thought, *It's okay for you, but not me, eh…!*

"Wait 'til we get to the other side," he called over the din. He slowed down as we approached the Lockport side, and pulled the cycle as close to the bridge railing as he could.

"NOW!" he shouted.

I heaved the jar over the side, much as a quarterback laterals the football as he's being tackled. In the several seconds it took the jar to reach the water, Hickey made it to the far side of the bridge and turned around toward the Lock Haven side.

The night was clear, dark without a moon, cool, with no breeze. The stars glistened. A mile downstream, the lights on the Constitution Bridge sparkled. As we came back across the bridge to the spot where I had tossed the jar, we were greeted with a fireworks display shooting up from the river that rivaled any Fourth of July celebration I'd ever seen.

Fiery balls of sodium hissed straight up into the sky, some bending in giant arches back towards the river with tails of brilliant white flame. We were about thirty feet above the water. Some of the blazing balls flew to the top of the bridge, probably another thirty feet to the scaffolding above us. Fragments sputtered down onto the roadway.

The sky around us glistened with sodium balls bursting into flame like giant fireflies, flames streaming behind them like shooting stars, they shot to the top of the bridge, some all the way back down to the water. Many balls blew out and fell back into the river, only to explode all over again, creating a circus-like display of hurly-burly lights, hissing and humming through the air.

"HOLY SHIT!" Hickey shouted, slowing down to take it all in. I too gaped at every flash and stream of light dancing all around us.

Suddenly, a ball bounced off the machine, its fire not yet spent. Another hit me on the arm. "Ouch!" I screamed. It left a nasty burn mark, which hurt like the dickens.

"Let's get the hell out of here!" Hickey shouted.

I knew he was anxious that the cops not see this dazzling display from the city side of the bridge. If they did, they'd come racing in our direction to cut us off, so we had to hide somewhere real quick.

He gunned the old Indian, and off we went like a squirrel up a tree. As I hung on for dear life, now with both hands finger-locked around his waist, I looked back over my shoulder to watch sodium balls still popping and fizzing all over the place. Hickey drove like a madman straight over the bridge, past the courthouse, and made for the first alley, half a block straight ahead. He swung right into it, quickly stopped in the darkest shadows, and abruptly shut off the noisy engine.

The sudden silence jarred me. Putting an index finger to his lips, Hickey shushed me and jumped off the machine. We both froze as we heard patrol cars on the streets either side of us. We cringed as beams from the swirling red lights bounced off nearby buildings.

"Come on!" he whispered, and grabbed the handlebars, while I swung around to the other side to push from the seat. We muscled the bike hurriedly up the alleyway toward his house. At some point we had to cross over to the alley that went past Hickey's shop. He knew the cops would stop by to see if he was there.

We rolled the bike as quickly as we could, especially when we crossed a main street, but we had to stop at least twice in the shadows as squad cars passed by on the main drags. Thank heaven no officer thought to check the alleys. Of course, they were not only *looking* for us, but *listening* for the thunderous sound of the old Indian.

I gotta hand it to Hickey—he knew—he had it all figured out. I shivered at the thought of getting caught. What would my mother say? And Dad? Forget about it.

By the time we got to his shop, sweat dripped from every pore. Inside it was very stuffy from the afternoon sun. Hickey immediately swung the large front doors open and switched on all the lights, inside and out. The evening air made me shiver. He quickly disassembled the Indian's hot gearbox, with much swearing about burnt hands and arms touching hot engine parts. After spreading the parts on the floor, we found rags to wipe away our sweat, and sat down to try to appear cool.

As if on cue, we heard tires crunching on gravel, accompanied by those sickening, twirling lights from atop the squad car, splashing red on sheds and trees alike. The squad car stopped right in front of the shop door, engine and lights still running.

Slowly the officer got out. He deliberately walked around the front of the car, so that his sidearm, ammunition belt, and badge all glinted in the headlights. His large, athletic frame overpowered the open doorway of the shop. With his dark, *Cool Hand Luke* glasses, we couldn't tell where he was looking. A tense eternity passed as he stood there, thumbs locked in his gun belt. He leaned against the doorframe, staring at us. Was he trying to figure out what to do? Were we his quarry from the chase?

Having wiped away my sweat, I tried very hard to appear as calm as Hickey. I couldn't look at the officer. Ignoring what Hickey was doing, I picked up a part and pretended to look for another one to fit it. Hickey looked as though he had lost a piece of something or other. Neither of us spoke.

Suddenly, as if he hadn't noticed him before, Hickey looked up and flashed one of his winning smiles at the poker-faced officer. "Oh—hi there, Officer Collins. Come on in." Hickey motioned him to come in and take a seat as if he had been expecting him to drop by and hang out with us—which wouldn't have been the first time. Hickey knew the entire force as well as they knew him.

Officer Collins just stood there, stone-faced, looking at us, without a word. He seemed to be deciding what to say. Slowly, a knowing smile crept over his face, but at the same time he tried to suppress it. Finally his body relaxed, and with a broad, okay-you-got-me-this-time smile, he raised his right hand slightly in mock salute, and nodded toward us.

"You boys have a good evenin'." His sun glasses swept the room.

Shaking his index finger towards us, he continued, "Stay out of trouble now, y' hear?"

"Sure thing!" Hickey beamed.

"No problem, sir!" I offered.

As he slowly dipped his head toward us, we could see reflections in his CHL-aviator glasses. With his right eyebrow raised, he turned back toward the car, shaking his head. He retraced his steps, got in the squad car, turned off his top light, and once again we heard the slow crunch of tires on stones down the alley.

When the tire-scrunching faded into the darkness, we heaved a joint sigh of relief.

• • • • •

My sense of spirituality seemed to drift away with each new Hickey adventure. Those were the years of rebellion, a teenage expression of independence and self-discovery. I had always been a model student as well as a churchgoer, but I wanted to experience the freedom that Hickey enjoyed. He was his own man, beholden to no one. Yet I realized that his lifestyle had trapped him into a no-start future. You can't disregard schoolwork the way he did and expect to have a brilliant career.

On the one hand, I admired how he flaunted authority, yet, I realized that palling around with him would not help my academic future. Nor did it contribute toward my spirituality. These adventures were to me like the sirens to Ulysses, except I was not strapped to the mast. I also agonized over my baffling sexual desires that I believed were totally antithetical to the Christian faith. *But why? And what should I do about them?*

My irrepressible need to impress girls propelled me to change my "snobbish" image. I believed, or wanted to believe, that to pal around with Hickey would make me more attractive to girls. Yet at the same time, my intellectual side could not abide the pop culture that most teenagers loved and followed. I hated their music, especially Elvis. He represented the culture that undermined classical music. Plus, it annoyed me to see girls gah-gahing over him.

Of course I was jealous. Girls didn't go crazy over me. They didn't like the music I liked, or want to talk about science, or what was happening in the world. All they wanted to talk about was who's dating whom. Some made fun of me for being *square*, calling me an *egghead*—a contradiction in terms, it always seemed to me—and I wasn't even at the top of my class. I was only seventh out of over two hundred students, but they treated me as if I *thought* I were Number One. If only they knew how insecure and stupid I felt.

These internal struggles frayed the faith I had felt in David's company. *How could Christ let me flounder like this if He were everything He's supposed to be? Shouldn't He take away my anxieties and fears? Shouldn't He calm my raging hormones?*

My confusion about sex, I believe, came from my mother's own conflicts about it. On the one hand, she would insist that sex was "natural," but on the other, she would use words like "dirty" or "off-color" to describe jokes with even the slightest sexual implication. She sent very confusing messages about girls, sex, and dating.

As an example of her messages, once she told me that if I kissed a girl on the back of her neck, I *had* to marry her. I thought she was serious. But if I pressed her, she would deny everything and walk away. Small wonder I was confused and inhibited around girls until I was in my twenties.

The feeling of freedom I had when I was with Hickey felt strangely akin to the bliss I felt listening to music with David Wolfe, and later on my own phonograph.

One oasis from my teenage turmoil was my friend, Edward "Ed" Cox.

Chapter Five

Tree Stumps

Ed Cox and I went through the Trinity Methodist Church Sunday school together from kindergarten up. We were also schoolmates all through the Lock Haven High School system. His father had been a pastor, but having divorced his first wife—a no-no for pastors in those days—his dad was forced to leave the pastorate. The Cox family lived in a cabin near Rocky Point, a few miles north on the other side of the Susquehanna River from Lock Haven. They had a tough time until Eddie's father finally landed another job.

Ed was an inch or two taller than I, blond crew cut, blue eyes, body trim and fit, with a ready smile to those he knew. Shy and retiring, he appeared to strangers as either aloof, or as a tough guy, but he was anything but. He lived his faith, and the Lord's good name often came to his lips—in the opposite way any tough guy would use it. Unlike Hickey, Ed had a faith you could count on. It was simpler than David's, less cerebral. We didn't have to discuss it—he lived it, simply and honestly.

One stifling day in May 1956, Ed and I were walking down the muggy hall to English class, sweat beading on our foreheads.

He said, "Bob, what are you doing this summer? I mean, do you have a job?" He took off his glasses to clean the sweat off of them. He wiped his brow with his short sleeve.

"No, not at this point," I said. "Mom says Mr. O'Connor may want me to take care of his lawn this summer, but that's not for sure. Why do you ask?"

"Well, my dad and I have cleared a field of trees so we could raise some corn. He hopes to sell some of it. Thing is, this job is too heavy for him. He's not doin' too well, especially after clearing all those trees. Besides, things are kinda tough for us right now—he just lost his job...."

"Oh, I'm sorry to hear that. Is there anything I can do?" I wiped my brow.

"Well, yes there is. There are a bunch of stumps left, and he wants me to clear them out. But this isn't a one-person job. Have you ever pulled stumps?" Beads balanced on his upper lip.

"No, but they have stump-pullers, don't they?" We stopped outside the classroom door.

"Oh sure, but we can't afford that heavy equipment, or to pay somebody to do it for us."

"So, what do you have to do?" I shooed away a bug. I was glad I had short sleeves that day. I hate the heat, especially when I have to wear school clothes.

"We have a tractor that can pull them, but we have to cut the roots first."

"Okay. That shouldn't be too hard—I think." I looked at him intently.

"Bob, I won't lie to you. It's a tough job. I had to do it once before when Dad cleared a field. It takes two guys to do it—at least. If we could get more, well...I'm not so sure that would work. More guys would just get in each other's way. I'll show you when we get there...."

Since I didn't have a paying job for the summer, I agreed to help Ed out as soon as school let out. It was a particularly hot summer that year. The first Monday we had, I got up early and put on my oldest shirt and dungarees. I also had an old pair of army boots, not very comfortable, but high and sturdy. Ed had told me it's very dusty work, so wear old clothes and boots. Since I wasn't getting paid, Ed said he'd pick me up in the mornings and drive me to and from the field, which was almost directly across the river from us.

"I could swim straight across," I joked with him. "Save ya a few miles." I chuckled.

"Yeah, right," he quipped. Actually, the field was further north than I thought. I would've had to walk quite a distance after my swim.

On the first day, he drove two miles south from his house to the Lockport Bridge, and then two miles north on our side of the Susquehanna to get me, then all the way back again.

When we arrived that first morning, I soon learned that digging around those tough hardwoods, hacking at their roots, then pulling them out with a tractor, with roots splintering and spraying dirt all over, was indeed grinding, dangerous work. The sun beat down on us mercilessly, making everything hotter and sweatier. The second day I splashed on suntan lotion and bug spray.

At first I was not a happy camper; the work was *much* harder and dirtier than I thought. My old boots weren't much help. They quickly filled up with dirt. I kept having to stop and empty them. "Damn it!" I said under my breath.

Ed's good cheer and ready smile helped to soothe my sweaty brow, but perspiration kept messing up my glasses, getting into my eyes, and making it a nuisance to see. After working for my father, Ed's steadiness calmed me down. He loved to talk about the Lord, and despite all their financial troubles, he and his parents felt truly blessed, he said. This "attitude of gratitude" was a new experience for me.

We carried lunch buckets to the field each day, and took a break long enough to eat our sandwiches. On the first day, we discovered to our everlasting delight that we both loved peanut-butter sandwiches with sliced banana on top.

On one of our lunch breaks, Ed told me a story about how his mother attempted to kill a rattlesnake with the shotgun, but instead, blew away a side of their front porch. The snake got away, but the porch took quite a hit. "Knocked one whole side of the porch off, including the roof support." Ed and his father had some extensive rebuilding to do.

That summer, Ed, by living out his faith each day, brought me back to a more Christ-centered frame of mind. He was a good spiritual model and faithful friend, a counterpoint to my adventures with Jim Hickey.

After that summer I didn't see Ed until our fiftieth high school reunion in 2007. He looked almost as he did in 1957. God bless him—I looked very different from the way I looked in 1957.

Having a friend like Ed was great, but what I longed for in high school was a girlfriend. I dated several girls, both in the senior class and lower, but none seem to click with me, or I with them. I was never interested in the one or two young ladies that showed an interest in me. And vice-versa.

Then there was Leslie.

Chapter Six

First Love

"Oh, woe is me. Whaddam-I-gonna do? Nobody wants me. Nobody loves me. Poor me."

Such was the pitiful state of my love life—or lack of it, throughout high school.

There *were* two cute girls that lived on Susquehanna Avenue. Opal McGee was one, but she paid no attention to me. We used to fight as children, screaming at each other as she walked past our home. I think I threw something at her one time, and she started up our terrace to beat me up. She could have. Johnnie was there to defend me so she ran away.

After that Opal took to the other side of Susquehanna Avenue to get past our house. We never spoke at school. She ended up marrying Johnny Wert, the guy who broke my arm in the second grade. Sweet justice I suppose. Hey, my arm, the right one I always called "my broken arm," kept me out of the service. Didn't have to go to Vietnam.

But it also kept me from becoming a violin virtuoso, according to Mr. Brown, my violin teacher at Mansfield State Teachers College. Funny how things determine your life. I wanted to be a violin virtuoso—well, for a while, but I wanted to be a lot of things: a singer, a pilot, an engineer, a scientist, a preacher, a teacher, an astronaut (before the word was coined)…a lot of things.

71

Another dying flame in high school was Gayle Bittner. I remember walking her home once. Yes, once. She lived just up the street from us on the other side. I doubt we said more than two words to each other. Lovely girl, long, dark hair, dark eyes, classic face, great figure—lovely, timid smile. Once. That was it. Don't ask me why. 'Cuz I don' know.

Then I met Leslie. "Met?" No, actually I *saw* her for the first time…in their family limo—or at least, that's how grand their car looked to me. Actually, I'd never seen a limo, but their long Lincoln Continental *looked* like a limo to me.

As I came out of our house onto Susquehanna Avenue on my way to school, she happened to ride by one cool morning in the fall of 1956, the beginning of my senior year. Brown leaves scampered across the road as I began my trek to school. Red and orange ones were still on the trees. You could smell the fall in the air. The slight chill felt good after a hot summer.

I caught a glimpse of her as she gazed out the back window. I stopped to follow her with my eyes. My heart went into overdrive. Never had I seen such an enchanting face. I waved, thinking she noticed me. Then she caught sight of me waving to her, and she quickly sat back out of sight.

Whoa? What did I do wrong? Who was this angelic beauty? Where did she come from? Would I ever see her again? How could I find her? I wondered what had she been looking at so intently out the window. At first I thought it was I, but obviously…yeah, right. How could I find out…? Wait a minute! My yearbook.

I could hardly wait to get home after school to look through my yearbook for that unforgettable face. That's how I discovered her name was Leslie Pete. I found her picture way in the back of the book: she happened to be on the girls' basketball team. She stood in the back row. Her face jumped off the page at me when I recognized her.

Oh my gosh! She's only a sophomore. I'm a senior.
I don't care—I've got to make her acquaintance.

So, for the next several weeks, I made a point of getting out on the street at the time I figured she'd come by. On those rare occasions when she did, I'd wave at her, and soon she began to wave back, beaming that enchanted smile at me. At least I dreamed it was for me.

I also took to looking for her in the halls at school.

Then one day it happened. I spied her, scurrying toward me, probably to a class. She didn't see me, so I smoothly edged into her lane, kinda blocking her path. She'd have to step around me to get past.

She was dressed in a flowing dark blue skirt and white blouse, which highlighted her ample bosom. It was buttoned to the top, giving her an air of respectability. A gold chain entwined around a bright yellow scarf held a jeweled pendant in the front. Her blue eyes twinkled despite a cautious smile, her dark auburn hair neatly bobbed.

"Hi, Leslie, I'm Bob Mitchell."

She smiled at me, looking puzzled. She took a step to get around me, but I said, "I'm the guy who waves at you on Susquehanna Avenue."

"Oh my goodness," she said, and blinked quickly. "Of course I recognize you. So you're a student here too? How do you know my name?"

All my senses flew into gear to make a good impression. I had anticipated this question, and had prepared a reply so I wouldn't have to grope for an answer.

Her disarming smile never stopped. She just looked a bit surprised, pleasantly so.

"Since I saw you passing by, I looked you up in the yearbook." I wondered if she was impressed with my homework.

"Ha, ha! You're very clever. Why would you do that?"

I blushed, realizing I didn't have an answer for that. I thought she'd say something like, "I'm impressed." I had a response for that: "So am I." So I thought quickly and said, "Ah, because I wanted to meet you." It was all I could think of.

Her eyes and smile were beginning to melt me. Especially my brains.

"Oh. So you live on Susquehanna Avenue…" she said thoughtfully, trying to make sense of this conversation and my reason for waylaying her in the hall like this.

"Yeah, we're neighbors." I smiled, palms out as if to say, *Welcome to the neighborhood.*

The lilt of her laughter charmed me, but with a toss of her hand she danced around me and hurried off, "Gotta go—late for biology class. See ya."

I whirled around to look after her. Damn, she didn't look back. I took a deep breath and tried to pull myself together. As I trudged to my next class, I argued with myself about the success—or lack thereof—of this meeting. Neither judge nor jury showed up for this one.

Later I assured myself that I would keep trying. I convinced myself she was worth the struggle. Whenever I managed to encounter her in the hall, I spoke to her, however briefly. I maintained my practice of waving to her on Susquehanna Avenue. Little by little, she seemed to thaw a little.

• • • • •

Then one day after school she, along with several friends, walked into the drugstore where I worked. Her strong, exuberant voice caught my ear immediately.

At first I wanted to hide behind my tobacco counter, afraid if she found me working here, she'd think me a peasant—beneath her, anyway. By this time I knew she was from money, so I imagined a divide between us as depicted so well in old Charlie Chaplin movies.

I now knew that her father owned and operated the only upscale women's fashion store in town, The Smart Shop. They lived in the posh hill section north of us called Sunset Pines. I imagined her home to be a palace like the ones you'd see in high society magazines. They were Jewish, and my father hated the Jews. (I'll deal with that subject later.) All this made me feel like the poor boy on the other side of the tracks, even though we lived just down the street from them.

I summoned up my courage, and came out to the soda fountain area to greet her.

She turned to me and burst into a glorious smile. "Bob, what are you doing here?" Her noisy friends, still gabbing loudly, crowded into a booth as she stepped toward me.

I eyed her appreciatively in her classy, deep maroon skirt, black patterned blouse, buttoned to the neck, sporting a billowing white neck scarf. Her fragrance enchanted me.

Deep down I wanted to take her in my arms and kiss her, but I pushed that urge aside, stepped toward her, and said authoritatively, "I work here. Hey, it's great to see you, Leslie." I indicated an empty booth and gestured her to sit down. "Can I get you something from the fountain? A Coke? Some ice cream?"

She looked surprised, shook her head, and eagerly slid into the booth as I sat down opposite her. That was against company rules, but I didn't care. Leslie was more important than rules. We talked for a while about school, her activities and mine. Since there were only the two of us in the store at the moment—neither of us noticed that her friends had left.

Janet, the soda fountain attendant, came over and offered to get us drinks. She took our order, and as she turned back to the soda counter, she winked at me as if to say, *Moving up in the world are you, Bob?* She apparently knew who Leslie was.

My eyes followed her for a second so Leslie wouldn't see my blush, then I turned back to her. It felt so good, being with her. And yet, I couldn't discern what was going on behind that lovely mask. How I wished I could see through it. She gave nothing away. I sensed something hauntingly superficial about her—or was it just my nerves? I didn't seem to know what to say to get her to talk about herself. Was she deliberately not letting me in?

Since I couldn't get her to talk about herself, I blabbered on about myself, not knowing what else to say. After a while I had to get back to my post. Janet, bless her heart, had covered my counter for me while I sat there.

Then something totally unforeseen happened: Leslie mentioned that she was planning to walk home. *Ah*, I thought, *this is my chance to be alone with her.* So I nonchalantly offered to walk with her. When she accepted, my heart leapt a mile—*Get a grip, Robert.* My hopes soared. *Did she too want to be alone with me? Did she feel something, anything, for me? Please Lord, let it be so.*

"I get off at seven. Is that too late for you?" I asked.

She looked at her watch, "6:30. Hu-m-m."

"Can you wait 'til seven?" I asked, trying not to plead. When she looked down at her watch again, I said, "Maybe I can get off earlier. We don't seem to be very busy right now."

"No, that's all right. I'll wait," she said, and reached into her bag and produced a book.

She'll wait for me! "Great," I said as nonchalantly as I could. I took a deep breath, reached across the table, and softly rested a hand on hers. I squeezed it ever so lightly, hoping she'd get the message. Her eyes met mine as I rose. Her eyes followed me back to my tobacco counter. As I crossed the floor, I turned back and noticed she hadn't moved the hand I'd touched. I grinned at her. She parted her lips ever so slightly as our eyes met. A smile just enough for her dimple to appear....

Dare I hope...?

That was the beginning of our long walks home. The more we talked the more we discovered that we had much in common. She loved music, philosophy, religion, and art—all the things that I loved. *Oh God, is this Heaven or what?*

On one evening walk, I asked her about Judaism.

"What do you want to know?" she said.

"How come you Jewish folks don't accept Jesus?"

"We accept him as a man—just not as a god. My dad says that Christianity has too many gods."

"No, we don't," I retorted, my brow bunched slightly.

"Don't you have what you call a *Trinity*?" she said as if in debate. "That's three gods right there." She looked steadily at me.

"No, it's not really. The Trinity is one God in three Persons." I met her gaze, loving it.

"My dad says that doesn't make any sense. How can three persons be a god?"

"That's a good question, Leslie. It does sound kinda crazy, 'specially when you put it that way. I don't know. I'd have to ask someone. Do you know David Wolfe? He could answer that."

"I've heard the name, but I don't know him. Why, is he Jewish?"

I laughed. "No, not David. He's a Baptist, and knows a lot about the Bible. I'm sure he could give you a good answer. You know, I haven't talked to him in a long time. Tell you what. Next time I see him I'll ask him."

And so our conversations went. Another night as we walked Leslie told me about concerts her folks took her to, such as to a Williamsport Symphony Orchestra concert. She said, "They played a Beethoven symphony—I don't remember which one—and, a piano soloist played the Grieg A Minor Piano Concerto. I also recognized Mr. Kleckner, the high school band director. He sat right up in front of all those string players. He even played a couple of terrific solos."

"Yeah," I said. "He's their concertmaster."

"How did you know that?" Her eyes widened in surprise.

"Well," I began, "You said he sat up front and played solos. That's what a concertmaster does. But I also knew that because I took violin lessons with him for two years."

She stopped walking, put a hand on my arm to stop me, and turned me to face her. She was laughing. "Bob, you studied violin with *Mr. Kleckner*? You never told me that. Do you know how *good* he is?"

"I never heard him play in public, but he always seemed real good to me. Anyway, that was a few years ago—until I broke my father's violin." I almost said, "*cheap* violin." "Mr. Kleckner hated that old thing because it was a beast to tune."

She giggled. "Why?"

"The pegs didn't fit properly. Mr. Kleckner always hassled me about getting them fixed."

"Why didn't you?"

"Dad always got mad at me when I mentioned it. He claimed he never had any trouble with them. I think he just didn't want to spend the money… ." I was on a roll. "Yeah, Mr. Kleckner is a real good teacher. I learned a lot from him. When I started in the band, in junior high school, he taught me to play an old E-flat upright. From there I 'graduated' to a mellophone. When Cissie graduated from high school, I inherited her French horn."

"Cissie?"

"Oh! Sorry. Cissie's one of my sisters, older. Well, it wasn't hers, actually. It belonged to the school. Anyway, I became the first chair horn player. We sat right under Mr. Kleckner's nose in band. Sometimes, when he got excited, I thought he would clip me on the head with his baton."

Leslie laughed. "Didn't you tell me you also play the piano?"

"Yeah, I still take lessons with Mrs. Kamp. It's been four years now."

"And here I thought you were just a singer. Everybody knows that." She looked at me, shaking her head slightly. "Bob, you amaze me. I didn't know you were so talented."

I blushed, shrugged my shoulders, and lowered my eyes. Tongue-tied, I didn't know how to react because no one had ever paid me such a compliment before. I doubted she had any idea how much her words meant to me. How could I thank her? In my confusion, all I could do was look back at her adorningly. How I wanted to take her in my arms and…! *O-o-o-h*….

And so our conversations went—all over the place. We enjoyed being together. She had a way of getting me to talk about myself, but I never really cracked the code that would get her to speak about herself. For example, I didn't find out until much later how into sports she was. At the time, I was oblivious and afraid to ask for fear she'd think I was prying. How I wish I hadn't been so naive. Most people love to talk about themselves.

She was not allowed to walk the final hill up to her home, a long, lonely trek up a straight, steep drive, considered too dangerous for a young lady to be alone there. She was to wait at the bottom of the hill under the street light where people could see her and call for help if necessary. There was also a gas station on the opposite corner, always open it seemed, so it was considered safe for her to wait there. Her mother or dad would pick her up at eight o'clock on the dot. Sometimes I got out of work early, so on those evenings we had fifteen or twenty minutes together under the street lamp.

One particularly comfortable evening, my heart throbbed as we stood under the darkening sky. A gentle breeze caressed us. The stars began to shimmer above us, the street lamp's soft glow fell gently on her hair, warming it to an amber glow. Her white skin softened to a creamy hue, her lips seem to throb with passion. I imagined playing in a movie with her where I could take her in my arms and kiss her. I took a small step closer, her eyes expectant, and I slowly began to lift my hands toward her—but there was no screenwriter to give me the right lines….

"My mother knows I'm here—she'll be down soon, I'm sure." The spell snapped. "She's never late, and she never lets me climb that hill," she explained needlessly.

I lowered my eyes in disappointment. When I looked up, she was smiling at me.

She looked up at the stars. "It's really nice tonight, isn't it?"

I was close enough to touch her; she didn't move, I followed her gaze to the stars.

"She'll be here in a few minutes," she whispered leaning toward my ear. We were so close. I wanted throw my arms around her and declare my love, but for some stupid reason I was afraid she'd be offended. I had endlessly rehearsed the words to ask her to the Senior Ball. All the way up Susquehanna Avenue, I looked for the right cue.

Hey, stupid, this is IT! I lovingly placed my hands on her upper arms.

"Leslie, would you do me the honor of accompanying me to the Senior Ball?"

A hushed moment. Even the gentle breeze stood still. Her fragrance tantalized my nostrils. Goose bumps all over. Our eyes tried to read the other's thoughts and feelings.

"The Senior Ball?" Her mouth slowly dropped, eyes widened. "Oh!" She took a deep breath. "Bob, that's right! You're a senior."

How could she not know? "Yup," I confirmed, trying not to lose the moment. Words had vanished from my mind. I had believed all along that she was *expecting* me to ask, but if she didn't know I was a senior…?

Her face beamed as the realization sunk in. The Senior Ball was a big deal—and she, being a sophomore actually believed nobody would invite her. At first, I thought she'd say, "I'll think about it." But my entire body, my whole being glowed when she said breathlessly,

"Oh, Bob, I'd love to."

I looked into her eyes, and she returned a gaze like mine. At first I blushed, just as I did when I met Aunt Kay on that Christmas years before. The Jewish connection between these two favorite women didn't occur to me until later. But at this moment, I felt a mystical bond to both of them—and to Judaism.

I pulled her slowly toward me for our first kiss. Her hands came up to my chest, our bodies almost touching. She smiled, waiting for me to make the first move, but I hesitated, *Dare I do this? Oh God, Leslie, do you have any idea how much I adore you?* I leaned in for the kiss; her lips waiting for mine.

Whoosh…! Just then, we felt the breeze of the big car arriving. The passenger window purred down. Mrs. Pete called out, "I see you two are enjoying this lovely evening."

We quickly dropped our hands and stepped back. Leslie turned to her mother, trying to appear nonchalant, and said, "Yes, Mother, we are," her eyes glowing at me. She winked at me and said, "Thanks again, Bob. I really appreciate your keeping me company." In a lower voice she added, "I'll let you know." All her body language at that moment was shouting, YES, but she didn't want to commit until she had permission.

She turned, opened the car door, and got in the back seat. "Good night!" She threw me a kiss her mother couldn't see.

As the car glided away, I stood there feeling terribly alone, and began to fret about whether or not her mother would let her go to the ball—with me.

·   ·   ·   ·   ·

Although I don't remember how she accepted, I shall never forget that warmly pleasant spring evening when I drove up to the Pete mansion in Sunset Pines and stepped out of my chariot, a light blue 1939 Ford coupe, polished for the occasion, imagining myself as the Prince in *The Student Prince*. As I approached the house, the flowers in front greeted me with a scintillating fragrance. I thought of the scenes between the Prince and Kathy, the barmaid, with whom he fell so passionately in love.

·   ·   ·   ·   ·

Oh, how I had wanted them to live together happily ever after,
But it was not to be.
Oh, how I wanted to sing to Leslie as the Prince
Poured out his heart to Kathy!
But hold, my faltering heart, tonight is my dream of dreams.
Away with yearning and sadness! This night she'll be with me.

·   ·   ·   ·   ·

I rang the bell. Mrs. Pete opened the door with a radiant smile, and welcomed me into their home as an honored guest. Mr. Pete sidled up behind her, smiling at me over her shoulder.

Mrs. Pete said, "Bob, you look so handsome in your tuxedo! And what an exquisite corsage. For Leslie, of course. Come in, come in!"

I stole a quick glance around the room, trying to take in the large, cushy sofa and matching chairs, the exquisite wall paintings, a large green plant in one corner, and the spotless beige rug on which I stood. Even my nose luxuriated in the posh aromas of furniture and flowers around the large, toasty warm living room. I had never been in such an elegant home. My imagination ran wild, wondering fleetingly if all Jews were this rich.

The Petes don't seem to mind that I'm a Christian.

Mrs. Pete must have thought I was speechless from nerves, so she tried to make me feel welcome. "She'll be down in a minute. Would you like to sit down while you wait? Can I get you something to drink? Make yourself at home."

· · · · ·

Not accustomed to such hospitality, I suddenly remembered all the nasty things my father said about Jews. "*Not true!*" my mind shouted. "*Not true at all.*" Fighting back tears of anger and sorrow about what happened to the Jews in Nazi Germany not that long ago, I tried desperately to banish all my father's poison from my head.

Dad not only hated Jews, but he was bitterly envious of Mr. Pete's success in business. I know he had tried from time to time to get Mr. Pete to order all his store forms from him. But Mr. Pete bought only business cards from Dad, who took it personally. "Those damned Jews take all the business away from good Christian folks struggling to make a living." I deeply resented this ridiculous, indefensible slur. My face reddened at the thought.

· · · · ·

Mrs. Pete, noting my discomfiture, eased it with her warm, hospitable charm. She sat down next to me on the sofa, and with her graciousness, I soon found my voice. We chatted like old friends.

I'll never forget the moment Leslie appeared at the top of the steps, a vision of loveliness a 1950s Hollywood musical couldn't top. Her flowing, light blue strapless evening gown, trimmed with lacey white bands, cast a spell over the three of us as she slowly descended the staircase. A thin silver necklace with a small sapphire adorned her neck. It sparkled from the light below. The gown highlighted Leslie's brilliant blue eyes and elegant white shoulders, her dark auburn hair cropped at the neck like Audrey Hepburn's in *Roman Holiday*. Leslie's entire face glowed like a morning sunrise.

Mrs. Pete watched my reaction to Leslie, as she too warmed at the winsome sight of her only daughter. Mr. Pete was struck with awe.

As Leslie reached the midpoint of the stairs, I had already risen to greet her, corsage in hand, eyes fixed adoringly on her. As she stepped onto the floor, eyes fixed on me, she crossed directly to me with not even a glance at her parents.

Noticing the corsage, she asked coyly, "Is that for me? Oh, Bob, it's beautiful! Would you like to pin it on me?" Noticing my hesitation, she added with a knowing smile, "It's customary, you know."

Her gown had a low-cut bodice, so I froze at the thought of where to pin it. Still smiling, she took my hand and led me to a full-length mirror across the room. As I stared down at the top of the gown, my hands started to shake at the thought of touching her so publicly in such an intimate place. She giggled at my dilemma.

"Here, let me help you," she said, and guided my hands. Her soft skin felt warm on the backs of my fingers as I slipped them under the stiff bodice to protect pricking her breast with the pin. Her glee-filled eyes danced back and forth from my eyes to my hands. She giggled, but she never blushed. I did.

With proud grins, her parents wished us a very good time. They knew from the high school instructions that we would be out all night, first for the ball, and then for prearranged movies, ending with an early morning breakfast. These events were planned because of wild parties in previous years that last year had resulted in the tragic death of a student and serious injury to several others. The school administration made attendance at all the events this year mandatory. Everything was well-planned and well-chaperoned.

"So, we'll see you in the morning?" Mrs. Pete asked, yet she said it more like a command. "What time will you bring Leslie home?"

"Gee, I don't know exactly, they didn't say." I thought for a moment. "I guess around six o'clock."

"We'll expect you at six, then."

I escorted Leslie to the car, held the door for her as she tried her best not to wrinkle her gown getting into the front seat. After closing her door, I turned and waved to her parents as they stood on the front steps. I hustled around the front of the car, got in, and started the engine. Leslie rolled down her window and waved to her parents as we pulled away.

The ride to the dance hall and the early activities at the dance itself have largely faded from my memory. However, I do remember that the planners did a superb job. Everything they arranged for us for the entire night came off without a hitch.

The ball was held at a large downtown hall, the grand Masonic Lodge on Main Street, as I recall. Leslie and I had never danced together before, but we enjoyed it immensely. As the ball progressed, we danced closer and closer. I felt that she loved me as much as I loved her. Her fragrance, her hair brushing my face, the occasional kiss to the cheek, and the warmth of her body against mine lifted me right up to the stars.

Later, as part of the planned entertainment, we drove to the local drive-in theater, where we watched the preselected movies. We held hands and kissed more than a few times, even on the lips. Nothing passionate, but warm and tender. I didn't tell her how much I loved her, afraid the bubble might burst.

True to my word, I chauffeured my love to her front door promptly at six the following morning. After warmly kissing me, she floated into the house where her mother waited. Mrs. Pete greeted me with an appreciative grin, then they both disappeared inside.

I'm sure she did exactly what I did when I got home—went straight to bed.

This was one of the most memorable nights of my life. I relived the romance of the *The Student Prince* in my head. We danced the night away. We laughed. We giggled. We joined in the games. We enjoyed the movies. We talked of everything from music to religion and the stars above. My heart sang to her just as the Prince sang to Kathy, the impossible-to-have barmaid. Yes, my memories have dimmed, but the passion remains deep inside my musical soul.

I could have converted to Judaism that night, just to be with Leslie. Knowing her and meeting her family that night set in motion a life-long quest to learn about Judaism. All of it has shaped my future life—and ministry.

One afternoon two weeks after the ball, I was working at the drugstore. When I stood behind my tobacco counter, no one could see me unless they were directly in front of the counter because of all the displays hanging in the front of the counter. Nor could I see out, except right in front of me.

Three or four girls came into the soda fountain area, chattering away about boys. I immediately recognized Leslie's mellifluous voice, and I started to go out to greet her. But I froze in my tracks when I heard her telling her friends about her latest love interest. I naturally assumed it was me. I really wanted to hear what she would say. But the more I heard, the more confused I became. When she finally mentioned the fellow's name, my heart dropped like lead ball. *Gary? No way! Leslie, how could you?* I was crushed.

· · · · ·

Well, it was my own fault. All along I had suspected she didn't feel the same about me, but I got so many mixed signals I didn't know what to think. I really believed that in time she would come to love me. I *knew* I should have called her, but I was afraid to. Just saying that makes me cringe. The problem was I couldn't *afford* to date her. That's why I kept arranging to meet her wherever I could—at least to talk with her, and walk her home. Even when her mother came to pick her up, Mrs. Pete never offered to drive me home. *Come to think of it, I doubt they knew where I lived. What was I to them? A nice, friendly buffoon perhaps?* Leslie had seemed pleased about meeting this way, so I was sure she felt *something* for me. But that afternoon in the drug store shattered all my dreams. I was broken to smithereens.

· · · · ·

What could I say to Leslie now? I certainly couldn't confront her in the drugstore in front of her friends. That would embarrass her, probably enrage her, and wreck everything. So what do I do now? It seemed too late to do *anything*.

No one to turn to. Not my parents—I could just imagine Mom shrugging her shoulders and saying, "Well, what do you expect *me* to do about it? It's your problem, not mine. I can't help you." She'd walk away.

Dad'd probably laugh. The only person I could talk to was Johnnie, but he was across the ocean in the Navy. David and I never talked about love. I'd be embarrassed to call him at this point. Hickey? Forget about it. Both Joan and Cissie were married by this time, and gone. Besides, I never confided anything in either one of them. I could never share my feelings with my family. They'd tease me to death.

· · · · ·

Sometime after that, Leslie came into the drugstore again. Um-m. Of course, she had no idea how I felt. So I nonchalantly asked if I could walk her home again. She, not knowing that I knew about Gary, accepted as she always did.

It was early evening on this hot July day, but a river breeze caressed us as we walked together. The air carried that pleasing aroma of freshly cut grass from the other side of the river. Leslie was dressed in her favorite color of blue—Bermuda shorts this time, and a thin tan blouse. Kind of daring, I thought, because I could see her bra underneath. Oh, how I loved all her feminine charms. Her hair was longer now, and wafted gently in the breeze. I luxuriated in the scent she wore.

The sun had set, and some stars began to appear. *A romantic evening shaping up, maybe…?* My feelings for her hadn't dimmed, but I still rankled about her last drugstore visit. I hadn't phoned her because I was angry and afraid her mother or father might pick up. What would I say to them? I'd have to hang up without speaking.

As we walked, we chatted about school this past year, even smiled as we reminisced about the Senior Ball. We talked about each of our plans for the summer. Since I had just graduated, she asked where I planned to go to college. "Are you going to study opera?"

Good grief! Impossible. What could I say? I shrugged and said, "No, we can't afford that. I've decided to go to Lock Haven State," pointing at the main entrance at the foot of Susquehanna Avenue as we walked passed it. "I guess I'll study math."

"Math? You never mentioned that before."

"No, it's recent." I really didn't want to go into all the arguments I'd had with my parents. And it was painful to admit that I couldn't pursue opera.

Funny, I'd never mentioned anything about the ministry to her. Well, that was far from my mind anyway.

I knew she could go to any college she wanted to, and that made me jealous, so I changed the subject. Besides, she had two more years of high school to go. So, I asked her about her summer plans, but I really didn't listen to what she said. My mind drifted away, trying to think if I should broach the subject of love again.

By the time we reached the streetlight, I decided I just *had* to tell her how much I loved her. At first I tried to be casual about it, and she seemed to respond. But then as I got more serious, she seemed to pull away.

Suddenly she blurted, "I can never marry *you*, you know!"

What? It felt like a punch in the stomach. I didn't like the way she emphasized *you*. "Why not?" I asked, kind of irritated.

"Because you're not Jewish." She flippantly tossed off the line with a rueful smile.

I must have looked pretty forlorn, because she immediately softened, her eyes sympathetic. She knew she had to tell me what I couldn't bear to hear.

I stood there stunned. My grand plan to woo her—zapped, shot to hell. I stared at the ground. I hissed air through pursed lips, then looked up at her. "What's my not being Jewish got to do with it?" I truly didn't understand.

"My parents would never let me marry somebody who's not Jewish." She said emphatically.

I wondered if she had actually struggled with this. Over me. Over her feelings for me, whatever the hell they might be. I paused, thinking how her mother seemed to have approved of me, or so I thought. "Why not?" This was a demand.

She softened. "Oh, I don't know, exactly. I guess it has something to do with anti-Semitism." She seemed at a loss for words.

"Anti-*what*?" I didn't know this word at all.

"Anti-Semitism." She looked at me quizzically, not believing I hadn't heard this word.

"What's that?"

"It's a word for people who hate Jews."

I wanted to shout, *But I don't hate Jews! I love you. I love Aunt Kay. How could I hate Jews?* But the words stuck in my throat as I thought of all the nasty, horrible things my father had spewed out about Jews. In fact, all the vicious comments he had made about Leslie's father suddenly slapped me across the face, and that closed me down once again.

Dad's horrible words flashed through my mind as Leslie and I stood there under the cool, moon-lit sky. Her familiar perfume drew back all my passion for her. How I longed to embrace her, but I feared she'd pull away, slap me, or something. Even so, I inched closer and fixed my eyes on hers, longing to find the right words to make her love me.

At first I thought to tell her that my father's bullcrap hadn't rub off on me, that I have nothing against Jews. *In fact, if they are all like you, my darling Leslie, I couldn't do anything but love them as I love you.* But...I stopped, and suddenly realized she knew nothing of Dad's stupid, vicious, and ill-informed prejudices. *Damn him. Damn his damned prejudices!*

At that moment, damn it, the dreaded Lincoln Town Car had to make its appearance. I wanted to shout, "Go away! Leave us alone. I want to make love to your daughter, damn it."

The shadowy window silently slid down, Mrs. Pete smiled at us from the driver's seat. She leaned toward us and called out to me, "Thanks for watching out for Leslie."

I waved back in acknowledgement, mustering a smile. *She didn't call me by name. Does she remember it? Did she ever really know it?*

Leslie hopped gaily toward the car with a wave and beamed, "See ya!"

Shit. Is this the end? Frozen to the spot, I forced myself to say, "Goodnight."

I wanted such a different parting: *Goodnight, my love, my darling, my life...* I imagined kissing her passionately...no, no, no...shit, shit shit.

The limo that wasn't a limo purred off into the night like a cat licking its whiskers.

I looked up at the moon and began to cry. *Oh God, what's wrong with me?*

• • • • •

A brief Leslie aftermath when Mom died in 1993:

Joan and I came to Lock Haven for the funeral. We stayed at a downtown motel whose manager happened to be Leslie's younger brother, Ronnie. When I saw his name on a plaque behind the registration desk, I asked the attendant if she knew whether or not he was Leslie's brother.

She replied, "Oh sure. Let me get him for you."

I gave Joan a surprised look.

The attendant left and soon reappeared with Ronnie in tow.

When I explained to him that I had dated his sister in high school, he said, "I don't remember you, but that's okay. Would you like to talk to her?"

Again I was startled by how quickly things were happening, but said, "Sure!"

He picked up the desk phone and dialed her number. When Leslie answered, he handed me the receiver, "Here she is."

I took the receiver timidly, not sure what to say. "Leslie?" I asked hesitantly.

"Yes." Her rich voice sounded the same as it had some forty years prior, just a bit deeper. "Who's this?"

"Bob Mitchell."

"Bob…M-m-mitchell?" she repeated. "I don't think I know any Bob Mitchell."

My heart sank—as of old. But I bravely proceeded to explain who I was and that I had dated her—you—in high school. She acknowledged that my story sounded vaguely familiar, but she really couldn't remember who I was—until I described the Senior Ball.

She said slowly, "Oh, yes. I sort of *do* remember that. But I still can't picture you."

None of my efforts to take her back to those years helped jog her memory. We said our goodbyes and hung up. By this time Ronnie had left, so I thanked the attendant, and we also left.

I guess all my worst apprehensions about her feelings for me way back when were correct. Sometimes I wonder what would have happened if she had loved me as I loved her. Would I have married her? Would I have converted to Judaism?

My heart still says, "Of course!" But who can say? At that time passion ruled me, and I like to think that I could have endured all the family slings and arrows hurled my way. It's sort of tantalizing to imagine how her family might have reacted to such a match, even if I had converted and become a good Jew.

My guess today is that they too would have resisted as passionately as my family would have. I can see Mom crying her eyes out, and Dad raging like a typhoon. I can't imagine what Leslie herself would have had to endure with her family.

Yet, somehow, I believe God had a hand in all this. My love for her birthed a life-long desire to know more about Judaism. Little did I know then that later in New York City, when I began to sing at the Hebrew Tabernacle Synagogue in the late 1960s, I would sing there for nearly thirty years, and meet all manner of Jewish people, many of whom became good friends. Dr. Ruth Westheimer was a member of that congregation, and invited us, *das Chor*, (the choir), along with other guests, to her apartment just north of the synagogue for occasional soirees after temple services on Friday nights. She was an entertaining, generous hostess, full of wit and charm.

An octogenarian, Milton Marx, who was ever-present at Hebrew Tabernacle, was thrilled when Joan and I asked him to be Godfather to our first son, Rob. He took it very seriously.

I remember fondly both Mrs. Meyer and Mrs. Dittman, who helped me learn my German songs and operas.

More than one Jewish acquaintance quipped, "Bob, you know more about Judaism than I do." Indeed, I pursued many a theological line of inquiry that sought to bring Christianity and Judaism together, as naïve as that sounds. But the effort taught me much about both faiths.

Eventually, I gave it up because Christianity and Judaism both have so many internal theological divisions dating from ancient times. If neither faith can bring its own many parts under one umbrella of faith, how could anyone bring these two monotheist giants together? I had other worlds to conquer.

Ah, youthful dreams! Yet without them, how could we ever move forward?

•　•　•　•　•

Well, Leslie, to paraphrase a song from *The Student Prince*, "Deep in my heart, dear, I *had* a dream of you...." A dream I have never forgotten, never forsaken, a bittersweet dream, a never-to-be fantasy of love. Nevertheless, Leslie, my dear, you shaped my life in a way you never could possibly have imagined, and I don't regret a single, precious moment I spent with you. *Baruch ata adonai.* ("Praise be Thou, O Lord.")

Chapter Seven

Brotherly Love

When we were little, Johnnie and I hated being inside. We stayed in the house only for rainy days—and punishment. Even if it rained, we loved to run through showers in our bathing trunks, catching drops on our tongues, splashing puddles as high as we could, and sliding down wet grass. Mom would keep us inside only for terrible thunderstorms.

In hot weather we swam at Price Park, later renamed Hanna Park, along the Susquehanna River (West Branch). The park was a mile north of us, and walking there was half the fun. In summer, we didn't wear shoes, and we toughened our feet by walking up to the park, as well as on the rocky beach itself. The town occasionally spread sand on the beach, which lasted until the first heavy rain. Those rocks made my feet so tough that in high school I could run on the college cinder racetrack in my bare feet. The college athletic field was a short jaunt through the woods in back of our house.

In high school I spent a lot of time running on that track, but when we were little, we played "cowboys and Indians" in the field and adjacent woods, bounced rubber balls off the red brick fieldhouse wall, or swung on the swings next to the old school house diagonally across from the fieldhouse. Sometimes our neighbor across Susquehanna Avenue, Eddie Ryan, joined us. We loved our summers, hot or not.

In winter, we built snow forts and organized neighborhood snow battles—even with the girls, if they dared join us. We loved to sled down Chestnut Street.[8] It ran along the side of our house—we called it *the alley*, because it wasn't paved and seemed to us like the alleys downtown. Most small towns in Pennsylvania have alleys.

Cissie's friend, Jolene, hated it when we called *her* street, Chestnut Street, an alley. After all, her address was 4 Chestnut Street, she would heatedly remind us, the only house in Lock Haven with a Chestnut Street address. "It's a *street*, not an *alley*," she would yell.

"Yeah? Well it looks like an alley. It's not paved," we yelled back, standing next to each other like goons, hands on hips.

"That makes no difference." With crossed arms and a rigid body, Jolene held her ground. Cissie stood off to the side, unsure which side to take.

"Yes, it does." And so the argument would continue.

Jolene didn't like us sledding on her street. "It makes it slippery for my mother to get her car in and out," she complained.

"It's our street too!" we'd counter. "We can sled on it if we like."

"No you can't."

"Yes we can."

Again Cissie stood off to the side. Just then Joan would came out. She was the oldest among us, and a tomboy. She loved sports (Cissie not so much), and she'd join the fray.

"What's the problem?" she asked.

The reply was a cacophony of "We want to sled…." jumbled with, "The boys are making Chestnut hill too slick for my mother's car…."

Joan would throw up her arms and retreat into the house until the storm blew over.

Cissie just stood there.

We had lots of snow in the forties and fifties, so there were plenty of opportunities for winter sports: snowballing and sledding. We hauled our sleds past Jolene's house, whether she liked it or not, through the woods to the Catholic cemetery located atop an expansive, wooded hill, this side of Hill

---

[8] Today unnamed on Internet maps, but the LHU Ropes Course Trail transects it.

Street and Sunset Pines, and sledded down the narrow walking trail. It was quite a ride.

Since we were the only ones who used that trail, it was often overgrown with bushes or roots, or sometimes gutted from storms. If a tree had fallen across the trail, we created a detour around it, making some dangerously sharp curves. Rocks, deep ruts, and downed trees made it that much more fun for us.

Across Chestnut Street from Jolene's house stood a majestic oak tree sporting a trunk five, maybe six feet thick, overlooking the entire Susquehanna valley. We called it, *Sergeant Oak*. The ground on either side of it sloped, one side to Jolene's street, the other, toward a thorn hedge that bordered the Smith property. Passage on the Smith side was quite narrow for the sled to fit through; passage on Jolene's side at top speed severely tested the sled driver's maneuvering skills.

By the time we reached Sergeant Oak, we must have been traveling close to twenty miles an hour. The angle of the trail was such that we were forced toward the tree. We had to make a *very* quick decision as to which side of Sergeant Oak to go. Since he refused to step aside for us, no matter how fast we were coming, Johnnie and I both have a number of scars testifying to his victories and our stupid miscalculations, especially when we rode piggyback. (We had only the one sled.)

"Lean!" Johnnie, the driver, shouted at me, riding on top of him.

"Which way?" I yelled back, tightening my grip on the sides of the sled.

"Right!"

"No, you said we'd go left..." I screamed, that was the agreed-upon option before we started.

Bam!

I slid into Mr. Smith's thorny hedge, while Johnnie had a direct encounter with Sergeant Oak.

"Ouch. Oh-o-o...."

"Are you all right...?"

Never had any serious injuries—just lots of cuts, scrapes, and bruises.

Johnnie and I had a love-hate relationship growing up. He believed I was the pampered baby of the family, while I resented his bossing me around. He felt entitled to do so as the older brother. This often led to pushing, shoving, and wrestling. (We rarely punched each other, and never struck the other in the face. The object was to get the other in some sort of a submission hold. Which rarely happened.)

As an example, one time inside the house, an argument led to a fight at the top of the front staircase. Two steps down from the second floor hallway was a landing with an outside window, at which point the staircase took an L-turn and continued to the first floor. As we tussled, we fell down the two top steps and crashed into that window, cracking two panes, one quite severely. Fortunately we didn't go *through* the window, or we would have fallen to the ground some twenty feet below.

But the cracks where our heads or elbows connected with the glass looked like large spider webs. We sustained minor cuts and got a severe tongue lashing from Mom, and a worse one from Dad when he got home. He decided our punishment would be to repair the window at our own expense. He said, "It'll teach you a lesson. Plus, you'll learn how to install a windowpane." For that, Dad was a patient, but exacting teacher.

These stories show the two sides of Johnnie's and my relationship. We could play together as great pals, then suddenly break into a squabble over something. I guess it's what you call normal.

I'm happy to report that in the autumn of our years, though we are separated by the Atlantic Ocean, we have come to realize how very much we mean to one another, especially since Joan and Cissie both died in 2012, two months apart.

Johnnie played the trumpet in the high school band, so I wanted to play trumpet, as well. And it was Johnnie who first awakened my interest in classical singing. He took singing lessons from Mr. Fontana across Susquehanna Avenue. He was a local operatic baritone legend, and when he started giving Johnnie voice lessons, I had to get in on it. I was a constant thorn in Johnnie's side that way.

Johnnie sang in the high school chorus, as did both Joan and Cissie before him. Johnnie and Cissie also played in the high school band, so I followed in their musical footsteps, including church choirs and high school band. After a year or two in the band, I began taking piano lessons, paying for them with the money from my paper route.

Mrs. Kamp, my piano teacher, happened to live on my paper route. She was the organist at Trinity Methodist Church. Studying piano with her led to singing in the adult choir. She was strictly a classical music person, and her dedication to it rubbed off on me, so that by the time the singing bug bit me, I had no use for anything but classical vocal music. The singing of Mario Lanza, especially in the movie, *The Student Prince*, mentioned in the previous chapter, inspired me to sing opera above anything thing else—even though I had never heard an opera. (I can't explain it....)

My desire to sing began to push everything else in my life to the side. It even outweighed the spiritual pulls on my life, I blush to admit. When I joined the Youth Fellowship at Trinity, the girls redirected my attention. There were certain girls there I wanted to date. Diane Graves, for one, the lovely daughter of the high school vocal music teacher, whose smile caught my eye. But she rarely showed up—at least, not when I was there. Diane was two grades below me, reminding me of my disappointment with Kay Hickey. But I did meet Diane at the local Y where we danced occasionally. But as with Kay, we couldn't find common ground. (Her mother was to become my first private voice teacher.)

· · · · ·

In high school, Johnnie made friends with the son of the Methodist pastor at the other end of Lock Haven, near the Piper Airport. His name was Stan, and he, like Hickey, loved cars, and spent every spare moment working on them. He had a shell of a car that he was rebuilding. Four wheels loosely connected to a frame, with the engine loosely perched on it, *loosely* being the operative word for that junk heap.

Add to that a steering wheel and the pedals necessary to operate it: accelerator, clutch, and brake. A tattered driver's seat, a rocking chair, not even bolted down, completed the wreck. Passengers could find space on what remained of the flooring, but were on their own to stay aboard when the rattletrap was in motion. Remember, no sides on the car.

95

One cool, summer Saturday night, Stan decided to take his monster for a spin, and invited Johnnie and me along. He told us he *had* to drive it at night—so as not to get caught.

"Get caught?" I asked. "Whaddaya mean?"

"Are you kidding?" Stan said. "The monster violates every law in the book. I'd probably end up in jail if they stopped us on the road in this thing."

"Oh."

We needed a full moon to see anything because the beast had no lights. Worse, there was no muffler. It made a racket like an angry jackhammer. Not many people lived at the east end of town near the airport. He probably figured if anybody was out and about, they would be at noisy bars too drunk to hear anything. One bar nestled next to the airport, but from all reports of the racket within, they wouldn't hear a thing even if the Russians dropped a bomb next to them.

I didn't want to go on this adventure because I had to sing a solo in church the following morning. It was already late, and quite cool. A full October moon with a crystal clear sky, no breeze. And I didn't have a jacket with me, so I said, "Guys, I gotta sing in church in the morning."

"So?" Johnnie said, looking at me as if I were a traitor.

"I can't stay out this late."

"Why not?" Stan asked rather defensively.

"Well, for one thing, I need my rest to sing."

They both groaned and looked at me with jeering faces. "Don't be such a baby."

"If I'm out in the cold, I'll probably wake up with a sore throat," I said, now becoming irate.

"Ah, fer cryin' all night, Robert," Johnnie said. "Don't be such a pansy-waist."

That was Mom's word for a coward. It was our word for a battle cry.

"You're just a chicken, that's all," said Stan, who was more amused than angry. He sided with Johnnie to persuade me to come along, but while Johnnie was getting pretty heated, Stan took it all in stride, smiling to himself, *Let the brothers have it out.*

"No I'm *not*," I said hotly, but my resolve was faltering. I looked from one to the other. Seeing Stan smile about it calmed me down a little. I finally shook my head and said rather angrily, "Oh, all right, I'll go." I didn't want to be labeled a chicken.

Stan had a devil of a time getting the cranky engine started, but once it roared to life, the din of it scared the living daylights out of us. Since his house was on Main Street, where a slew of people lived, Stan realized the noise would not only disturb the neighbors, but also wake his father, a pastor, who, at this hour, would be in bed dreaming about the morning sermon. So he quickly shut the engine down. To avoid rousing the neighbors, we decided to push it several blocks and crank it up once we got down to the bridge—there weren't any houses there.

Once we were past the bridge, Stan got it running and we made haste toward the airport, which I thought was the destination, a half-mile down the road. Soon, the monster was cruising, if you could call it that, so Stan was inspired to put it through its paces.

I was surprised as he passed the airport. He took it just beyond, where the Susquehanna River splits for a mile or two, creating a fertile island (called Great Island), that consisted of farms with this road straight through the middle. Stan figured this would be the ideal place to test the limits of the monster, because the road was out of earshot—or so he thought.

He crossed the bridge and opened it all the way, creating a fearsome racket. Undeterred, he piloted the bucket of bolts back and forth several times, from one end of the island to the other.

The thrilling ride made me forget how cold I was. We all had grabbed for the nearest handhold just to stay on the beast. I had a firm grip on the windshield frame—there was no windshield in it. You could smell the corn and the occasional barnyard. I didn't look to see how the others managed to stay aboard. The wind blew my hair back and swept the sweat away.

The moon was bright enough so Stan could see the road. Our eyes were quite adjusted to the darkness by this time. I felt as though we were going to take off and fly right up to the shiny moon when the wind was at our back.

Dark houses began lighting up. Although we couldn't hear voices through the racket, we saw shadows of angry men waving, presumably shouting at us. One man had a flashlight. Why? Who could hear what they were saying? When we realized they were not shouting friendly hellos, Stan suddenly panicked, fearing someone would call the police. So we quickly hightailed it back to the mainland.

As we were coming to the lower end of the airport, we saw police lights coming our way. Stan immediately pulled off the road into a woodsy section at the east end of the airport and shut the engine down. We hid the monster as best we could in the dark woods. We watched with wide eyes as the police cruiser whizzed past us towards the island. I thought of that night with Hickey and the sodium balls, but kept my mouth shut. This wasn't the time to regale them with stories.

We waited. And waited.

"What are we waiting for?" I whispered to Stan, one hand on his shoulder.

"For the damned police car to come back so we can get this thing back to my house before my father finds out!" he hissed back to me.

By and by, the cruiser did return, speeding past us up Water Street, apparently hoping to catch us after speaking with angry residents. We dared not start the engine again, so we pushed the monster directly through the airport and down a taxi runway to remain out of sight—at least most of the way. We managed to get past the Constitution Bridge without being noticed and made haste for the alley behind Stan's house.

Johnnie and I lived about two miles from Stan, and it must have been at least three in the morning when we returned home.

With maybe three hours of sleep, Mom woke me up at 7:00 AM to tell us we had a phone call. Still in her nightgown, she was beside herself. I couldn't tell if it was fear or rage.

"Who's calling at this hour?" I asked dopily. I rubbed my eyes, trying to come back into the conscious world. I rolled back with the intention of covering my head with the pillow.

"Sheriff Milner down at the Police station!" she snapped, terror and anger in her eyes. "What in the world were you two up to last night? Where *were* you, Robert—you have to sing in church this morning! The sheriff wants you and Johnnie to come into his office right away. He sounded very angry."

The word *sheriff* stopped me in mid-roll. I looked back at Mom as my heart leapt into my throat, my brain froze. I pulled my feet out and plopped them on the cold floor. I couldn't face Mom, who was standing much too near, so I stared at the floor. Ever fearful of authority figures, my mind took a hiatus and my stomach was ready to retch from panic. *What am I going to do?*

Slowly my mind ground into gear. *Will they arrest us? Will they throw us in jail? What will I tell Mrs. Kamp? What can I say to Mom? To Dad?—good Lord!*

I dragged myself to my feet while Mom shouted orders. When I looked up, she had gone down the hall yelling at Johnnie to get up. Somehow, we both got out of the house without telling her anything significant. Fortunately, the sheriff's office was at the foot of Susquehanna Avenue, just down the hill. I dressed hastily, as did Johnnie, and we stumbled down the hill, each wondering how they found us out.

The sheriff, a burly, intimidating figure, turned out to be a very pleasant, understanding fellow, and he really wanted to avoid as much trouble for us as possible. He also didn't want us to acquire criminal records. We didn't want to rat on Stan, but we really had no choice. The officer seemed to know all about Stan, because this was not the first time his monster had caught their attention. The officer wondered how we disappeared so quickly from the road. Johnnie told him exactly what we did from the airport on.

I then said, "Sir, I have to sing in church this morning. Do I have to go to jail?"

He laughed, sat down heavily in his chair, and said, "Well now, we can't have you miss singing in church, can we? What time do you have to be there?"

"Ten-thirty."

"What church?"

"Trinity Methodist. Mrs. Kamp is the organist; Rev. Beam's the pastor."

"Okay, I think we can arrange to get you there on time. But first…."

Johnnie and I exchanged nervous glances.

He rose and walked around his desk to stand directly in front of us. Thumb and forefinger across his chin, he eyed me for a moment, and then launched into his favorite, friendly lecture on safety and the friends we keep. After this, he sent us on our way. On the way back up the hill, Johnnie and I spoke hardly a word. As we neared the backdoor, we looked at each other with the same thought, *What do we say to Mom? How about Dad?*

She was relieved to see us back so soon. She probably thought we'd be thrown in jail for at least a week for whatever we had done. Johnnie was good at persuading her that it was Stan's fault, that he had persuaded us to go along with his prank, knowing full well how dangerous and illegal it was.

Surprisingly, she did not press the obvious points, such as, why did you agree to go? Rather, she turned to me and ordered, "Robert, you get up those stairs right now and get ready for church. You need a shower. You don't want to have Mrs. Kamp mad at you, too." Mom couldn't handle other people's anger.

Somehow, Lord knows, I did sing in church that morning. But it was a challenge. The sermon put me to sleep, and only the organ bursting to life for the hymn after it woke me up. Standing helped. But soon after that, I nodded off during a long-winded announcement. I kept prodding myself to stay awake because I had to sing right after the man sat down. *Sit down already!* I wished I could open a trapdoor underneath him. I was more nervous than usual, and afraid my voice might not "work" after such a night, not to mention the stress of the morning. My senses dulled and I began to sweat. The longer he droned on, the drier and tighter my throat felt. *Shut up, for God's sake!*

At last…when I finally began to sing, adrenaline kicked in and got me through.

I never told Mrs. Kamp what had happened the night before. No need for her to know.

My singing wasn't the only force drawing me to the Church. God, in His formidable, mysterious ways, had His hand on me. Though I had no idea at the time, He had plans for me, and Johnnie's role in this had yet to be revealed.

Chapter Eight

Teenage Faith

Getting caught pulling pranks like that shakes a kid up, especially getting hauled in by the cops. A first for me. Very upsetting. My ego was fragile enough, thank you very much—I didn't need this slap in the face. Stan's out of my life now. Good riddance. Trying to figure out who you are and where you want to go, add parents tugging me this way and that…all this crap tested my relationship with God.

Did I even have a relationship? Was this latest incident with Stan a wake-up call? Which kind of life do you want, Robert, a life for yourself or for others? Are they mutually exclusive? What about singing opera? Must it be a life of self-indulgence? Can I be a Christian and still sing opera? Dad claims that artists are leeches on society. Maybe I should just join the military and be done with it. Yeah, go ahead and fly massmurdering machines. How about becoming a teacher? Or a pastor? How would I know if I'm called?

Singing. Yes, I sang in the Cherub Choir and then in the Children's Choir at Trinity Methodist. Music was always a vital part of my life, don't ask me why. Most of all, singing. Adults always said I had a pretty voice. Hum-m. Mrs. Kamp seemed to like my singing. I studied piano with her for four years. Although she never commented on my singing, she encouraged me—not sure why. Maybe because she always needed singers for her choir, or maybe she saw how much I loved it. Who knows?

It's true I felt a tension between my spiritual life and my desire to sing professionally. I shoved it all into the background. I had more pressing things on my mind. Grades. Girls. Grades I could handle, but girls…?

Somewhere along my high school continuum, Trinity Methodist acquired two new pastors, one after the other. The first was Pastor Marshall, and later came Pastor Beam.

Mom called them both "Pappy"—behind their backs, of course. She would never have addressed them that way, nor would she have permitted anyone else do so. Mom didn't want others to see her secret hypocrisy. She would have denied she had a different standard for herself than she held for others. I think deep down, she knew she was wrong.

Pastor Marshall came from South Carolina, complete with a drawl that Mom loved to try to mimic. He was a short man, but tall on energy, wit, stories, and exuberance. I can still see his bright features and unusually long fingers—which must have felt weighed down by so many colorful rings—dancing across the piano keys. His long, kinky hair wasn't as black and full as it used to be. He loved his jewelry, from neck to bracelets. His dark eyes lit up when he accompanied himself, especially when he sang Negro spirituals, which he loved. He really had the touch for that kind of upbeat music. I often wondered if he had African blood in him. He was rather dark complected…?

He usually dressed with brightly hued reds, yellows, and purples. Undoubtedly his clothes were strongly influenced by his African-American friends in the south. I suppose his upbeat demeanor and lifestyle—he often had a cigarette dangling from his lips, even in church—upset many a congregant at Trinity Methodist. All that brought his time with us to a premature end, sad to say. His southern ways worked against him as well. Prejudice was alive and all too well in the fifties, Lock Haven was lily-white at that time. I don't remember ever seeing a black face until we played Williamsport in football.

Mom, I believe unintentionally, helped to hasten his departure by complaining about his smoking. She truly liked the man, and I doubt she'd have wanted him to leave. But—she also smoked—not much, mind you—but insisted that pastors shouldn't. Especially in the church. She saw nothing wrong with her double standards, and she had plenty of them.

Mrs. Kamp often complained to me in my piano lessons about the smell of smoke from Pastor Marshall's office, not to mention his clothes. "It's disgusting," she ranted. "I hope you never take up the habit, Robert." She and Mom were not alone in their disapproval.

I can still hear his raspy voice ringing clear on the old Gospel hymn, "Standin' in the Need of Prayer." He would begin:

"It's-a me, it's-a me, it's-a me, O Lord, Standin' in the need o' prayer.

"O-o-h, It's-a-me, it's-a-me, it's-a-me, O Lord, Standin' in the need o' prayer!" [9]

His singing of this song engraved itself on my conscience. Somehow I had missed that spiritual spark in my life. I didn't pray as often as I should've, and I rarely thought to reach out to others in need. So, I would agonize, *Am I really pastoral material? I spend all my efforts on myself and very little for others. None at all, jerk. All you think about is your singing and what* you *want....*

Rev. Marshall understood very well that painfully thin line between saint and sinner. One day we were sitting in his office yakking. Although I could smell cigarette smoke in the air, he wasn't smoking. His desk was neat, except for the large, smelly, butt-filled ashtray. One butt had a thread of smoke twirling upward. Must not have snuffed it out all the way. Made my throat burn, like at home with Dad.

Shelves of books stood against two walls. The other walls were decked out with colorful banners, photos on the walls, a sofa on one side and a small table on the other with magazines and books scattered on top. Some of the pictures appeared as if they had been taken in Africa, but he told me no, in South Carolina. "Sometimes it gits jiss as hot as in Africa, though," he quipped. I didn't see his colorful robes; they must have been hanging in a closet somewhere.

"So, Robert, I understand y' wanna be an opera singer." His face broadened into a smile. He was very relaxed, not his usual hyper self.

"Yes," I said, nodding. I enjoyed his company and often sought his wisdom. "Well, Mrs. Graves and Mrs. Kamp both say I'll never make it into the opera, and I should find myself another vocation, like teaching music or somethin'."

[9] "Standing in the Need of Prayer." Hymnary.org. Hymnary.org, 2001. Web. 22 August 2015. http://www.hymnary.org/text/not_my_brother_nor_my_sister_but_its_me

"Another vocation, eh? That's what they say, um-m. What does Crik-, ah, I mean, your mother, say—and your father?"

"Pretty much the same thing. Dad wants me to take over his printing business…."

"Well, there y' go. Maybe y' can combine the two somehow."

I raised an eye brow. I echoed his "um-m," but with a different twist. "I can't see how."

"Who knows? Robert, y' gotta think creatively to come up with sumpin'. I don' spect y' t' figger it out as y' sit here. Go home and cogitate on it." He leaned forward and picked up a magazine. "Take a look at this magazine. It talks about receivin' God's call. Mebbe God'll call y' in a differ'nt direction than yer thinkin', but who knows? Mebbe he intends to use yer musical talents as well" He handed me the magazine.

I looked at it. The cover featured a pastor holding a violin with the words, "A Preacher's Music of the Spheres." Rev. Marshall said, pointing to the man on the cover, "The Lord blessed 'im with a ministry of music. Mebbe He'll do the same for you."

"Mebbe," I said, falling into his way of speaking. "Thanks, Rev. Marshall. I'll take a good, hard look at it." I laid it on my lap.

I launched into a diatribe about some of my foul-ups, and we talked about following one's own way and following God's way. How am I to discern which is which?

He assured me that if we listen hard 'nough, God will make his will clear. "He fergave me, after all," he said with a chuckle, and leaned back in his chair to tell me about his struggles to become a pastor. "Ya gotta keep prayin' and listenin', and God'll make his will known to ya."

His counsel gave me hope.

"Ya know," he continued, "it really doesn't take a whole lot to be compassionate to others. All ya really have to do is try t' see things their way. People are all differ'nt. We don't have to convert t' their way of thinkin', we just have t' make an effert t' see things the way they see 'em. When they see that ya care about them, they'll most likely respond in kind. If they don't, well, ya walk away, that's all. Ya tried. Ya did yer best, an' that's all the Lord asks of ya." He laughed. "I don' know how music fits into all this—that'll haf to be b'tween you and the Lahrd." He stood up and offered his hand. "Got some work to do. Great talkin' with ya, Robert."

I shook his hand, thanked him, and left.

·　·　·　·　·

In the fifties, prejudice against people of other races was well entrenched in Lock Haven. Just take my bigoted father for example. He had no tolerance for Jews or blacks. He'd just as soon shoot 'em as look at 'em.

Reverend Marshall's guidance taught me a tolerance that had never occurred to me, growing up in such an environment. When he preached on the subject, many congregants muttered and complained among themselves, or so I heard at home. I wasn't totally aware what was going on, but I knew something was very wrong about the way people hated other people, and just because of race or religion. Sometimes, I overheard Dad raving about the pastor and his "ridiculous ideas" to Mom. Rev. Marshall's call for racial tolerance became another nail in his coffin at Trinity Methodist. The complaints about him, I soon learned, were widespread in the congregation.

I wept when he left. I wept for him. I wept simply because of the injustice of it, it just didn't make any sense. None at all.

Pastor Marshall gave way to the Rev. Herbert P. Beam, who couldn't have been a greater contrast. Tall and lean, a full head of grey hair, a stern chiseled face, deep-set, brooding grey-blue eyes, broad, thick eyebrows, thin lips, square chin. He always dressed in black from his worn Fedora to his polished, but shabby shoes. All that black made his gleaming white clerical collar shine like a lighthouse beacon.

I never saw him in any other clothes, and often wondered if he showered and slept in this "uniform." Unlike many other pastors, especially Pastor Marshall, he never adorned himself with crosses, lapel pins, or any kind of jewelry. For many folks, he was a caricature of a country parson, much like the Fearless Fosdick in the *Li'l Abner* 1950s comic strip that satirized the famous New York preacher, the Rev. Harry Emerson Fosdick of the 1920s, 30s, and 40s.

Rev. Beam's commitment to his calling, his unflinching faith, and loving concern for his wife and flock, made a strong impression on me. I don't remember his sermons, but I can still hear his deep bass voice that could crack glass at fifty yards, and sounded like the voice of God when he raised it. He too took me under his wing soon after he arrived, recognizing in me some mysterious potential for the ministry.

Maybe it resulted from the stories Mom told him about Pop-Pop, I don't know. In any case, his dream was to send me to Drew University in Madison, New Jersey, to first major in English or History, and then continue my studies at the prestigious Drew Seminary for a Master of Divinity, and perhaps even a doctorate. His interest in me lifted my feelings of self-worth out of the gutter. Did he see something in me I didn't know I had? What was it?

· · · · ·

I should point out that I had not experienced a spiritual "call,"[10] a necessary requisite for entering the pastorate, but Rev. Beam was confident that a call would follow in due course. He even asked me (commanded me, more like it) to preach a sermon at Trinity one Sunday morning. I still remember my text: 1 Corinthians, Chapter 8, the section about meat offered to idols. The thrust of my sermon was to "take care lest this liberty of yours becomes a stumbling block to them that are weak." Given that today I can't remember what I preached about last week, that I remember this particular sermon after all these years suggests how much Rev. Beam's confidence in me meant.

I felt exhilarated standing in front of the congregation. It was meant to be. At the time, I took that as a sign that I was meant to be a performer, an opera singer. I didn't mention that to Rev. Beam, though.

Suddenly, I felt that my singing was to be sacrificed like a burnt offering if I studied for the ministry. Like Jonah, I began to run the other way. Little did I know how long that race would be. In that moment, I couldn't escape my longing for Ann Blyth, the actress who played the barmaid in *The Student Prince*. My understanding of love at that time was very nineteenth-century German Romanticism.[11] The biblical word, *agape*, the Greek word in the Bible for God's love, had no meaning for me.

---

[10] The term "call" is used two ways: 1. A personal sense of God "calling" an individual to a spiritual vocation, and 2. The formal invitation ("call") of a congregation to a pastor. This latter "call" is a written covenant, or agreement. (Technically in church terms, it's not a contract).

[11] In nineteenth century German romanticism, a lover puts the object of his love on a pedestal high above, unreachable; and yet, he had to try to win her.

Whether they liked my teenage sermon or not, they praised me if for no other reason than I was a future pastoral candidate, or so they thought.

On the other hand, I was attracted to Rev. Beam's plan because I saw the opportunity to study and learn, the chance to acquire knowledge and learn how to reason logically—like David Wolfe. I had always hankered to be well educated. (I dreamed of people addressing me as "Dr. Mitchell," or "Rev. Dr. Mitchell." Or, if I'd chosen the military, "Admiral," "Captain," or at least "Commander Mitchell." I loved the Navy—my dream was to fly planes off ships, combining flying with sailing the oceans.)

However, both parents insisted that I at least begin my studies down the street at Lock Haven State Teachers' College. "After all, both Joan and Cissie put themselves through Lock Haven State," they reminded me.

"But I want to go to Drew. It's a far better school."

"You can transfer later. The cost of living on campus at Drew *alone* exceeds the cost of tuition at Lock Haven. Doesn't make sense. You can live here at home and save a bundle of money."

"But Dad...."

"Think about it."

· · · · ·

Today, since my wife and I have raised two sons and helped them through undergraduate school, my parents' logic resonates with me now. But back then I really wanted to follow my dream of singing opera. I had folded my desire to sing into this pastoral plan because I hoped there would be vocal opportunities at a large university like Drew. Perhaps even opera.

· · · · ·

Rev. Beam was undeterred by the financial issue. "We'll get loans," he assured me.

"Yes, sir. Thank you, sir," I said.

With that hope I dreamed of going on for a doctorate and becoming a theologian. Teaching appealed to me more than preaching at that time.

Rev. Beam gave me the loan applications to take home to Dad, who I thought would readily buy into this plan. I carefully prepared the papers in the proper order, so that when I set them down in front of him, he could simply go through them and sign where necessary. I placed the documents before him with a big smile.

"What?" he yelled. "You wanna *borrow* money for college?"

"Sure, Dad. I'll pay it back. It won't cost you a cent! All I need is your signature," I pointed to the first sheet, "here…."

As he picked them up and scanned them, he said, "I've never borrowed money in my life, and I'm not about to start now." He paused and scrutinized the pages listing the costs. He looked up with the papers in his fist, shaking them at me furiously. "This is a lot of money. Why do you have to go to such an expensive college? Why can't you earn the money first, and then go down the street like your sisters did? Like any obedient son should?"

"Because Rev. Beam *wants* me to…and I want to become a pastor, like Pop-Pop."

"A *pastor*?" Dad stared at me. He rarely attended church, and had been out of the loop about what I might want to do with my life other than take over the printing business. "What makes you think you can become a pastor? Why don't you go for something constructive, like—well, I thought you wanted to become a scientist—or what happened to your opera singing? Damn it, Robert! Make up your mind. You think I'm going to risk my business as collateral for all your goddamn pipe dreams? How do you know you'll be able to pay it off?"

"I will, Dad…"

"Yeah, right. But how? Preachers don't earn this kind of money. And you'll never earn a dime as a singer, mark my words. Look, Robert," he said, swinging his chair around to face me, "I can't take that chance. When you default on one payment, they'll come after *me*, not you. That'll ruin me." He turned back to his desk. With the documents still in his hand, he shook them at me and continued, "No way. Now get the hell outta here. I have work to do!" He slapped the papers into my chest.

Later, Rev. Beam tried to reason with him, but got nowhere. Mom tried her wiles as well, but—the result was the same. Dad was adamant, and that was the end of my dream to become a pastor-theologian. I turned back to my dream of becoming a singer, which seemed even more elusive for me. Consequently, I finally decided to attend Lock Haven State Teachers College as my two sisters had, until I could find my way, whatever that would be.

• • • • •

In the meantime, Johnnie had graduated from high school and joined the Navy. He continued playing the trumpet, privileged to study with a trumpeter from the United States Naval Band while stationed in Washington. Later, he was transferred to the naval station in Norfolk, Virginia.

It was there that one of his buddies took him to a local evangelical church. For the first time in his life, he heard the Gospel proclaimed in the evangelical manner. Johnnie responded and became a "born-again" Christian. That his conversion was true and complete was demonstrated by his commitment to become a Baptist pastor and missionary in France. After he completed his studies, he and his wife, Beverly, immediately went to France, and have made that country their home ever since—over fifty years now.

On a trip home on leave from the Navy in my senior year in high school, 1956-1957, Johnnie was so excited about the Lord that he quite naturally wanted to share his faith with the rest of us Mitchells. Dad was amused and totally disinterested. Mom was horrified that he had been baptized *again*, after having been baptized by Pop-Pop Trautman. The Bible calls for just one baptism. Before long, whenever Johnnie's name would come up in conversation, she would say, "Johnnie's become a flaming Baptist." Our older sister Joan was intrigued by his conversion. I can imagine her smiling and wondering how she too could become a Christian. Cis resisted, as I recall.

I was wary at first. But soon I could see the spiritual logic of it. All the years I had spent with David Wolfe became clearer. Consequently, Johnnie led me to the Lord by walking me through certain Bible passages, explaining them, and assuring me that if I did not surrender my life to Christ, I would go to hell.

We also prayed together over the several days he was home. Finally, we prayed the Sinner's Prayer in which I acknowledged my past transgressions of

God's law. Afterward, I felt a warmth in my heart I'd never felt before, an assurance that all my past wrongs had now been forgiven. A warmth swept through my entire body. Tears came to my eyes, and Johnnie and I had a good cry on each other's shoulder. God's forgiveness was (is) real.

After that, Johnnie took me to First Baptist Church on Church Street in Lock Haven, where I met David again. He was very pleased about my conversion. Our reunion felt good.

Johnnie went back to the Navy and David went off to Wheaton College in Illinois. But the change in the Christian understanding, along with a very different worship style, began to gnaw at me. Moreover, I was sad and uncomfortable with having displeased Mom and Pastor Beam. The argument over baptism Johnnie had with Mom haunted me. He cited biblical references that clearly say we must become a believer *before* we can be baptized. The Bible says nothing about parents making promises for their children, he argued. I could not challenge his point.

Rev. Beam said very little about Johnnie's conversion. But when I asked him what he thought about it, I could tell he was angry by his sullen demeanor, and especially, his eyes. "They have no right to take our people away. Live and let live, I say. I hope your brother is happy."

•   •   •   •   •

Ecumenism as we know it today had yet to be born, and mainline churches felt threatened by this kind of evangelism. They still do, actually. Evangelizing folks from other Protestant denominations crossed an unspoken line: your mission field is *not* the church down the street. Mainline ministers, such as Rev. Fosdick, therefore, spoke harshly about evangelical practice and beliefs, discrediting their proselytizing tactics. This distrust fueled dissension all across Protestantism.

Catholics, however, were always fair game for Protestants, especially with the Evangelicals, who believe some misguided things about Catholicism. I think of Rev. Marshall's words, "We don't have to convert t' their way of thinkin', we just have t' make an effert t' see things the way they see 'em." Perhaps if we all did this, we wouldn't have so many denominations.

. . . . .

Through all the disappointment and confusion about faith, I gradually pushed my Baptist experience into the background, thinking that God had let me down. *What's going on here, Lord? You lead me up to the fountain for a drink, and before I can dip my cup you take the fountain away. What kind of crap is this?* I couldn't help the foul language. *Do you see how this frustrates me? I'm really pissed off at you, Lord, for letting this happen. So—I guess I'm back on my own again. Thanks a lot.*

Even though I lost my temper and turned my back on God, the profound effects of David's ministries, and Johnnie's, remained throughout my life. For the moment, however, my spiritual life took a back seat. *Jonah, I guess I'm still following you around....*

Chapter Nine

Career Confusion and Marriage

When I graduated from high school in 1957, the Korean War—then euphemistically called, "Conflict," had raged for two years. I hadn't paid much heed, but the mere fact that I was now eighteen, the war suddenly grabbed me by the shoulders. If I were to be called up to serve in the military, I wanted it on my terms: an officer in the sky or onboard a ship, not in the trenches. For that I needed at least two years of college.

Mom and Dad had already won the battle about which college to attend. So, I entered Lock Haven State Teachers College, (Lock Haven University today), as they had wished, uh-h, demanded. The money ruled the day. Besides, LHSTC was so close by, I could stay in my own room at home.

The funny thing was, I had decided to study mathematics. Part of that came from my new dream of becoming a pilot in the military, which I could do in the Navy, my favorite branch. There was a naval flying school in Pensacola, Florida that required two years of college. Completing their course would provide me with both a bachelor's degree and wings for flying duty in the Navy. My plan was to serve for the required time and then become an airline pilot. Cushy job, I thought. Maybe I could sing on the side. The first step was to complete the required two years at Lock Haven State, and then, off to Pensacola.

But that's not the whole story.

The Smith family next door had but one child, Sammy, Sam Jr. He was a year or two older than my eldest sister, Joan, and he was a merciless, and sometimes nasty, tease. More than once in my younger years, Joan wrestled him to the ground in my defense. By my last year of high school, Sammy had long since left home. I was the only one left in our house as well. Johnnie was in the Navy, Cissie was teaching in Austin, Texas, and Joan was married and living in Harrisburg, Pennsylvania.

Growing up, I had no idea that Sammy's father was a math professor at LHSTC—indeed, the longstanding chairperson of the mathematics department. His career spanned thirty-one years, from 1927 to 1958. The present Smith Hall is named in his honor.

In stature he was rather short and had a professorial image not unlike that of Einstein—except for his hair. His thinning grey hair tumbled over his ears, glasses perched halfway down his nose. He walked with a perpetual slump as if he were untangling a difficult mathematical problem. As children, we rarely spoke to him, and he didn't speak to us. But if I were to say, "Hi, Mr. Smith," he would look up, startled, and reply, "Oh, gut'n Morgan to you, Robert," in his distinctly Pennsylvania Dutch accent, with a smile and friendly wave. How he knew my name always puzzled me.

Mrs. Smith domineered the Smith household. She towered over Mr. Smith by a head. My childhood image of her was that of a drill sergeant with a rolling pin in her massive right hand, always at the ready to enforce her kitchen edicts. She was never without an apron covering her long flowery dresses, flat shoes, her salt and pepper hair bobbed in the back.

One time when we were small, Mr. and Mrs. Smith drove Johnnie and me in their tan, four-door Nash sedan, which to us was like a limousine. I can't remember why or where we went—perhaps they were babysitting us while Dad and Mom were busy, or involved in an emergency of some sort. Johnnie and I sat in the back seat.

Mrs. Smith was a jabbering traffic cop from the passenger seat, with Mr. Smith responding, "Ja," or "Ja, Elsie, I see it," in a quiet way that made Johnnie and me to look at each other and giggle.

Every time she commanded him to do something, we thought of Dad, who would have abruptly pulled the car over, cursing and swearing, and ordered Mom to drive it herself. (But Mrs. Smith didn't drive anyway, she said.) We were totally in awe of how remarkably unflappable Mr. Smith was. What a contrast to Dad!

On the way home she treated us each to a 3 Musketeers Bar, a first for us. Mom never allowed candy bars. "Rot your teeth," she'd say. I fell in love with 3 Musketeers bars, and to this day, when I see one on a rack someplace, I think of that ride in the Nash with the Smiths.

In my senior year of high school, I was having trouble with Algebra II, and one day I was whining to Mom about it, and she said, "Why don't you ask Mr. Smith?"

"Mr. Smith?" I pointed a finger toward Chestnut Street. "You mean—?"

She nodded.

I looked puzzled. "Ask him what?"

"Robert, for heaven sakes,[12] he teaches math down at the college."

"Really? I didn't know that."

"Well, where have *you* been for the last ten years?"

I blushed.

Of course, I wanted to take advantage of this unexpected resource next door, but I hesitated. What if he was like Dad? Anyway, he'd probably brush me off. And if he took me on, would he make me feel like an idiot—like Dad always did? But my need to make a good grade overcame my reticence.

Much to my surprise, when I approached him, he responded like a loving grandfather would. "Vell now, Robert, vat's the trou-bul? How kann I help you?"

When I showed him my work, he smiled and said, "You come ofer after zupper and vee'll see vat ve kann do."

•　•　•　•　•

When Johnnie and I were little, we rarely saw the inside of the Smith house, which Mrs. "Sergeant" Smith kept in perfect order. When we *did* knock on the back door, usually to ask Sammy to come out and play, she would invite us in, but we never got past the kitchen. She'd say, "You wait here. I'll see if Sammy is up." We loved waiting in her kitchen because of the scrumptious

---

[12] She always said "sake" with an unnecessary "-s."

baking aromas. Every time we were there, she offered us a cookie, a pastry, a slice of freshly baked bread—which melted the butter on contact—or a piece of pie. We always hoped Sammy would take his good-old time to come downstairs.

I noticed a door on the left, just as we entered the kitchen, always closed. Another door on the same wall across the kitchen was always open. They went freely in and out of that one, which led through the dining room. But that first door haunted me. What was behind it? I once asked Johnnie about it.

"How in blazes would I know? I've never seen it open either."

"Just asking. Geez!"

From outside the house standing on Chestnut Street, I could see the windows to that room, but I couldn't see into the room. Maybe it was a large, walk-in closet—with windows for some reason or other. I used to conjure up images of ghosts and goblins, bear and stag heads on the walls, maybe cobwebs strung from one head to the other. What was in that room?

· · · · ·

On the day of my first visit with Mr. Smith, much to my astonishment, he, not Mrs. Smith, met me at the kitchen door with a big smile and a modest greeting. "Vell, Robert, it's good to see you. Come in, come in." Without further ado, he invited me into that very room, the mystery one, through that first, mystifying door on the left. I think this was the very first time I ever saw that door opened. My heart raced in anticipation.

Following Mr. Smith, I stepped into another realm that didn't come close to my childish imaginings. The fragrance of pipe tobacco overwhelmed Mrs. Smith's heavenly baking aromas, which at first twisted my nose like a wet dishrag.

Now I know why Mrs. Smith always kept that door shut!

As I grew used to it, the tobacco odor reminded me of our neighbor on the other side of our property, old Mr. Messerly, the *late* Mr. Messerly, who, some years ago prior to his passing, refused to give up his pipes, although he was sickly and confined to a wheelchair. His vast pipe collection stood at attention in a rack easily within his reach. Tobacco, matches, and all the necessary paraphernalia knew their place in his scheme of things. His smoking routine fascinated me when I visited him as a small boy. I'm not sure why, except to say that Dad's smoking in our house was as routine as his cursing at a printing press. I've seen pictures of Dad smoking a pipe, and I remember finding that same pipe in a drawer after he died, but I myself don't remember him smoking it. Mom always said she loved the "smell" of a pipe. I think all these pieces put together awakened my interest in pipe smoking.

Here in Mr. Smith's magical room, I relived the sights and aromas of the late Mr. Messerly's living room.

Across Mr. Smith's room stood an elaborate desk, with a full pipe rack that seemed a mile long. On a side table sat a large can of Prince Albert tobacco, along with numerous smoking implements—I had no idea what they were for.

As I walked behind Mr. Smith toward the desk, I noticed several forest pictures hanging on the wall, as well as a sofa, several chairs, a coffee table, and a filing cabinet in one corner. There were no stag heads on the walls, and everything whispered of its resident's past. My heart glowed as though I had just met a grandfather I never knew.

•　•　•　•　•

Mr. Smith reminded me of my grandmother, Dad's late mother, who had lived with us, who was the only grandparent I ever knew. I've always remembered how she helped me memorize Lincoln's Gettysburg Address for a fourth grade pageant. Her patience touched me deeply. I struggled to memorize the difficult words, sometimes frustrated to the point of exasperation, but she had a quiet way of calming me down, and making me feel that I *"can do it."* She would patiently tell me about Gettysburg, she described the various battlefields, and the whys and wherefores of the Civil War. And so, with her love and serene wisdom having built me up, I recited those venerable words in front of the entire elementary school with a new sense of confidence in myself.

•　•　•　•　•

Mr. Smith smiled at me before he sat down, and motioned me to a nearby chair.

"Von't you pull it up and choin me?"

117

As he faced me, I felt surprised to be looking down at him. I smiled at my childhood remembrance, always looking up at him.

As we sat down, I realized why, as a child, I sometimes had trouble understanding Mr. Smith's speech. I had no concept of foreign languages as a boy. To me, he just "talked funny." My mother's imitations of his accent came to mind, and I flushed with embarrassment for a second, but I don't think he noticed. Mom had mentioned he was Pennsylvania Dutch. Suddenly—for the first time—I understood what she had been saying about him.

Later in college, I studied German, and learned that Pennsylvania Dutch is not "Dutch" at all, but a form of Platt Deutsch that German immigrants brought to this country hundreds of years ago.

"Vat kann I do for you?" Mr. Smith asked as he turned towards his desk against the wall. The work surface before him was slightly inclined, like an artist's desk. The top edge was level. The pipe rack occupied that part, and in front of it were scattered tablets, writing instruments, a large ashtray, and pipe implements. A flexible-neck light was attached to the edge of the desk. I knew that he knew exactly where everything was.

He caught me admiring the pipes and said, "Ja, I haf a pipe for efery day. I never smoke da same pipe d' next day. Dey need to dry out." It was my first lesson in pipe smoking.

I also noticed how he rolled the r's in his throat, and his o's were rather closed.

"So! Vat haf you got dere?" He pointed to my workbook.

I opened it to the problem I couldn't solve and handed it to him, pointing to the exercise. He held the page under the light and scrutinized it. He slowly set it down on the slanted writing surface and reached for paper and a pencil.

I scooted my chair up behind him to look over his shoulder.

"Venn solfink any problem, you must first decide vat 'x' equals," he calmly spoke as he wrote in a clear, steady hand:

Exercise 1 $\qquad$ Let $x =$ ____

"You must decide vat x equals based upon the information gifen. See hier?" He pointed to the values given in the example. He then walked me through the steps of solving the problem.

His manner and soft-spoken voice reminded me of Uncle Vin, and how he had explained phonograph sound technology to me. I enjoyed Mr. Smith's company, and how he patiently and clearly explained not only the math, but also anything I asked him, including the best way to smoke a pipe.

The lingering pipe-smoke aroma of the room captivated me. I observed closely as he fussed with tamping the tobacco just right, lighting it, then stamping it again, sometimes with his index finger, then relighting it.

One night he picked up the next pipe in line. He turned to his tobacco container, opened it, and began to fill the pipe. He noticed my watching his every move.

"You see, Robert, it's important to keep ze tobacco fresh, odervise the pipe gets too hot and it burns ze lips and de inside uf de mout, efen de t'roat." He picked up what looked to me like a large silver nail. With the head, he tamped the tobacco into the pipe. Nearby was a box of matches. He picked one up and struck it on the box, then held it to the pipe, which was now in his mouth. As he drew on the pipe, the flame was pulled into the tobacco, lighting it. He threw the match in the ash tray and began pushing the tobacco down with his right index finger.

"What are you doing? Doesn't' that burn your finger?"

He chuckled. "No, Robert, my finger is youss to it. But you can buy tampers to do ze yob." He held out his finger for me to inspect. It was black and calloused.

The pipe went out, so he repeated the process.

"Why are you lighting it, then putting it out, and lighting it again?"

"Ven I light it ze first time, ze tobacco expands from the heat. You haf to tap it down for it to stay lit."

"Oh," I said aloud, but thought, *that seems stupid. Why does the tobacco do that?* But I kept my counsel.

He lit it once more and the fragrance wafted all around the room. He laid the pipe in the nearest tray so that it remained upright. He picked up his pencil and proceeded with the lesson.

Whether I asked, or he anticipated a question, he patiently explained and demonstrated how everything worked, and the importance of keeping the tobacco fresh with a proper humidor. He showed me how he filled the humidor from the Prince Albert can.

I spent as many evenings as I could with him. I even found problems that were not assigned just so I could be with him, hours my father never allotted for any of us kids. Mr. Smith never expressed impatience, never made me feel stupid—a new sensation for me, and he never chided me for my dependence on him. Clearly he enjoyed our time together as much as I did.

By now, the answer to the question that began this chapter should be apparent—why did I decide to major in math? Since I had no choice but to attend Lock Haven State, after this high school experience, all I wanted to do was to continue working with Mr. Smith.

September of 1957 began on a high note with my first class at LHSTC. I even dreamed of a career as a mathematician, instead of a pilot. I had always wanted to be a teacher, preferably, a college professor. Just like Mr. Smith.

In the meantime, I became an occasional guest baritone[13] soloist at the Great Island Presbyterian Church, where Russell Gillam was organist and choirmaster. He was my choral teacher at LHSTC, where he directed the college choirs and taught vocal music. Cissie had enjoyed a good teacher-student relationship with Russ, and I picked up where she left off.

I also sang occasionally at Trinity with Mrs. Kamp, even though I dropped my piano lessons for lack of time and money. Today I wish I could play concert music, opera, show tunes, and even jazz, but I felt I had to make that tough choice.

Never in my wildest nightmares had I anticipated what happened in in early 1958. With no warning, Mr. Smith suffered a massive heart attack and died almost immediately. I didn't know about it until later. It was a shock not only to me, but also to everyone in Lock Haven and across the state college community. He was well known for his teaching skill and style. Many graduates of LHSTC owed their careers to him.

I decided to soldier on in math, at first, but did not like the teacher who replaced Mr. Smith, so much so, I decided to study music instead. I couldn't afford a conservatory, so again I settled for an alternative: to study music ed-

---

[13] It was not until 1960 at the Mannes College of Music in NYC that Mr. Singher declared me a tenor.

ucation at Mansfield State Teachers College, MSTC. I entered in September of 1958.

That Christmas Johnnie came home on furlough as if to awaken my spiritual life. I went with him to First Baptist Church, something I did only when Johnnie came to town. When he was not there, I continued to worship at Trinity Methodist with Mom and Dad.

Little by little, my spiritual life got lost in the distractions of college life. Add to that, I never got over my father's refusal to sign for the Drew University loan. Plus, I was angry with God for allowing that to happen. My father's philosophy, "You'll do what you have to do, not what you want to do," irritated me no end. Worst of all, so far he'd been right.

Doggonit, God, where are you?

By now, my sisters were gone from Lock Haven, Hickey was in the Air Force, Johnnie the Navy, and David Wolfe at Wheaton College in Illinois. Although Johnnie had led me to the Lord, I waffled about what that meant in the broad scope of my life. I'd thought about switching to First Baptist, but to join, you had to be baptized again. Remembering Mom's anger and disappointment with Johnnie's rebaptism, I said no. Was it cowardice? Anger at God? Loyalty to my mother? I couldn't—and still, can't rightly say. All of the above, or perhaps, none of the above.

Every summer I worked and saved enough for at least a down payment on my tuition, which was about $1,900 for the year, or perhaps even less, I don't remember. State colleges went out of their way to accommodate good students. Mansfield STC also gave me a work scholarship, waiting on tables in their dining hall for the two years I was there.

For my first year at Mansfield STC, I lived in Mrs. Cruttenden's house with two other students. She was one of several widows in Mansfield who took in college students to help maintain their homes. She was a grandmotherly figure, dignified, sweet, always smiling, a pleasant word of encouragement, ever-ready with a glass of milk and a slice of apple pie with cheese. Her house was down the hill from the campus, I enjoyed walking or running up and down to my classes.

[In 2011, I visited MSU as a guest of my fraternity, Phi Mu Alpha. Walking up and down those hills nearly killed me. I longed for my twenty-two-year-old legs and stamina.]

As I became more integrated into the student life at MSTC, I met another upperclassman who invited me to join a college group at the local Methodist church. This friend seemed fonder of off-color jokes than studying the Bible. Still, I joined the group of which he was president, but only two or three of us came to the meetings, plus, there was no grounding in the Word. It was pointless, so I dropped out. I worshiped at the Methodist church for a short while, but because of my experience with Johnnie, I decided to check out the local Baptist church.

Although I didn't know the difference then, this was an American Baptist Church, which has closer theological ties to mainline churches than to the evangelical community. What I remember was the pastor himself: an older man with a crown of blazing white hair, decked out in a well-weathered tuxedo, a black coat, and grey checkered trousers, complete with a ruffled-front shirt and bow tie. His sermons were long, boring, springing from the pre-WWII era, and I soon tired of all the churches in Mansfield, preferring my musical life and friends to this vacuous church scene.

• • • • •

During the summer of 1960, I bell-hopped at the North End Hotel in Ocean Grove, New Jersey.[14] That summer completely changed my life. I met a fellow singer, baritone James DeHaven, who persuaded me to go with him to New York City that fall to study voice and opera at the Mannes College of Music.

"Bob, you really *are* a tenor, you know," Jim's deep, resonant bass-baritone assured me one evening when we were singing at one of the many grand pianos in the various rooms and halls of the hotel. Jim was the most accomplished pianist—and singer—I had ever met. He played jazz as well as classical music, all from memory, even such difficult pieces as my favorite, Rachmaninoff's Second Piano Concerto—which I constantly requested of him. He also knew

---

[14] Read the complete Ocean Grove story in my Tales of a Tenacious Tenor, 2014, ASJ Publishing, Chapter 3

show tunes, and most anything I asked him to play. If he didn't exactly know it, he improvised. He was younger than I, yet his singing voice was so well trained and mature that I was certain he could sing in any opera house in the world.

"Really? You think I'm a tenor? All my teachers told me I'm a baritone," I said. Jim was at the keyboard, while I stood in the curve of the piano.

"They're wrong," his mellifluous voice chimed as he smiled broadly. "I hear it in the quality of your voice. Tell you what. Come to New York with me and let Mr. Singher decide."

"Mr. Who?"

The words "New York" sent shivers up and down my spine. I hadn't been there since I was a small boy, while staying with Uncle Vin. He drove us all around the perimeter of Manhattan Island. The idea of going "into the City" both excited me and scared me witless.

"Mr. Singher has been *the* French baritone at the Metropolitan Opera throughout the forties and fifties, as well as singing all over Europe and South America," Jim said.

"Wow, do you think he'd teach me?" I asked like a kid with his nose against a candy shop window.

"The only way to know is to go in and audition for him. Let's see what he says."

With swirling emotions, I agreed to go along. Jim's confidence buoyed me up.

When we traveled into the city later that summer, Mr. Singher confirmed Jim's impression of my voice, and, in due course, we both became students of his. My four years at Mannes were devoted to learning to sing properly as a tenor, to study and sing opera roles, and to learn how to get into the opera field.

• • • • •

This concentration pulled me farther away from the Lord, and I was blind to my spiritual life at this point. When I thought about it, I'd convinced myself that the Lord had blessed my singing. Here I was, studying at Mannes with some of the best opera professionals in the world. What more could I ask? Thus satisfied, I concentrated on improving my singing and learning the necessary skills for the opera stage.

The Lord has *got* to be blessing this.

• • • • •

When I first walked into the Mannes College of Music, [as of 2015, Mannes School of Music,] on that hot August day in 1960, the trees outside sagged in their resentment of the heat. The punishing sun brought rivulets of sweat from every pore. Jim and I hadn't eaten anything since breakfast, but my adrenalin kept me going. We came by bus—thank heaven it was air-conditioned—and Jim guided me through the scary, clanging, musty NYC subway labyrinth like a seasoned New Yorker.

Mannes College was then located on East Seventy-Fourth Street, a brownstone residence formerly occupied by David and Clara Mannes, later by their son, Leopold Mannes, who was president of the college at that time. We pushed through the large front door into a spacious vestibule with tables and chairs lining its walls. It was a bit cooler, but made clammy by the many people present. Perfume competed with less pleasing odors for attention.

Jim pulled our applications out of a briefcase and walked toward the rear where a sign marked, "Auditions" hung with an arrow pointing to the rear. Numerous people, young, old, men, women milled around a table in the center of the passageway which we had to navigate around through the noisy throng.

I don't remember anything after that other than singing nervously for Mr. Singher in a stifling studio on the third floor. Nor do I recall what I sang, but it was likely an aria or a show tune Jim had taught me. He played for me as well, providing familiar support.

Mr. Singher, said, "Well, my dear (he called everyone that), you're most certainly not a baritone. You are a tenor without high notes."

I looked at him, confused.

Noticing my anxiety, he quickly smiled and said, "But, we shall see."

The way he said it filled me with the confidence that he could make it happen. So I went away happy, making plans with Jim all the way back to his house in Ocean Grove.

• • • • •

In early September when I returned to start classes, my first contact was with the Registrar, known to everyone as Matty. Sitting next to her was a lovely student with a winning smile, flowing deep cherry-brown hair, with matching doe-like eyes. Matty introduced her to me as Joan Bishop, as she nudged her with a *now-there's-a-nice-young-man-for-you* glint in her eye.

"She played Cupid every time a young guy came through the door, but you were the last one, thank God," Joan told me later.

Soon after that meeting, Joan and I became fast friends, sharing the lunches she brought from home. We often took meals together, went to the opera, and sang in church choirs together. In those days, it was almost a ritual that every aspiring singer found a singing job in church and synagogue, both for the singing experience, but also to help pay the bills. Matty helped us by sending us to Dr. Hugh Giles, one of the organ professors at Mannes, as well as Organist and Choir Master at Central Presbyterian Church on Park Avenue. Joan was hired as a second soprano, and I, as a second tenor. We sang there throughout my four years at Mannes.

• • • • •

Joan's mother, Johanna Franken (Bishop), arrived in the United States from Germany in 1905 with her mother and father. Not knowing a word of English, they stayed with relatives who had come before them from Krefeld, an industrial town near Düsseldorf. Weavers by trade, they had come to work in family businesses where their experience was welcomed.

Johanna's father, Peter, had a lovely tenor voice. Little by little, Johanna learned English and kept the homes fires burning, taking care of her parents. She married Frederick Bishop in 1920; their first child, Freddy (junior) was born in 1928. Joan came along in 1939, the year I too was born.

Fred, Joan's father, was all-American, proud to have served in World War 1. He was a hard worker, and kept himself busy at home with chores inside and out. He was proud to "do" the dishes after every meal.

Joan grew up quite separately from her brother, he being almost twelve years older. At an early age, Joan studied piano, and in high school, began voice lessons. The family encouraged Joan to sing, always insisting she sing at family gatherings. No one doubted her lovely voice, pure and even from top to bottom. However, they, being uneducated, had no way of appreciating the full impact of her exemplary musicality and language skills. They simply called her "smart." No music seemed too difficult for her. In junior high school she came under the tutelage of Met Soprano, Helen Jepson. At that time Joan sang mostly coloratura music.

She had entered the Mannes College of Music in 1958, two years prior to me, and also studied with Mr. Singher. He once said to me, "Joan's French is absolutely perfect, without accent when she sings." When I told Joan about this extravagant compliment, she pursed her lips and hissed, "F-f-f! He never told *me* any such thing!"

Joan's lovely smile and captivating eyes enchanted me from the start. From the get-go, I realized she was very bright, and that unlike all my previous attractions, we indeed had much in common, especially music. From the start she was ready and eager to help me in Italian, French, and German, the three languages we were required to study at Mannes. I felt truly blessed by her.

One day that fall, Joan told me about a friend's concert. "Would you like to go?"

"Sure," I said without thinking, assuming it was a school thing and I'd meet her there. Suddenly from the look in her eye, I saw another purpose. "You mean to go *with* you?"

She blushed slightly, cocked her head to one side, and said, "Sure, *with* me. Why not?"

It was my turn to blush. I thought, *Is she asking me for a date? Our first date? Shouldn't I be asking her for a date? Robert, where's your head? Get a grip, guy.*

"You want to make it a date?" she said innocently. "Hey, that's a great idea. Sure I'd love to go with you."

Now wait a minute, I thought. *She's turned this thing around. I thought she was asking me. Stupid! Don't you get it? She's making it okay for you to ask her. DO IT, STUPID!*

"Would you like to go to this whatever-it-is concert with me?"

She smiled and put her arm through mine. "I thought you'd never ask. Sure, I'd love to!"

It was our first date, the first time we went "out" together.

Soon we found out about the score desk tickets[15] available to students, so we began to vie with other students for these free tickets, and soon became Met score-desk groupies. The desks were provided by the Met for student use. They were on a first-come, first-served basis, which meant getting to the opera house early, jostling one's way to the front of the restraining rope at the bottom of the ballroom-like, entrance steps, and then running like a scared squirrel up the flights of stairs to these Dress Circle desks. Having been a runner in high school, I was in good shape and usually got there first to claim the best desk.

The conducting majors didn't like us at all. One night, waiting for the attendant to remove the restraining rope, I complained how hard it was to see the stage from the desks closest to the stage due to the sight angle. By trial and error, I soon learned that the desks farthest from the stage were the ones offering the best view. One especially irascible conducting major complained loudly—so all could hear, "They're called 'score desks' for a reason, *singers*"— he spit out the word with venom. "They're for us conducting majors to follow the opera with a *score*, get it? They're not bleachers for you to worship your favorite singers."

I replied, "Then why come to a live performance when you can listen to a recording? We singers want to see the singers, yes, but we also want to see the staging, the costumes, the lighting, the acting, the chorus, the orchestra, the dancing—the WORKS—not just the *notes*, about which you conductor-types wag your batons aimlessly in the air."

At first, Joan and I were simply two students drawn together by our common interest. But sitting so close to one another at those score desks, it wasn't long before we both began to look forward to touching the other, first shoulders and arms, then fingers, then hands, then sitting as close as we could in those small seats, arms wrapped around each other.

One night at the opera a month or two later, as we sat stuffed together at one desk, I turned to look at Joan. When she smiled at me, looking straight

---

[15] Tickets available exclusively to music students at the major conservatories in NYC, available only through these schools. Schoolroom-like desks were installed along the left side of the Dress Circle at the Metropolitan Opera for students to use to follow the opera with either orchestral, or piano-vocal scores.

into my eyes, my heart fluttered, and I felt a surge of warmth through my body. I looked away, embarrassed. She couldn't have known my turmoil about the girls of Ocean Grove, one of whom I had committed to stay in touch with. I also didn't want her to know how naïve about love I was.

She reached a hand through my arm and gently clasped my forearm. I turned to her, and her eyes looked lovingly into mine. I placed a hand on her hand.

She smiled and rested her head on my shoulder.

I wanted to kiss her, but it might be too forward, and I'd ruin this precious moment.

We spoke not a word.

After the opera, I usually bounded down the steps two at a time—just to show off my athleticism, then I'd wait at the bottom for her. This time I walked down beside her as an interference against the unusually large and boisterous crowd. I hadn't realized how violently opera crowds can push you around, so I wanted to protect her from the jostling that could knock her down the steps. I took her left hand in mine, and wrapped my right arm around her. Her hand was as warm as mine. Grasping it tightly, she looked up at me, her eyes assuring me, "I'm with you, Bob."

Her father was waiting for us in the car at the agreed-upon spot. Traffic after the opera always created havoc. As soon as we saw the car, we dropped our hands. *We're just friends. Don't let Dad see us holding hands. He'll get the wrong idea and tell Mom. Then we'll be in for endless questions.* At this point, we didn't want people to think of us as a couple. We both had been hurt by previous romances, and we wanted to be sure that this was "it."

As autumn wore on, Joan and I saw more and more of each other.

"How's *l'Elisir d'Amore* coming along?" Joan asked as we tucked into our Yankee Kitchen steak sandwiches one day at lunchtime. This was a favorite hangout for Mannes students, just around the corner from the school on Lexington Avenue. My opera workshop class was working on scenes from *L'Elisir*, a comic opera by Gaetano Donizetti.

"Oh, okay, I guess. Linda seems to have as much trouble singing the Italian as I do, but she'd never admit it. She loves to flirt with me, but Adina doesn't flirt with Nemorino, she taunts him. Linda just doesn't get it. Maybe she doesn't understand the Italian."

"Oh, so she flirts with you, does she?" Joan set her sandwich down and looked at me with a raised eyebrow, eyes suspicious. "Do you flirt back?"

I looked down at my plate sheepishly. "I try not to."

"What do you mean, you *try* not to?" Joan suddenly angered by this response.

Trying to appear nonchalant, I shrugged my shoulders and muttered, "I don't want to be rude to her." Yes, I was flattered by Linda's attention. Not many women have flirted with me since Kay Hickey—that I was aware of—and I was unsure how to handle Linda. I never told Joan about how Linda had come to the library where I worked. She had on a very tight, black dress that revealed more of her than was comfortable—for either of us, but for different reasons. She filled it a bit too much. I had a dickens of a time getting rid of her.

At last, my library supervisor, who happened to be on my floor just then, came by and proclaimed, "Bob, what's this young lady doing in this restricted area? It's not for the public." I flushed with embarrassment, and Linda stood up from the chair she was using to display her cleavage, turned and started toward the steps. On her way, she'd swing around to smile at me every few steps as she sashayed towards the descending staircase.

(I didn't tell Joan all those details—only what she "needed" to hear.)

"She's got a thing for you," Joan said, staring me in the eye.

"Seems so. I don't quite know what to do about it," I said, shrugging my shoulders.

"Well, whatever you do, don't encourage her," Joan said as she picked up her sandwich.

"I don't," I replied defensively. I was uncomfortable with this interrogation. I dug my fork into my salad, determined to change the subject. "By the way, can you help me with the Italian in our new scene? I understand most of the words, but sometimes I don't get what the entire phrase means. Know what I mean? I guess it's the idiomatic use of the words."

"Of course. Do you have the score with you?"

Whew! Glad that's over. "No, we can do it later." Then I changed my voice to a more endearing quality as I said, "You know, sweetheart, I wish you were singing with me. Have you ever sung Adina?"

"No."

I put my fork down, rested my chin on my hands, and looked longingly at her. "I dream about us singing operas together some day at the Met. Do you ever think about that? Which operas do you think we could do?"

"Oh, *Boheme*, of course." She beamed at me. "I already know Mimi," she added enthusiastically.

"Yeah, you said that before. How did you learn it?" I genuinely wanted to know because I had never learned an entire opera role before. The opera workshop was only scenes.

She responded enthusiastically, "I listened to the record over and over again, and soon I could sing it without the record. I know everybody's part, not just Mimi. Before I came to Mannes I'd studied it with Helen Jepson. I know Marguerite in *Faust*, too."

"Wow, you know that whole role, too?" I was truly impressed.

She nodded as she put her fork down and looked at me with an endearing smile.

"I'm impressed," I said, wondering if her smile meant what I hoped it meant. "I feel like such a dolt, knowing so little about opera. I don't even know a whole tenor *aria* yet…. A couple of *baritone* arias," I chortled.

She reached across the table and took my hands. "Bob, you're learning. You'll do fine. You haven't had the training I've had. You have such a beautiful voice. I can hear you singing Rodolfo, Alfredo, and Faust, and all the romantic lyric roles. I do *so* look forward to singing them with you. Except *Traviata*."

Tears began to swell behind my eyelids. I looked up at her, smiling warmly at me. "Why not *Traviata*?"

"That role is just not me," a tear rolled down her cheek.

I choked out a "I'm so sorry about that, but thank you," and mouthed, *I love you.*

"I love you, too," she said softly, as our eyes held each other's.

Suddenly, some of our friends burst into the restaurant, and, spotting us, exclaimed boisterously, "Ah, the love birds! Don't you two have classes to get to?"

Joan, facing the door, looked up, smiled at them, and then looked at her watch. "Oh my Gosh! I've got to get back to the office." She left some money on the table, came around to me, kissed me quickly, and said, "I'll see you tonight."

I got up and hugged her. "Five o'clock?"

"On the dot." She bolted for the door, waving at our friends as she departed. "Hi, guys. See ya later."

"What's her rush?" one of them asked, as they all exchanged glances.

"She works in the school office," I explained. I picked up my books and headed for the door. "We just met for lunch, is all. Gotta run, too. A class. See ya." And out the door I went.

By winter of 1960, Joan and I were very much in love and even thinking about marriage. But our parents were not at all keen on the idea with me still in college.

The familiar refrain was, "Why don't you wait until you finish college and get a job?"

In order for us to marry, I had to demonstrate to both families that I could earn a living and support a family. Of course I wanted to do that through singing, but my teachers and coaches said, "You're not ready."

So I knew I had to get a job with a future.

I remembered how Dad had said, "You'll do what you have to do…."

Yes, Dad, I know.

All through school, I worked for the New York Public Library, first as a page in the Art Collection at the Forty-Second Street Branch. But before the end of my first year, I was promoted to a clerk position at the music branch, located on East Fifty-Sixth Street, just off Lexington Avenue. I shared an apartment on East Eighty-Second Street with Jim DeHaven, my baritone friend from Ocean Grove, now also a student at Mannes. It was a bit of a walk to school, a longer haul to work, but all of it feasible since I loved to run. There was always the bus or subway in bad weather.

• • • • •

In fact, the year in which I took a class in music history, running the eighteen blocks from Mannes College became a necessity. Mrs. Catherine Miller, Chief Librarian of the music branch, and my boss, put me in charge of the NYPL Orchestral Collection, a unique collection of orchestral music made available to amateur orchestras. Pick-up was only on Wednesdays from 12:30 p.m. to 4:00 p.m. My regular schedule was seventeen-and-a-half hours a week, three-and-a-half of which *had* to be these hours. My class in Music History ended at 12:30. The eighteen blocks suddenly seemed very long indeed. I'd need Superman's cape to get there!

"Do you think we could push the opening time back just a smidgen?" I asked Mrs. Miller.

"No," she said, solidly but politely. "Why not ask your professor to let you out early on Wednesdays?"

I asked Dr. Braunstein, my music history professor, and suddenly his European manners deserted him. "Vat? Leef early? Nefer!"

Mrs. Miller, a softy at heart, relented and agreed to look the other way if I opened the collection no later than 12:45 p.m.

No problem, I thought, but it put my running to the test for two semesters. I was in excellent shape in those early days. At 135 pounds, my trousers were a boy's size.

· · · · ·

From the get-go, Joan was convinced I was starving, so early on she appointed herself my Florence Nightingale by bringing me lunch every day. We were inseparable and did everything together—except live together. It simply wasn't done in those days, at least not in families like ours. Our itinerary expanded to movies, concerts, and of course, the opera. We dreamed of becoming the darling couple of the opera world, singing together in performances of *La Boheme*, *L'Elisir d'Amore*, *Faust*, *Manon*, *Romeo et Juliette*, all of which featured the leading soprano and tenor roles as lovers.

It wasn't long after Joan launched her lunch campaign that first winter in 1960 that her mother wanted to meet me, so I was invited for a Sunday dinner at their home in Fort Lee, New Jersey.

Equipped with careful instructions from Joan, I took the bus to the Palisades Amusement Park—now occupied by high-rise apartments—where Joan greeted me with a radiant smile. Like a little kid, I couldn't wait to see her and to be in a home again, especially with the holidays approaching, knowing I couldn't afford to go home to Lock Haven. Seeing where she grew up made me feel so much more a part of her life, and I was sure she was *it* for me.

My mother's admonitions about being polite and respectful when in other folks' homes gave me the jitters, but all went well. Mr. and Mrs. Bishop, Fred and Johanna, made me feel very much at home, and the dinner was fabulous. The conversation concentrated mostly on my background and family. Occasionally, I asked questions about their family, which they answered generously. At the end of the evening, Mr. Bishop drove me back into the city, with Joan along for the ride.

"Where to?" he asked, much as a New York taxi driver might ask.

"One Sixty-Four East Eighty-Second Street," I chimed from the back seat, surreptitiously holding Joan's hand. I didn't want Mr. Bishop to keep looking in the rearview mirror to check on us.

"East Side, eh? *Upper* East Side," he said with confidence.

"Yes, Sir, Upper East Side." I could see the wheels churning as he tried to decide which way to go: George Washington Bridge or Lincoln Tunnel. He turned north out of his driveway, so I knew he had chosen the bridge. He drove right to the apartment without further instructions from me.

For our first Christmas together, Joan and I decided to treat ourselves with our favorite opera, *La Boheme*. One of Joan's favorite singers was soprano Renata Tebaldi. Joan had heard her many times and owned several of her records. When I found out that Ms. Tebaldi was singing Mimi on Christmas Eve that year, I said, "Let's splurge and buy good seats so we don't have to run up the steps for score desks. That'll be our Christmas present to each other. How 'bout it?"

"Why Bob, that's a great idea!"

After work one day on the way home, I stopped at the Met box office and purchased tickets. They were center balcony, perfect view of the stage. Eugenio Fernandi was the tenor—how I wished for Jussi Björling, but he had passed away in September. His death shocked the opera world, as he was only forty-nine and very much in his prime. I was more devastated than most, he being my operatic idol. I never heard him in person. Joan had seen him in *Faust* before I arrived in New York.

Mom Bishop had planned a dinner for us and had invited the family, Freddie, Joan's brother, with his wife and kids. She was not happy about our scooting off to the opera, but Dad Bishop chauffeured us to the Met that night and home again after the performance so that we could enjoy as much time with the family as possible.

He dropped us off under the marquee of the (old) Met entrance on Broadway. Even with the bright street lights, we could look up and see stars above, adding their twinkle to the scene. A remnant of snow shone softly. We waved goodbye to Dad as we entered the main entrance. Only then did we take each other's hand. "You warm enough?" I asked her.

She nodded with a warm smile.

The people ahead of us crowded into the ticket stalls and carpeted grand staircase with its columns and stately balustrades. The restraining rope was already down so we made our way upstairs. I led the way to the coat counter and helped Joan with her coat. I couldn't help noticing the dark red velvet dress that snugged her figure. My face reddened when she caught me ogling her, but her eyes beamed, "Glad you like me."

"Lovely dress," I said, my eyes being pulled down to her curves.

"Thank you."

I wrapped an arm around her to escort her to our seats in the Dress Circle. By this time sweat beaded on my brow from climbing the steps, not to mention the sweltering stairwell. I was enchanted by her perfume and whispered sweet nothings in her ear as if to dispel the less appealing odors emanating from the throng jostling us along. Her eyes twinkled in acknowledgment. Conversation was impossible with everyone yakking in the confined space. When we got to our seats, we noticed an elderly couple in the row just behind us, crabbing about this and that. Clearly they wanted the whole world to know about it.

I thought, *Oh no, that's all we need....*

Neither Joan nor I had heard Signor Fernandi sing before, but we already knew he could not measure up to the great Björling whom I had always longed to hear in person, and now never would. From Fernandi's first notes to the end, he didn't come close. In addition, both Tebaldi and Fernandi avoided the thrilling high-Cs by taking the music a half-step lower. But Puccini's rapturous music under Thomas Schippers' direction carried the day. For me, it was the first time I'd heard a live performance of this opera. Joan too loved this music, and it had an electrifying effect on our budding romance.

When the first act love scene began with Mimi's knock on Rodolfo's door, I reached over and took Joan's hand. She squeezed back and laid her head on my shoulder. One of the two curmudgeons in back of us made rude, indignant noises, so Joan quickly removed her head. It's the way we were brought up. But we continued holding hands, and slowly slid down in our seats as she whispered the translation of the words into my ear, "Oh lovely maiden, your sweet face reflects the moon's glow; you awaken all my fondest dreams of love...."

I slowly turned my head to her, my cheek brushing her lips. Soon my lips united with hers, and we eagerly kissed rapturously as the music soared into its climax.

Ha-rumph!" grumbles the old biddy behind us.

Embarrassed, we broke off and looked toward the stage.

"*No, per pieta*, (No, please)" Mimi pulls away coyly as Rodolfo tries to kiss her. Rodolfo asks Mimi if she'd like to accompany him to the Latin Quarter. She agrees. He offers her his arm grandly and slowly escorts her out. They continue singing offstage.

When the last note of the act sounded and the main curtain whooshed closed, the entire audience burst into applause and cheers. Most everyone rose to cheer for the two protagonists. We scooched down again to enjoy more wet kissing, touching and sighs.

• • • • •

Mr. Bishop enabled me to visit their home frequently by picking up the two of us in the city. He was retired and loved to chauffeur us; he'd meet us at Mannes or elsewhere in the city after a concert or an opera. It involved him in our lives, a happy union all around.

As 1961 progressed, I became a weekend fixture in the Bishop household. Joan's parents even fixed up a spare room in the attic for me so I could stay over on the weekends whenever possible. It felt cozy to have a family to come home to again.

However, a slight rub began to surface. At first subtle, but soon became clear that I was not the Bishop's first choice of a husband for their only daughter. They would have preferred someone with better prospects, one who had a good job with a solid career path. "Do you really think you can make a living singing? How can you support a family that way? Maybe you could teach on the side…." And on it went, sounding all too familiar. I even got the starving-artist routine.

Johanna loved me nonetheless, and fed me very well—too well, in fact. Uninvited pounds snuck up on me over the next couple of years because Mom Bishop dispensed her love on a plate. Okay, I acknowledge my part in my expanding waistline, but eating when I was growing up was a privilege, seconds were discouraged. "Save some for another day," was the Mitchell maxim. How could I say *no* to my new mother? Besides, Mom Bishop knew the way to a man's heart, "Here, Bob, have some more!"

I thought I had died and gone to heaven, (a popular cliché in the Bishop household).

At first, Fred Bishop and I didn't relate especially well. He had been a laborer all his life, working around heavy, noisy weaving machinery that messed up his hearing, but accounted for his muscle-toned, slim frame. He stood only about five-foot-seven or so, but was very proud of his exceptional strength, which he attributed to his job. He was in his late sixties when I came into the picture, with a full head of salt and pepper hair, bright hazel eyes, and a bashful smile.

We also had nothing in common—except his daughter. As with most fathers with daughters, I suppose he was suspicious of my intentions towards her, although he never said so. He kept a keen eye on the two of us, making sure we didn't go off to a secluded spot to make whoopee. (We didn't until our wedding night, I swear.) Over time Dad Bishop and I became quite fond of each other. Soon I was calling him Dad, and Johanna, Mom.

Johanna was an inch or two taller than Fred, with short brown hair. Her passion was the weather. Maybe more of a fetish. She kept a daily log—if it rained or poured, or windy, or cool, or hot, she wrote it down. In detail.

I never saw her in slacks; she always wore a dress, most of the time with an apron over it. The kitchen was her domain. She loved to cook and bake. It always struck me as ironic that she, German-born, loved to cook spaghetti and meatballs, not *vero italiano*,[16] but I loved 'em anyhow! Maybe it was because I loved her so much. And, her pound cake was to die for.

Though Joan and I spoke of marriage, we never broached the subject with them. Not yet.

For Christmas 1960, I had given Joan a turquoise ring as a token of my intention to marry her. It was also to show Dad Bishop that my intentions were serious. The Bishops were not enthusiastic about this announcement, but, little by little, they resigned themselves to its inevitability.

The following summer I worked very hard back in Lock Haven to earn enough money for tuition.

• • • • •

For several summers, I worked for a family friend we knew as Johnny Yost. No one ever called him "Mr. Yost," even though he was a funeral director and devoted to Trinity Methodist Church. He and his wife lived across the street from the church, above the funeral parlor in a large white Italianate house, which probably had belonged to a very wealthy family before Johnny bought it for his business. With a large, closed-in front porch, and added sections in the rear, Johnny kept it in pristine condition, including the yard, always mowed, bushes trimmed, everything hunky-dory.

"Got to make a good impression," Johnny said. "Business depends on it. When people ask me how I do it, I tell them, 'I'd be happy to keep your house the same way.'" That's where we came in—we did all the work.

Johnny was a compact man with a quick smile, and an ever-ready wit. He loved to joke and do crazy things. For example, I remember him standing in the balcony in the back of the church tossing a fifty-cent piece down to the collection plate during the offertory. The clang resounded above Mrs. Kamp's soft music. I can still see him up there leaning down, carefully taking phantom practice

---

[16] "true Italian"

shots at the plate. His gaudy suspenders appeared to keep him from falling. When he finally took the shot, he rarely missed the plate. Sometimes the coins would bounce off with a thunderous clang, but I never saw him miss the plate altogether.

Dad knew that Johnny Yost hired young men for some kind of labor, he didn't know what, and told me to ask him for a summer job. Before I got around to asking, one day after completing my first year at Lock Haven State, Dad sent Mom and me to deliver some funeral cards to Johnny.

When we arrived at the side business entrance of the funeral home, I pushed the bell and we walked in. A door across the room opened and Johnny appeared. In his wake a strong flowery aroma wafted across the room. Must be a viewing in there. He beamed at Mom, then spotted me and said, "Robert! Whadda *you* doin' here? Or do you go by Bob? Hey, whatcha doin' this summer? Don't you graduate this June?"

"No," I said. "I graduated last year—I'm in college now," I jabbed my thumb over my shoulder in the direction of LHSTC. "Family calls me Robert. Most everyone else calls me Bob. Either is fine."

"Okay, Bob." He looked at the boxes we'd brought. "Still workin' for your dad, I see."

"Well," I hesitated. "Not exactly." I really didn't want to get into my squabbling with Dad. So I simply said, "Y'know, I actually *do* need a job for the summer—for college next fall."

"Oh, yeah? You up to some hard work?"

"I'm always up to hard work."

"Tell you what…you available right away?"

I shrugged quickly. "Shuure."

"Be here tomorrow morning at 7:00. Wear old clothes you don't mind gettin' dirty. We'll see if you can handle a bit o' hard work." He chuckled as he ushered Mom and me back to the door. "Gotta run now. Viewing." He indicated with his head. "Good to see you, Cricket. Thanks for bringing the cards." He smiled as he practically pushed us out the door.

The next morning, I showed up promptly at 7:00 at Johnny's barn-sized garage in back of the house. I was greeted by the motleyest crew of toughies I had ever encountered. *Good Lord, what have I gotten myself into?* They looked at me as if a skunk had just walked in. I wondered if they were from Sugar Run Road just north of Lock Haven, a valley where folks without options eked out livings as best they could. I'd had some nasty run-ins with some of those mulish kids.

Just then, my face lit up as Eddie Cox walked in, looking and smelling too clean for the work I thought we'd be doing.

Boy, am I glad to see you! "Whadda *you* doing here?" I said as I extended my hand, smiling broadly.

We shook hands heartily.

"I'm working for Johnny this summer—I guess you are too, right?" Ed said with a big smile. Clearly he was as surprised to see me as I him.

I took him aside, and asked, "What's this job and who are these guys?" cocking my head towards them, now milling around the hearse, whispering among themselves.

"Oh, they come from Sugar Run and downtown, the other side of the tracks. They help Johnny out in all his businesses. They're okay. Once I shared my lunch with them—that broke the ice. Now we all share our lunches."

"'All his businesses'? What's *that* about?"

"Didn't you know? Johnny has a landscaping business, a carpet cleaning business, along with his funeral parlor. We don't work inside much." He rubbed his clean-shaven chin, smelling of Old Spice. "He'll do pretty much anything around the house his customers want."

"Hu-u-m," I shook my head. *I had no idea.* "I thought he was an under-taker."

"Sure, we all know that, but he's got his fingers in a lot of pies in this town."

Thus began my two-year, part-time career with Johnny Yost Enterprises. I was assigned to the landscaping detail. It was hot, dirty, gritty, sweaty work. But Johnny paid my way through several years of college, God bless 'im.

● ● ● ● ●

Toward the end of the first summer, 1958, Johnny brought me into the house to help clean and arrange the various funeral rooms. Dick Lucas, who was Johnny's "inside" man (*inside* the funeral home), became my mentor. My first job was vacuuming the viewing rooms. I helped bring in flowers, remove old ones, set up and break down chairs for funerals, move tables and caskets, empty or full, and did outside chores, like sweeping sidewalks and watering the flower gardens.

The embalming room was in the barn,[17] and the completed bodies had to be rolled into the house viewing rooms through a passageway built for that purpose. Johnny himself did the embalming and preparation work on the bodies. Dick and Johnny placed the body in the casket, Johnnie saw to the last stage preparations, hair, dress and makeup, after which Dick and I would roll the prepared casket to the viewing rooms.

Sometimes on breaks, or after a Saturday or evening viewing, Dick would invite me to his apartment upstairs in the barn behind the main house "for a beer." His lovely wife would join us for chatting, games, or the uproarious stories Dick regaled us with, some made up, some not—but it was impossible to tell the difference. He also taught me how to smoke cigars, of which he was very fond. He certainly rounded out my post-adolescent-pre-college upbringing.

When Johnny saw how eagerly and responsibly I worked, he began to send me home to clean up, change into a dark suit, and drive the flower car for funerals. During my first year of college at LHSTC I lived at home, so when Johnny got real busy with funerals—they always came in droves, feast or famine—he called me in to help. One day he pulled me aside.

"Bob, what are you studying at Lock Haven State?"

By this time Mr. Smith had died, and I had a bit of a quandary about my future. I didn't know what to say to Johnny. I looked away from his penetrating eyes.

"Do you like working for me?" he asked with his most winning smile.

I looked back at him. "Sure, Johnny. I love working for you. You're not at all like my da—" I stopped short, and dropped my eyes.

Johnny smiled. He knew Dad for many years, and had almost single-handedly kept his printing business afloat. It was an awkward moment for me, but not for Johnny. He dove right in. "Yeah, your dad can be a pill at times, but he's got a good heart."

---

[17] Which was the site of the original funeral business Johnny had bought. He later bought the house on Main Street, turning the first floor into viewing rooms. He also built a closed-in ramp connecting the two buildings.

I raised my eyes to look at him again, amazed. I was afraid he'd reprimand me for not standing up for my father. He put a hand on my shoulder.

"Listen," he went right on, "the reason I asked is I heard you say something about leaving Lock Haven State. Why don't you consider going to mortuary school? You've got one year under your belt. You need only one more. Well, in your case, it may take a bit longer because of required courses, but the point is you only need an associate's degree, and you could be earning money. I have plenty of business. You could work for me." He leaned his head back in a characteristic "Johnny" way, looking up at me with impish eyes, lips curled to reveal his top teeth. He was so close I knew he had bologna for lunch.

"What about Dick?" I asked.

"Dick's good, but he doesn't have a degree. Besides, I don't think he'd want to take on the whole bailiwick. With a head like yours and your outgoing personality, you could become very successful in this business."

One day a few weeks later, Johnny called me up and said, "Get dressed. I'll be right there to pick you up."

Pick me up? Johnny never, ever picked me up. What's this about? Not daring to question him, I said, "Sure, Johnny. I'll be ready." I assumed he meant for me to dress for a funeral. But why would he pick me up? It was my job to get to his house, not the other way around.

He pulled into Chestnut Street in the old Buick hearse that he kept in sparkling condition.

Oh my God! What's going on? I came out and jumped in the passenger's seat. Afraid to ask questions, I said, "Hi, Johnny." But I couldn't resist knowing, "Where'r' we goin'?"

"To the hospital," he said, looking straight ahead, all business. He pulled forward enough to back into Dad's favorite parking space next to our back porch. He wielded the hearse around and turned left out of Chestnut Street.

I looked at him, questioningly. He turned to me and smiled.

"Dr. Lindsey just died. We're going to pick up the body," he said matter-of-factly.

Gulp! This was totally out of the blue. My heart froze at the thought of a corpse, but my mind raced, *Why does he want me along?*

As if reading my mind, Johnny said, "Dick's picking up another body in the panel truck. Like I said, when it rains, it pours. I need you to help me."

"What do I do?" I said, trying to keep from vomiting.

"I'll show you. Don't worry." He looked at me and began to laugh as he turned left into the back of the hospital, just up the street from our house. "You should see your face. You look as if you just saw a ghost." He then roared at his own joke. I felt my face turn crimson. Johnny glanced over and laughed all the harder. Soon I was laughing, too. My nausea disappeared.

He stopped at the Emergency door, saying, "C'mon," as he bolted out his door. He hustled to the back of the hearse. I helped him roll out and extend the wheels of the gurney. "Follow me," as he took off like a greyhound down the hall, leaving me to push the gurney obediently behind him.

I had never seen a corpse before. A naked one shocked me *throughly*, as the poets say. I helped Johnny get the good doctor into a body bag and load him onto the gurney. When we got back to the garage, I started to wave so-long.

"Where do you think you're going?" he demanded, with a twinkle in his eye.

"Oh, I thought I was done," I said as I started for the door. I had forgotten he picked me up. It was over a mile to walk home, but that would have been a lark for me in those days.

"No, no. The job's just beginning," he laughed. He motioned me back to the hearse and together we slid the body out. We then rolled it into the embalming room and slid it out of the bag onto the cold, metal embalming tray. Johnny chatted incessantly between directions. He saw my distress, and from years of experience, had adopted this endless verbal stream as an antidote for trainees. It didn't help much. My mind was getting foggier with each new procedure.

First, we had to drain the blood. The squish of large needles inserted into the groin area and jugular vein not only made the room start to spin and turn white, it triggered my stomach to roll once again. By the time we got to the needles, my legs felt like jelly and spots danced before my eyes. When Johnny lifted a long, quarter-inch thick, silver tube with a beveled point on one end, I asked weakly, "What's that for?"

Johnny connected the other end to a hose and said, "Oh, this is the most important thing we do. If we don't get all the air and fluid out of the lungs, the body will secrete fluid out of the mouth or nose during the viewing. We can't have that happen, can we?"

I gulped, trying to stop my stomach from sending its contents flying across the table. The spots blurred into a solid white, my ears muffled every sound—except the *ska-runch* of the needle-tube as Johnny inserted it just under the breastbone and pushed up it into the lung area.

The last thing I remember before collapsing to the floor was Johnny's face concentrating on directing this medieval instrument into the unsuspecting corpse. Dreams of torture chambers and white-coated attendants standing by—we both had white surgical coats on—danced in my head as gleeful, unkempt soldiers produced horrible screams and chilling cries for mercy....

The next thing I knew, Johnny was standing over me, laughing, "What'r' ya doin' down there, Mitch? What's the matter? Can'cha take it?"

His calling me "Mitch" made me think of my father, not happily. Although he would never say it out loud, I believe he thought my father rather a dolt. He gave him so much business because of us kids. And Mom, whom he secretly admired.

"Just kidding," Johnny smiled as he stooped down to help me up. "Don't worry. Happens to everyone their first time. 'Cept me. I guess I was always the exception."

"How's Dr. Lindsey?" I asked dopily, Johnny still holding me up.

"Oh, he came through fine. Better than you, in fact. He didn't feel a thing."

This was reason number one why I didn't become an undertaker. I didn't think I could get used to the embalming process.

The summer of 1961, after my first year at Mannes, I took five hundred dollars of my tuition money and bought Joan an engagement ring. Never mind how I would pay my tuition—I was in love. The only thing that mattered was surprising her.

Time had run out for me to return to New York by car, so I took the rest of my money and grabbed a flight out of Williamsport through perfectly clear sunny skies to the Newark Airport, where Joan was waiting for me, alone, in Dad Bishop's car, all the windows wide open. Without a breeze, that didn't help much. The sun opened its furnace doors that day. Joan, nearly melted, moved to the passenger seat to escape its fury, intending me to drive.

As soon as I got into the car, I said, "Close your eyes!"

"Close my eyes?" Sweat dripped off her face, she tried in vain to wipe it away. Puzzled at first, she quickly became a little girl anticipating a present. She dutifully folded her wet hands in her lap and closed her eyes, drops sliding down her cheeks.

After lugging my bag from the baggage area to the parking lot, I felt as if I had walked into an active volcano. I longed to be in my bathing trunks—I hated to sweat up my clothes like this, especially in front of my love. I reached for my pocket but my clammy hand caught on the top edge. I struggled to get my hand in and wrap fingers around the small packet. It seemed like waiting for water to boil to extract my moist hands from my trousers. Of course the stickiness pulled the small item out of my fingers. My red face must have turned crimson. I reached to the floorboards to retrieve it.

Though I had carefully planned this moment, I blanked when it came, and my pretty speeches went *zap!* With trembling fingers I lifted the small box out of the packet with my fingernails, then lifted the top to reveal the sparkling, emerald-cut diamond. I held it in front of her face.

"Okay, you can open your eyes now."

Her face glistened as she opened them.

"Oh-h-h...!" was all she could utter. Her jaw dropped. Her face could have lit up Broadway. She turned to me, tears mingling with perspiration. She fell into my slippery arms and we enjoyed the wettest kiss we ever had.

"Oh, Bob! It's beautiful! Thank you, darling. Dear Lord, I'm so happy! Thank you!"

My tears streamed down blending with sweat to create a miniature Niagara Falls on my cheeks. We no longer noticed the heat soaking us.

She handed the box back to me. "Aren't you going to put the ring on my finger?"

I fumbled with the box, trying to extricate the ring, nearly dropping the whole caboodle, but managed to get it on the correct finger of the correct hand—she made sure of that.

Whether or not I actually popped the question, or she said, "Yes," it was a done deal—and has been for over half a century now.

· · · · ·

Even with the expense of the engagement ring, the college tuition dilemma worked out: Joan paid for it as an engagement present.

My parents were delighted with their new daughter-in-law. Dad loved to argue with her, and Mom couldn't have been happier with Joan. They hit it off right from the start. Mom and Dad had been devastated when both our sisters' marriages ended in divorce, they were delighted with the excellent partners both Johnnie and I had found.

The Bishops grew to love me very much, as I loved them, and their misgivings about my future job potential seemed consigned to the back burner. They knew that somehow, Joan and I would make it. They took me into their family as another son. I think we both, in-laws and I, always treasured our union.

The following year, on September 9, 1962, Joan and I were married at the Methodist Church of Leonia, New Jersey.

Joan, who had graduated from Mannes in June of 1962, later told people, "I got my *BS* in June, my *MRS.* in September, and two years later when Bob graduated, my *PHT* (Put Hubby Through)." Unlike me, Joan never aspired toward a Ph.D, although she could have earned it a lot quicker than I could have, that's for sure.

She worked as a secretary, and I continued my job as a clerk for the New York Public Library, still in charge of the Orchestral Collection. Meanwhile, Joan and I set up housekeeping in West New York, New Jersey, on the corner of Sixtieth Street. Our apartment building overlooked the Hudson River and the New York City skyline, just across from Sixty-Sixth Street in Manhattan.

· · · · ·

Harry's spiritual challenge to me paled in comparison with that of Dr. Eckstein, my philosophy professor at Mannes. Although philosophy was a required course, I jumped at the chance to take it. I loved it so much I took another course with him. I grew to like and respect Dr. Eckstein very much. He was both an intellect and a gifted raconteur. I was as drawn as much to his being Jewish as I was to his vast knowledge and homespun stories about everything. He once told me that he had come *that* close—snapping his fingers—to becoming a rabbi, but ultimately could not buy into the God-stuff. So he took his Ph.D. in philosophy instead of finishing his rabbinical studies.

"Look at me now," he said, flicking his ever-present cigar. "A poor college professor, when I could have been a rich rabbi," reminding me of the great tradition of Jewish comedians from vaudeville to television.

He questioned my belief in God, supporting his arguments both scientifically and philosophically. I was pretty much overwhelmed by his rhetoric, so I began corresponding with my childhood friend, David Wolfe, who was then teaching at a Christian college in Ossining, New York.

"I suggest you ask Dr. Eckstein what his metaphysical assumptions are," David wrote.

"His meta-what?" I replied.

"His ontological assumptions. You see, I suspect he assumes there is no reality apart from what our five senses perceive. That's basic to science. You have to find out whether or not he allows spiritual or non-material data into his ontology."

It took a few more letters for me to understand what he was talking about. The triangular conversations went back and forth, and I tried my best to represent what David said to Dr. Eckstein, but of course I was no match for the professor. I felt torn, and indeed Dr. Eckstein's persuasive ability was beginning to undermine my faith in Christ. I wished that David could come and argue with him in my presence, but that was just my fantasy. It couldn't happen for a host of logistical reasons.

•　•　•　•　•

On the spiritual side of things, the exposure to classical church music through singing at Central Presbyterian Church helped shape both my musical and spiritual life. During the six years I sang at Central Presbyterian and the four years I studied at Mannes, we covered the history of sacred music from Palestrina to Bernstein. I learned the Catholic Mass from singing it in several languages. In Music History class, we were required to learn all the parts of the Mass. I learned, for example, that the third section of the Mass, the Credo, is what we Protestants know as the Nicene Creed. These musical experiences served as a counterpoint to Dr. Eckstein, and helped my soul cling to these vestigial remains of my faith.

Singing every weekend and often during the week in church and synagogue also helped bolster my faith. Often I was deeply moved by musical settings of biblical texts. One such example we sang at Central Presbyterian was Mrs. H. H. A. Beech's anthem, "Let this Mind Be in You," set to Philippians 2:5-11, which begins with a bass solo. "Let this mind be in you which was also in Christ Jesus…." I can still hear Chester Watson's rich bass voice dramatically rendering this passage that ends on a very low note with the words, "…even the death of the cross."

This was followed by a glorious soprano solo sung by Marjorie McClung, who sounded like a true Wagnerian soprano in this music. The choir came in on v. 9, which begins with the word "Wherefore," in this setting of the King James Version. Dr. Hugh Giles, our organist and choirmaster, a native of Georgia, always cued us by singing, "Where-foh." That became a favorite byword between Joan and me.

Both the soaring beauty of the music coupled with the gravity of the text moved me deeply. The sacrifice Jesus made for us came alive in a new and profound way through this music. Many years later in seminary I was to learn that this passage is known as the *kenosis* of Christ, the *emptying* of his heavenly prerogatives to become fully human. To this day, I cannot read or hear this passage without thinking of Chester Watson and Marjorie McClung singing this glorious anthem, which, by the way, seems to have disappeared from the church musical literature, sad to say.

• • • • •

When I graduated from Mannes in 1964, I was still working for the New York Public Library. By this time I had only two performances of complete opera productions under my belt. I felt as if I'd come to a **Y** in the road, music or what? Certainly a singing career was not an option without years of further study. What was the other prong of the **Y** to be?

Chapter Ten

Career Crossroads

Mezzo-Soprano, Janice Matisse, promised to help me with my singing career that "Amazin' Summer of 1960"[18] in Ocean Grove, New Jersey. She, a devout Christian, loved to sing for the Lord, but also enjoyed an concert and opera career. I looked her up when I got to New York City in the fall, and she sent me to her good friend and pianist-accompanist, Hugh Waddy. Hugh taught me to sing Gospel music, about which I wondered if God had opened a new career path for me. After working with Hugh for a while, he connected me with several church groups for which I sang a number of concerts and other occasions.

Through Janice and Hugh, I later met other Christian celebrities, most importantly, Jack Wyrtzen, founder of Word of Life Ministries, and Metropolitan Opera basso, Jerome Hines, well known in Christian circles.

Both Hugh and Janice contributed their talents to both Mr. Wyrtzen's and Mr. Hines' evangelical endeavors. One such public gathering occurred on Long Island in which Janice and I sang to Hugh's accompaniment. I sang Gaither's song, "Because He Lives," complete with an interpolated high-C (meaning the composer didn't write it). The audience loved it. Jack's son, Don, who was just starting out as a Christian Gospel composer, was there and gave me a copy of his song, "Unbounded Grace," which Joan and I later sang as a duet many times.

---

[18] For the complete story, see Chapter 3 of my Tales of a Tenacious Tenor, 2014, ASJ Publishing, available on Amazon, Goodreads, and other venues.

Later, Hugh put me in touch with Mr. Hines to audition for his opera production on the life of Christ, *I Am the Way*. Mr. Hines composed the music, sponsored, and directed the production, which he took all over the country. He reserved the title role for himself, which I imagine limited the number of engagements he could accept, given his busy opera schedule.

One cool fall day, Joan and I drove into Manhattan to pick up Hugh, and then proceeded to Mr. Hines' New Jersey home. Mr. Hines greeted us at the door, and grandly ushered us into his posh living room filled with cushy furniture, heavy drapes, and a very thick rug which I almost tripped on. The rooms oozed a luxury I had never before experienced. A flowery fragrance filled the room. I wondered where it came from. The finely crafted furniture wore thick suits of Mariana chocolate colored embroidered silk with a cream white shag wall-to-wall rug, so thick it almost entangled my feet. Elaborate curtains covered the windows, holding the room to a hush as we entered. With such sound inhibitors I wondered how I could sing. I hoped we would talk here and sing in a studio somewhere else.

Talk we did, or more accurately, Mr. Hines talked about his life, his faith, his singing career, etc. He would pause here and there to ask me questions about where I studied and sang. His face could not hide his condescension to my answers. I already knew his life story from his book, *This Is My Story, This Is My Song*, but I didn't want to dim my chances of working with his company by saying, "Yeah, I already know all this, sir." Let him tell his story. I have to admit, however, that I really didn't like the man—he was much too pompous and self-aggrandizing, I thought.

"God has blessed me mightily," he rumbled on in his deep basso, and proceeded to relate how Sol Hurok, the most influential impresario in the world at that time, heard him at the Hollywood Bowl. "I was very fortunate that due to World War II, most of the great bassos were either banned from the Met for being Italian or German, or they simply returned to their homelands, which left the American field wide open." He grinned, "For me."

Tell me something I don't already know. I did my homework…sir.

"It was a great era for American singers, and many made the most of it—including me," he continued. "Mr. Hurok signed me immediately and arranged for me to sing a small role with the San Francisco Opera. How many young singers get a break like that? He wanted to groom me to take over the now depleted basso field in this country. Soon I went to New York and the Met. The rest is history.

"You, on the other hand," suddenly towering over me, "are not so fortunate in today's world of tenors, with the likes[19] of Domingo, Bergonzi, Gedda, Tucker, Corelli and, well, even singers like Barry Morell—but you know who they are as well as I do."

Yes, indeed I do.

"I believe that talent always finds its way to the top," Hines droned on. "If you have talent, then you'll make it." Joan and I glanced at each other, perceiving his clear implication that I *lacked* the talent to sing with major companies, *because* I hadn't already done so. "You'll never make it here in America. You should go abroad. I'm sure some small opera house in, say, northern Germany, would take you."

As this homily progressed, my anger and embarrassment mushroomed inside me. I wanted to both throttle him, then melt into my comfy chair. *Is he really telling me I have no talent—before he even hears me sing? I can't stand such artistic snobbery!* Any confidence I may have had when I walked in the door was just flushed down the tubes, as they say. I wondered if my face was red—I certainly was sweating—I wanted to run and hide.

Joan's face glowed with anger. Her eyes drilled such a hole through him I wondered if I could see through him, pun intended. One good came out of this ridiculous scene: her fury, blended with mine, gave me the courage to stand up and sing.

After his long speech and all too brief interrogation, he finally invited me to do just that. He pointed to a large Steinway grand off to the side of the room. Hugh sat down at the keyboard and I took my place in the curve, and took a deep breath. Because of the heavy curtains, the fluffy rug, and thickly cushioned furniture, I felt as if I were singing at the bottom of the sea. I could barely breathe, nor could I hear or even feel my voice. *Did he make me sing in here on purpose? I wondered if he ever sang in this room. It was ghastly for singing.*

---

[19] Pavarotti catapulted to fame at New York's Metropolitan Opera in 1972, long after this scene.

It became another pitiful audition. Mr. Hines then proceeded to grind salt in my wounds by critiquing me at length: my voice, my technique, and by emphasizing my very limited prospects for a career. He was also blunt in telling me he couldn't use me in his opera, *I Am the Way*, which was why Hugh had brought me here in the first place.

All in all, a dismal, downer experience.

At my next lesson, Hugh apologized for my Hines humiliation, then promptly told me about a Christian operatic tenor by the name of William "Bill" Harness. As it happened, Bill was enjoying a stint at the Metropolitan Opera, and happened to live next door to my cousin, Paul Trautman, in Teaneck, New Jersey. Hugh invited me to a concert in which he accompanied Bill. I was especially moved by Bill's rendition of "Moses," a choral piece composed by Gospel singer, pianist, and composer, Ken Medema.

Afterward, I spoke with Bill, mentioning my cousin Paul, which brought a big smile to his face. "You know Paul? He's my neighbor."

"Yes, so he told me. He and I are cousins."

"Really!?"

He clearly wanted to talk to me some more, but the crush of people cut our conversation short. "Stay in touch," he said as he shook the next person's hand. I was elated, but when we got outside, we noticed there was no contact information on the flyer, nor did Hugh have his number, nor did Paul.

Nevertheless, Bill had made such a strong impression, especially with "Moses," that I bought the music to the choral version, the only arrangement I could find, and began working on it. The piano part was fiendishly difficult, but Hugh played it with aplomb. Thank God for Hugh, who was willing to work for a modest fee. "I do it for the Lord," Hugh said.

Sad to say, I never sang it with Hugh. The only time I sang it in public was before a large audience in the mess hall of Northern Frontier, a Christian camp high in the Adirondacks. My accompanist was a young woman whose name I've forgotten. She played it astonishingly well. The occasion was a fundraiser for the camp.

•　•　•　•　•

Now that I was a college graduate with a Bachelor of Science on my resume, I decided that I needed a professional level job. Since I was working at the New York Public Library, I briefly entertained the idea of going for a Masters in Library Science, but we couldn't afford that. Plus Joan said, "Is that what you *really* want?"

I hesitated.

She grinned and looked me square in the eyes and said, "I thought so."

The *New York Times Classified* was the bible for employment in those days, and they came through for me: as a trainee in the New York State Employment Service, (long since abandoned). I was sure my singing career was just around the corner, so I stayed with them for a couple of years while trying to make that happen. I continued my vocal studies, coaching and singing opera productions.

. . . . .

While all this was going on in my life, things were not going well for my parents back in Lock Haven. Dad's largest printing client, a large paper manufacturer, decided to do their printing in-house, so the major source of Dad's income was abruptly cut off. This company was the largest industry in Lock Haven at the time, and was sort of a cash cow for Dad that kept him safe and secure. He was devastated at this loss, and furious with everyone from God on down. I believe it shattered what little faith he had left.

As I remember it, this multi-million-dollar company then hired him as a truck driver, perhaps as compensation, knowing that they pulled the rug out from under his tiny business. He had done all their office and label printing for well over twenty years. There was no contract—Dad had walked into their office one day, sold them some business cards, and convinced them he could produce the shipping labels for them as well. The man who shook Dad's hand on the deal had left the company, but they continued to use Dad for a number of printing services. As I recall, there was a change of management, and he had become a casualty of that.

I don't think Dad realized when he took the new job that he would have to lift heavy boxes of paper, sometimes to carry them from his truck to a loading dock or warehouse. Dad had already suffered two heart attacks over the years, the second of which had occurred only a few years prior. He certainly wasn't up to this kind of labor, even in his mid-fifties.

I don't recall the exact sequence of events, but Mom had called me to tell me how "awful he looked," and how worried she was about him. Dad's physician had refused to issue a medical statement for Dad to be reassigned to a less physically taxing job. I never learned why. There was some "technical problem" the doctor had about issuing it. Mom asked me to intervene, being the closest, geographically speaking, of their children. I called Dad from my desk at the Employment Service.

"Dad, what's the matter with Dr. Paterson?" This physician had been on my paper route in high school, so I knew the man personally. "Surely he knows your medical history, and can ask the company to reassign you to something less physically demanding. Why won't he issue you a medical pass?"

"I don't know. He just won't do it." I could hear the frustration in Dad's voice, and how frail his voice now sounded. That really upset me.

"What do you mean, he *won't* do it? He must," my voice rose. "He's a doctor, and he has to tell them that you must stop carrying these heavy loads of paper. Your life is at stake. How much do those boxes weigh, anyway?"

"Oh, they're not all that heavy. I can handle it."

"Thirty pounds? Forty pounds? Fifty pounds?"

"Robert, it's none of your goddamned business. I can't afford to lose this job. You wouldn't understand." Some of the old feistiness crept back into his voice.

"Damn it, Dad!" I shouted, responding more to his crankiness than to the issue at hand. "If you continue in this job, you're going to have another heart attack. Can't you see that?"

"So what if I do?" he countered. "Then you won't have to put up with me anymore."

"Dad, for God's sake, get a grip on yourself. Do you want *me* to call Dr. Paterson on your behalf? This whole situation makes me livid. There's something fishy about it, and I want to get to the bottom of it. Don't you?"

"No, damn it. Robert, there's nothing wrong. I told you—I need this job, so you stay the hell out of it," he said, and slammed the phone down.

My desk at the Employment Service was just one of dozens lined up in rows in a large room of employment interviewers like myself. Even though the room was always boisterous, my nearest colleagues were starting to look at me to see what the matter was. I returned the phone to its cradle quietly, and shrugged my shoulders at them. "No problem," I said, then waved a hand of dismissal.

The following Monday my office phone rang. "Hello," I said, expecting a client call.

"Robert?" said a strange voice I didn't recognize.

"Yes…. Who's this?" I asked tentatively. I wasn't used to being called Robert at the office. Everyone called me Bob. This had to be family. There was something familiar about the voice, yet I didn't recognize it. As I tried to think who it might be, she continued….

"This is your Aunt Mary."

"Aunt Mary? My goodness!" At that instant, I couldn't imagine why Aunt Mary would be calling me at work. So far as I could remember, I had *never* spoken to her on the phone, at any time. My mother had my office number, but how would Aunt Mary have it? "Where are you calling from, Aunt Mary? I mean, it's good to hear from you, but…."

"I'm calling from your house—I mean your mother's house, Robert. It's about your father…." Her voice trailed off in sobs. My heart sank. *I was afraid of this.* I heard Mom's voice crying in the background. She said something, not into the phone, but then took the receiver from her sister.

"Dad died," was all Mom could say before she began to cry again.

I was stunned, even though I had been afraid of getting a call like this. I took a deep breath, and sighed. I started to speak, but Mom said through her tears, "We think he had a heart attack. He died right here on the floor. I found him this morning. Mrs. Grugan came down…. I know he had been carrying heavy boxes at work…." Her voice dissolved into tears once more.

That made me furious. I was about to shout, "*I told him so…*" but before the words came out, I checked myself, and said, "Oh, Mom, I'm so sorry. I know what he meant to you…we all tried to help him…." Tears now came to my eyes, and my voice began to falter. *Damn.*

"I can't talk right now—I just wanted you to know," she said.

"Thanks for letting me know. I'll call you la—" She hung up before I could finish.

Johnnie recently sent me the following account of Dad's death:

"Mom told me that Dad spent his last weekend getting his books in order, almost as if he knew the end was not far off. On Monday, June 6, 1966, she came downstairs, and found Dad sitting on the floor in the living room with his back against a big hassock they had there. She told me that he sat there frequently, as it was the only comfortable way for him to sit, because his back bothered him so much. But this time, he was already dead when she came into the room that morning. At first, she didn't know what to do. Then she thought of our neighbor, Mrs. Grugan, who lived right behind us on Chestnut Street, remembering that she was a registered nurse. Mrs. Grugan immediately came down and confirmed his death. I think Mom said it was about 9:00 AM when she found him."

Some years after Dad died, a cousin of Joan's reminded me at a family gathering that Dad had died on June 6, 1966, or 6.6.66. Supposedly the biblical sign for Satan.

"What are you saying?" I asked the cousin somewhat defensively.

He shrugged his shoulders, as if to say, *Oh, nothing.*

I replied in my sternest, sermonizing voice, "I'm aware of the Kabbalistic tradition that includes various systems of numbers purported to explain the origins of the universe and all that has happened since, but I'm not persuaded by such approaches to life. Numbers assigned to letters—it's too arbitrary and capricious for me. I believe God's plan for our lives is clear in His Word, and it doesn't include this sort of wizardry."

• • • • •

Dad was a troubled man all his life. Some of the stories about his youth caused me to wonder how he was as good as he was. In my view, he was not a particularly good father, because he was "old school." Dad's always right, and Dad's always first in line. He was cruel at times, and even brutal by today's standards. He occasionally spanked Johnnie and me, sometimes with a belt if he felt the infraction were grievous enough. He was judge, jury, and executioner. Mom supported him in this, and used to spank us herself sometimes, or if she thought what we did was too pernicious, she asked Dad to do it. At the same time, she was our only support in the family, and we often used her to be an intermediary with him.

But the physical punishment was not as bad, and not nearly as persistent, as his psychological treatment of us. Speaking for myself, he had inculcated in me, I think perhaps even deliberately, an internal fear from as early as I can remember, with criticism, constantly reminding me how I didn't measure up, and by calling me—and my siblings—nasty and totally inappropriate names, some of them unrepeatable in this book. His mantra was, "Words can't hurt you." Little did he understand how wrong and destructive that was. Words can indeed hurt others, especially those spoken by the people closest to us.

Even those not so close…I have never forgotten how deeply the moniker a junior high school classmate laid on me cut me to the quick: "Mitch, the Bitch." He thought he was being funny, his rhyme *ever so clever*, but I was devastated the first time he called me that—in the playground in front of all our classmates. My gut reaction was to run. The next time he called me that, I became so infuriated I threatened to beat him up, even though he had pinned me in wrestling class. My fury was so intense I scared him into refraining from such behavior in the future.

Nevertheless, this insult has haunted me ever since. I believe now it wasn't the words themselves, but rather, it was the dissolution of whatever confidence I was born with in the face of such ignorance and cruelty. I lay this damage squarely at the feet of my father, whose inappropriate fury and withering names bullied me throughout my childhood. The encouragement denied me as a child created a vulnerability, a near-vacuum in my self-respect that has dogged me throughout my life—even with years of psychotherapy.

And yet, Dad worked very hard to provide for us, which I suppose was his definition of being a good father. When I got older, he loved to engage me in long debates over anything and everything. His method of arguing, however, was very frustrating, in that he didn't follow a logical path, but would wander from subject to subject until neither of us knew what we were talking about. Often we would end up shouting at each other, walking out, slamming doors, and the like. Sometimes he threw things across the room, never *at* me, thank heaven. Even so, his behavior distressed me. I think this model rubbed off on all us Mitchells because we all rattle on endlessly and erratically. (Just ask Joan.)

Yes, I was sad when he died, and yet I felt Mom's loss of him more than my own. I grieved for his troubled life, and that he was never satisfied with his lot. He always longed for something else. A piece of that rubbed off on me as well, and drove me from this to that in my life. I believe the difference between Dad and me is that I always found satisfaction in what I did while I was doing it. Dad never seemed to derive satisfaction from anything, not when he was doing it, or in retrospect. He didn't seem to enjoy even his family. Mom would have hotly disputed that, and did, claiming he loved his family more than anything else. Sadly, I rarely saw that—well, sometimes, like when he took the family for long rides in the country, or had cookouts in the backyard. But his painful legacy still haunts me occasionally: "Goddamn it, Robert, you'll never amount to a tinker's damn." I still struggle with *was he right?*

• • • • •

After three years and still no singing career that could support Joan and me, I decided to look for something in industry, where the pay was better. Joan and I also talked about starting a family. Since the New York State Employment Service had trained me to be an Employment Interviewer, I began sending out resumes to ads in the *New York Times*. One response came from the T. J. Lipton Company (Lipton Tea), whose home offices were located in Englewood Cliffs.

Yay! No more commuting on the bus to New York City. I could walk *from our Englewood apartment, though I preferred to drive up the long hill, especially on a cold, snowy morning.*

Lipton responded to my application by scheduling a battery of interviews and psychological tests, mandatory for managerial jobs in those days. The testing and interview process went well, and they hired me.

My immediate boss was an attractive blond lady, always neat and well turned out, by the name of Alice Jennings. A formal announcement went out to the Englewood Cliffs office on formal T.J. Lipton stationery, dated August 4, 1967, and signed by the manager, Dick Driscoll:

Effective August 7, 1967 Mrs. Alice Jennings is promoted to the position of Sr. Employment Interviewer for Englewood Cliffs.

The note goes on to review her background. Then, it announced:

Mr. Robert P. Mitchell will join the Personnel Department on August 7th as an Employment Interviewer and assume those responsibilities previously assigned Alice Jennings. Bob is a graduate of Mannes College, New York City and has been associated with the New York State Employment Service for the past eighteen months.

The note went on to review my professional experiences, and concluded:

Both Alice Jennings and Bob Mitchell will report to Mr. John Sinnott, Employment Supervisor.

Notice how they omitted "of Music" after "Mannes College." They wanted to conceal the fact that my degree was in music rather than in business.

Alice took great pains to show me the ropes at Lipton, as well as train me to succeed her in her previous job. She helped me set up my files, contacts, etc. I began by recruiting clerical staff, for which my experience at NYSES had prepared me. All went smoothly—at first.

· · · · ·

One of the unanticipated perks of the job was business lunches, which Dick Driscoll loved to host. He encouraged me to join them, and also taught me the art of drinking martinis. At first, they were too strong for me, but I soon mastered the dubious art of "liquid lunches." At home, Joan and I enjoyed wine in the evening. Liquor was too expensive. But, as I grew accustomed to ordering martinis in restaurants, I decided that I needed to learn how to make them at home. So we invested in the necessary tools and ingredients to indulge ourselves—or more accurately, myself.

Joan was uncomfortable with it from the beginning, but I grew to like martinis, perhaps a little too much. After my Ocean Grove days of loose drinking in Asbury Park, it all came back. Naturally, I thought I could handle it, but occasionally I overdid a bit.

One year at an employee dinner, martinis gushed forth from a fountain. I thought I was in seventh heaven. Who could afford such luxury? Not I. Determined not to let such a boondoggle go to waste I frequented the magnificent fountain. There was a steady stream of the martini liquid flowing from it. I grew concerned about where all the wasted martinis were going. Did they recycle them? Well, I did my best to not let any more of them go down the drain. *My God, martinis are expensive.* I looked around for someone to help me stem this waste. *Nobody? I guess I'll have to do it myself.*

That night, I could hardly see to find my car in the parking lot, much less to drive. I had never been so drunk in my life. I had asked for more coffee, but it was all gone. I drank water hoping to flush my system. That helped a little, but I still couldn't see straight. I found a phone in the lobby and called Joan.

"Honey, ish me."

"Bob! Are you all right?"

"No. I had too mush to drink…. I dunno how the hell I'm gonna get home. I tried to get shome coffee to shober up, but they clojzed the damn bar on me."

"I'll come and get you."

"How? I got the car."

"I'll call my parents…." The desperation in her voice rose exponentially as she thought of my driving in such a condition.

"No, no. Ish too late to call 'em…. Don' worry. I can drive." I didn't want anyone to know about my stupidity, especially Mom and Dad Bishop.

"You don't sound like it…."

"Ishss all right. I can do it." I hung up.

The only thing I remember about that insane drive home is narrowly missing two head-on collisions when I wandered into the left lane. I got lost a couple of times because everything was so blurry, but somehow I made it home. When I opened the front door, I vomited all over the carpeted front steps, and passed out—in my own mess.

Joan cleaned up my mal de mer, and me. That incident, I believe, injected a low grade poison in our marriage that never left. After more than fifty years, it amazes me that our marriage stayed afloat with all my stupid nails weighing it down.

In retrospect, I can say candidly, and ashamedly, that it was more my desire to sing than my love of the Lord that kept me from ruining my life altogether with drink. The dark days after a binge always affected my voice, my breathing, and my stamina, not to mention my memory. Plus, I knew if I called in sick too much, I would be looking for another job….

· · · · ·

I began the story of meeting Harry in the opening pages of the book. Here's how we met:

It was a cold, rainy day in about 1966 as I rushed to get out of the rain. I was soaked by the time I reached my office at Lipton in Englewood Cliffs. It's a large parking lot, and I had to park far away from the building. As soon as I got to my office, I furiously tossed my totally wasted umbrella in the trash basket and hung up my rain coat, grabbing a scarf from another hanger to wrap around my collar to get warm. Rain on my neck arouses an unnatural fury in me—it's invasive.

As if to squeal, "Gotcha!" the rain continued to pelt my picture windows, which were desk-level to ceiling. I glared at the drops which taunted me as they ran down the panes. I could almost make out dewy fingers wagging at me as they passed. Turning my back on them in disgust, I plunked myself into my chair behind my desk.

No sooner had I opened the first folder to begin my day, a colleague from the insurance section of Lipton stuck his head into my office. I had seen him around, but didn't know who he was. He was darkly handsome, like movie actor, Glenn Ford, short, always nattily attired with a tie, sport jacket, and complimentary trousers. His dark hair was short and neatly combed, every hair in place. He noticed my nameplate sitting on the front of my desk.

"Robert Mitchell!" he exclaimed, pointing at the sign. "Hmm. Could you be related to *John* Mitchell?"

"*John* Mitchell?" I repeated. "There are lots of John Mitchells."

With so many Mitchells in the world, at least a third of them must be named John. Also, Vice President Richard Nixon's presidential campaign manager was named John Mitchell, and his name was much in the news. At first I thought he was joking.

161

"Yeah, but how many missionaries in France are named 'John Mitchell'?" he countered.

"Oh," I said, stabbing my finger toward him, "that one's my brother!"

A crack of lightening followed by an explosion of thunder caused us both to recoil.

Harry said, "What did you say?"

"That's my brother...Must be."

"Really? Your *brother*?" his jaw dropped.

"Yeah.... Hey, wait a minute. How in the world do you know my brother?"

"Well, John is one of our missionaries from the Hackensack Baptist Church. We support him. I've known him for years. By the way, my name's Harry Ireland."

Now it was my mouth that dropped open. "Small world...I've known him all my life."

That scene began a life-long friendship that lasted right up until Harry's untimely death in the mid-1980s. Harry, like my brother, was totally dedicated to the Lord. When he found out more about me, he decided that I wasn't *really* a Christian—my lifestyle and "worldly manner" suggested to him the Lord was not first in my life. Harry didn't even know about my drinking—at least I think he didn't. Despite my protests to the contrary, he undertook me as his special case. It took nearly a dozen years of persistence for him to get the job done.

Harry and his family became good friends to Joan and me. We often visited their house on the south side of Bergenfield after we had moved from Englewood to the north side of Bergenfield, and they were frequent guests at our home, as well. Their lovely daughter, Ruthann, later babysat our kids. Harry invited us to his church, to prayer meetings, to Bible studies, to any religious event that came down the pike. Many of these activities took place at Harry and Ceil's (Cecilia) house. They also had a son, Harry, Jr., a younger brother to Ruthann.

At Lipton, Harry and I saw each other occasionally for lunch in the cafeteria. His work took him in a very different direction from mine. Although Harry had been with Lipton much longer than I, a year after our first meeting, he stopped in my office one day to announce that he was leaving the company.

I was shocked. "Good heavens, what happened?"

"I got a better job out in Parsippany." He explained what he would be doing there. He appeared uneasy, and some of what he said didn't quite add up.

"Harry, you're traveling quite a bit further for less money. Why?"

"There are some bad things coming down the pike here at Lipton. I advise you to get out as well. Now, while you still can."

"What?" I was aghast.

"I can't tell you anything now, but a shakeup is coming down from top management. It looks like they want to 'clean house.'"

"Clean house? What the dickens are you talking about? My job's going very well."

He stopped talking and looked out in the hall to see if anyone was listening.

Truth be told, I couldn't believe him. I tried to get him to say more, but he put a finger to his lips, "Shhh."

Later I tried to get Jack Sinnott, my boss, to tell me what was going on. He said little, but assured me that all was well—nothing to worry about. I trusted him, largely because one day not long after Harry's visit, Jack came into my office and asked me, "Bob, how would you like to become a recruiter of professional people instead of your clerical ones?"

"Are you kidding, Jack? Of course!"

Thus began a program of training as a professional recruiter. Jack envisioned me going to college campuses and conventions to get the very best people for Lipton. They needed chemists, bio-chemists, and bio-engineers, that sort of people.

A few months later, when Harry's warning was all but forgotten, Jack popped into my office with a job requisition for a biochemical engineer for the tea division labs. We discussed it and I got right on it. There was a lot to recruiting besides interviewing candidates: advertising, contacting employment agents, placing ads; I also looked at universities with graduate level biochemical engineering programs.

My singing career wasn't going anywhere, and I didn't have time to pursue it anyway. So I threw myself into this task, thinking that a new career was opening up for me.

Candidates were not easy to come by. It was a specialized field and we were looking for the specific background of tea testing. Jack decided the college route wouldn't do because the company wanted someone with experience. He also began to pressure me to get the job done.

At last I found a candidate I liked. He interviewed well. The lab people also liked him. So I decided to send him for the psychological testing that all professional and executive candidates were required to undergo—just as I had done.

The results came back with one or two negative comments. Jack himself looked over the portfolio, including the test results. I can still see him coming into my office one morning, portfolio in hand, looking very concerned. "I have serious reservations about your candidate, Bob," he began. "I think you should get another one. We're running out of time. You'll have to get someone in here really fast."

I thought for a minute, looked him in the eye, and said, "Jack, there *are* no others. This one is the only one I have. There simply are no tea testers out there on the market. Besides, the lab boys think he's great and will do an excellent job for them. What's the problem with the psychological evaluation?"

"It shows this man is not stable."

"How so? There were some low marks on some of the psychological questions, but the lab boss said they didn't apply to his job and I was to overlook them. Besides, he's a bird in the hand. If we start again, it's not going to happen as quickly as everyone wants. It just *won't*."

Jack exploded. He didn't like my questioning his judgment. He also said I shouldn't have showed the report to Lewis. I wanted to say to him, *You can't have it both ways. Nor can you drop this candidate and pull another one out of a hat.* But I didn't say it. I also thought to remind him that he hired *me* despite my psych report having some reservations, but I didn't say that either. I clammed up, as I always did when confronted by authority figures. The last thing he said to me as he slapped the portfolio on my desk and marched to the door was, "Well then, the decision is yours. *You'll* have to deal with the consequences."

Was he setting me up for a fall?

That thought chilled my bones. I agonized over this day and night. Joan tried her best to advise and comfort me. I stopped drinking altogether. Harry's admonition to "trust in the Lord" never crossed my mind, but I clearly remembered what he said about the department being cleared out. *Was I to be the first victim?*

As soon as I could arrange it, I made the candidate an offer and he accepted. The lab people seemed happy, yet Lewis, the lab manager, told Jack that I had made the offer. "Wasn't that *my* responsibility, according to personnel policy?" he fumed to Jack, not me.

Jack came running into my office yelling, "Lew just chewed me out because *you* made the offer. He was severely pissed. Goddamn it, Bob, it's not *your* job to make offers to candidates. Only the department head can do that. You know it's against company policy…." On and on he went. I wanted to say, *No one ever told me about company policy, nor was it part of my training, and most certainly no one told me about who gets to make the offer. What difference does it make anyway?* But he stormed out of my office just as harried as he came in.

The next day, Jack stepped more slowly into my office looking very drawn. With a sense of *I told you so*, he said, "Bob, I'm sorry, but your breach of responsibility went straight to the top. The vice president has ordered me to fire you." In those days, you could fire people on the spot.

What? I felt as if some sort of a stun gun had zapped me. I couldn't speak. Despite Harry's dire warning, I had refused to see it coming. In hindsight I should have asked to see the policy about hiring. Shoulda…coulda done a lot of things. Too late now. I couldn't help the feeling they set me up to fire me. I couldn't believe that Lewis would have betrayed me like that, but I didn't dare go see him about it. Besides, I didn't think of this until long after the fact, and following many conversations with Joan, who gave me a laundry list of things I shoulda done. Too late. I wasn't given an opportunity to react. Clearly, it was *fait accompli*.

Jack continued, "I tried my best to defend you, but even my boss was outraged. Lew was really ticked."

Yeah, right. Why didn't Lewis complain to me first? We could have worked it out. He seemed a reasonable man to me. Did he know this would cost me my job? Do I smell a conspiracy here? Again, my lips couldn't move.

"I'm sorry, Bob, very sorry." And he turned and left the room.

You're in this too, Jack. Which bridge are you trying to sell me?

Needless to say, I was devastated. I had never been fired from a job before—or since, as it has turned out—at least not until I became a pastor—but that's for another book. I felt totally humiliated. Of course, it was my own damn fault. I can hear my father's voice screaming at me, *You'll never amount to a tinker's damn, Robert. I told you so.*

That specter haunted me for weeks.

After some time had passed, I got a call at home from Harry. "I knew there was trouble at the top," he began. "Since you left, both Jack and Dick have also been fired. You were the first to go, the sacrificial lamb. They cleaned out the entire Personnel Department. It had nothing to do with that hire you made. I don't know what the problem was, but somebody at the top wanted to shake up the entire Personnel and Insurance Departments. To what purpose, no one seems to know. But I hear that's exactly what they've done. You were the first to go. Jack needed an excuse to fire you. I wonder if they deliberately tricked you into making that offer so they could nail you to the wall. It's also possible that they made up the story about the department head being angry. I wouldn't put it past them. And you know what? The guy you hired is still there."

I wondered how Harry knew so much about what happened, but I was afraid to ask. Since I was already gone, what difference did it make?

The Christmas of 1967 was glum, and in early 1968 it was back to the *New York Times Classifieds*. In the meantime, I was on Unemployment Insurance. I hated reporting to the Unemployment Office each week, but we needed the money. We still lived at the Linden Lawn apartments in Englewood. One of the bright spots for me was that I could ride with Joan on the bus into New York City in the morning to look for a job.

By this time, all thoughts of becoming a pastor had landed on a distant planetoid somewhere out there, probably Pluto.

Even my singing had taken a back seat. Both Joan and I left Central Presbyterian Church on Park Avenue to be soloists and section leaders.

Through an agent, I had become a soloist in a Presbyterian church in Scarsdale. During this period, I also sang Belmonte in two small productions of Mozart's *Abduction from the Seraglio*. There were other now-forgotten productions as well, the point being that even my much sought-after opera career morphed from "the little engine that could" into "the impossible dream." The performances I was doing made no career traction for me, zilch.

Spiritually, my life was a wasteland. My interest in church was primarily as a weekend job to earn extra money, as was the synagogue work. Even so, Harry loomed persistently in the background to nag me back to the Lord.

Like Jonah, I ran the other way.

Chapter Eleven

Singing or Scholastic?

The New York Times Classified came through again in the spring of 1968. After many interviews with an equal number of rejections, I thank God Joan brought this particular ad to my attention. I responded, and immediately landed an interview at Scholastic, Inc., whose corporate headquarters were in my former New York Public Library stomping grounds, at the old Hippodrome Building[20] on the corner of Sixth Avenue and Forty-Third Street.

Carol Rafferty, Scholastic's Employment Supervisor for the New York office, was dressed in a smart, conservative grey business suit. She greeted me warmly, with a friendly smile and a firm handshake. Though she was a bit shorter than I, it seemed that our eyes were on the same level. It was hard to gauge how old she was. With youthful charm and buoyancy, she also exuded motherly vibes. Her lively sense of humor lightened the conversation, and made me feel at home. In a word, we hit it off.

She needed an employment interviewer to recruit clerical staff, artists, and writers. She liked my credentials from T.J. Lipton and the New York State Employment Service. (In those days, T.J. Lipton was forbidden by law to report that they had fired me.) "With your background in music, how did you come to be an employment interviewer?" Carol began.

---

[20] The original Hippodrome Building was gone, but the current building was commonly referred to as the Hippodrome Building.

"My teachers told me I'm not ready to sing opera, so I had to find a job. Not many options for a music graduate. My wife saw an ad in the *The New York Times* for training interviewers at the New York State Employment Service. All you needed was a bachelor's. I applied. They took me and trained me to interview. I've always loved meeting and talking to people, so it was a good fit."

"Why did you leave the employment service?"

"One of my colleagues advised me to look in the private sector. They pay much better, he said. Lipton was only a mile from home. My friend was right. They do pay much better."

"So why did you leave Lipton?"

"There was a reorganization in the Personnel Department. I was last in, and first out."

She smiled again as if to say, *been there, done that*, and rose from her desk. "I'll be just a minute. Wait here, please."

She recommended me to her boss, Paul King, Director of Personnel, a true eccentric. Tall, dark complexion with thinning, grey-flecked hair, his small potbelly belied an otherwise athletic trim. Wild, dark eyes peered over half-rimmed glasses. His clothes always looked as though he put them on as he was flying out the door. My interview with him was very different from Carol's. He pressed me hard on every subject.

Next, I had to make an appointment with their psychological testing agency ASAP. The tests were grueling, and, in my opinion, invasive, with too many opportunities for misinterpretation. I survived them and Paul offered me the job. I accepted with a wide grin. When I phoned Joan, she cried for joy, and I joined her.

From my first day on the job, I didn't see much of Paul. Carol was my immediate boss, mentor, and guide. But every now and then, Paul would burst into my office. I can still see him erratically wandering around my desk, talking non-stop, with exaggerated hand gestures. "Those damn magazine people, they always want their cake and eat it too…" gesturing erratically. I thought surely he'd knock something off my desk or hurt himself somehow. He had quite a strong baritone voice—I thought he could've been opera singer. His theatrical histrionics would make any stage director sit up and take notice.

Paul was in charge of Corporate Personnel. That included New York as well as offices and plants in New Jersey, Missouri, Ohio, California, Canada, and even overseas. There were three large operating divisions: Magazines, Book Clubs, and Text. My job was to hire clerical and beginning editorial and art personnel for the New York Office.

I had no idea at first that the artists and editors were protected by a labor union. For Paul, the unions were the greatest thorn in his side. My only connection with them was the benign editorial union in New York, which rarely caused any grief, certainly none to me. Yet Paul was always fussing with them about something or other. He would try to draw me into the fray, but I usually managed to sidestep it. Much ado about very little most of the time, although occasionally there were serious disputes over money and benefits.

I had to walk a tightrope, to please Paul as well as to keep my editors and art directors happy. All these folks, and their staffs, belonged to the editorial union. My job was to recruit any staff they required, professional and clerical. I recruited clerical help for the entire New York office.

Carol recruited managerial, supervisory staff, and high-level artists and writers. Paul recruited divisional executives for the entire company, domestic and foreign, except positions the Board of Directors themselves created, typically executive and corporate vice-presidents, divisional presidents (although I don't recall any of the latter during my tenure), and the like.

Many employees, like me, had long careers with Scholastic, a company that was proud to acknowledge our loyalty. They did so through the Five Year Club, which held an annual Five Year Dinner in the fall. As its name suggests, employees had to work five years before they became eligible.

Obviously, I was not eligible in my first year. The bash that year was held at the Tenafly Country Club in New Jersey, the same place that hosted the Lipton dinner a year or two prior. It didn't matter where in the US or Canada you worked, if you had the five years under your belt, you were invited.

Paul himself invited Joan and me to sing because he was desperate for inexpensive entertainment—he was terrified he'd run over his budget. "Your fee," he said, "is your dinner."

We happily accepted because we could sing whatever we wanted. Our favorite duet was the end of Act 1 in Puccini's *La Bohème*. Our accompanist for the occasion was Nogah Bar-Illan, sister of world-renowned concert pianist, David Bar-Illan, (who many years later became Netanyahu's Director of Communications and Policy Planning, a top spot in the Israeli government). We had been close friends with Nogah and her husband, Bruce Revesz, a trumpeter in the New York City Opera Orchestra, since our Mannes College of Music days.

We sang right after the dinner. Then Maurice "Robbie" Robinson, founder, President, CEO, and Chairman of the Board of Scholastic, stood up to give his annual speech. His first comment was, "I can think of a lot better ways of making love than singing Italian opera!"

Everyone laughed heartily—except Joan and me. We were incensed and embarrassed. When I later complained to some colleagues about the insult, they said, "Insult? No, Robbie didn't *insult* you. He was just trying to be funny."

Stapled to my 1968 Five Year Club list of attendees is a note, typed by Robbie himself on his own stationery, which reads:

October 30, 1968

Dear Bob,

It was a delightful surprise to learn that we had such a source of harmony in our own Personnel Department! You and your lovely wife, Joan, gave us all much pleasure last night. As time goes along, you will discover, I am sure, that we have many musical aficionados on the staff.

Thank you for your generous contribution toward making this year's Five Year Dinner a truly memorable occasion for all of us.

Cordially yours,

M. R. Robinson

Mr. Robert Mitchell
Personnel Department
6th Floor

At first, I thought this was an apology, but over the years, I have come to believe that he simply didn't realize how the remark struck us. Robbie was a fine gentleman, too kind and refined to hurt anyone. He went out of his way to be helpful to everyone who worked for him, from the people who cleaned to the top executives. When he came to the Jersey office, he always stopped by my office, stuck his head in and waved, "Hello, Bob. How's it going?" He never forgot my name no matter where we encountered one another. That impressed me profoundly. I have often thought of Robbie's amazing gift with people, and wished I had his ability to remember people's names, especially after I became a pastor thirty years later.

I loved recruiting artists and writers. Interviewing them and working with the Scholastic staff who hired them energized me—they were a fascinating bunch. Most job applicants had teaching in their background. In fact, I looked for classroom experience because it uniquely prepared applicants to communicate effectively with students. Scholastic's goal had always been to present contemporary events so that kids could better understand the world they live in.

There's a quote from Robbie that struck me by its use of the philosophical term *non sequitur*, which David Wolfe had taught me years before. Robbie wrote in an open letter to his son Richard, who succeeded him as President and CEO of Scholastic:

> "…you know how I feel about 'straight thinking' and my oft-repeated request that we teach kids about the non sequiturs by which they are so often led mentally and emotionally astray…."

His words have followed me through my careers as a Christian minister and educator. When we see the mindless, pugnacious manner of public discourse, thinking people everywhere should stand against it much more than we do. Far too much advertising, news reporting, public debate, and popular literature are characterized by *non sequiturs by which [we] are so often led mentally and emotionally astray.*

Robbie's dream became my dream. Much of my preaching and teaching has been centered in this ideal. When I later taught ethics at the Marist College in Poughkeepsie, New York, my syllabus stated, "All non sequiturs[21] and ad hominems[22] will be challenged. Please avoid them."

Thank you, Robbie, for the gift you gave us.

Occasionally, the people I interviewed for Scholastic made lasting impressions on me. One day a lovely young lady sat down in front of me. She handed me her application. The scent of her perfume reached my nostrils. Her nails were painted a soft red that made her skin glow. Her ocean-blue eyes connected briefly with me, then she looked down demurely.

I studied her material for a moment. "Oh, I see you are both a teacher *and* a writer."

She beamed. "Oh yes, I think I loved to write from the moment I could pick up a pen. Teaching followed quite naturally."

Her eyes sparkled under long lashes. She smiled when I asked, "How so?"

"We learn best from story, especially as children. My mother always read stories to me, and I loved to read myself. Even when I was very young, I wrote stories [she enclosed the word with finger quotes] for my friends and we acted them out in our homemade theater."

"Homemade theater?"

"Oh, it was under a tree in our back yard."

I smiled and nodded, admiring her creativity. "What sort of a job are you looking for?"

"Oh, if I could proofread or edit for either your magazines or books…I want to learn from the ground floor up," she said earnestly.

Serious applicants came into my office toting portfolios packed with their writing or artwork. It wasn't really my job to evaluate their work, but through trial and error I soon learned that reviewing their material provided me a win-

---

[21] It doesn't follow, meaning, the argument is illogical
[22] To the man, i.e., personal attacks

dow into their character and skills. Obviously, my impressions determined whether or not I'd send the applicant to an editor. I took that responsibility—and the power to change a person's life—very seriously.

I read a bit more of Ann's material, I liked her clear, engaging style, so I referred her to an opening in the Book Division. The interviewing editor was ecstatic. She told me, "Ann has *real* talent. Hire her."

That lifted my self-esteem. Obviously, I was happy for Ann, but she affirmed my judgment and talent for this job. I said to myself, *I've got a future here.*

· · · · ·

Becoming a pastor hardly crossed my mind anymore. If it did, I tossed it off with a shrug.

After candidates were hired, I didn't see much of them, especially after I moved to the New Jersey office several years later. But I often wondered what became of Ann. Was she still with Scholastic? I would tell people, "I hired her." Of course that wasn't strictly true, but at the same time, *if* she hadn't got past me, how would she get hired? She wouldn't, simply because my job was to screen out applicants. Such power puffed me up—but also scared the hell out of me.

A dozen or so years later, Scholastic tapped Ann to head up a new project known as *The Babysitters' Club*. The project became so successful that Ann eventually left Scholastic to set up her own company, which supplied Scholastic exclusively with the Babysitters' material.

One day in New Jersey, I bumped into a friend of mine from the Accounting Department in the employees' lounge. He seemed quite anxious as he fussed with the vending machine.

"You're looking stressed out today, Larry. What's up?" I asked, waiting behind him to use the machine, occasionally sipping my coffee. No one else was in the lounge at the time.

He finally got what he wanted out of the machine, and turned to me with an excited face. "I just made out a check to Ann Martin for a million dollars!" I couldn't tell if he was happy or nervous about it. We both whistled as we shook our heads. I told him that she was one of my great hires.

"Are you kidding me, Bob? She was pirated from another company." He took a vicious bite out of the candy bar for which he had fought the machine so valiantly. His nervous face had a glaze of sweat over it. I wondered what he was so anxious about. The million-dollar check?

"Huh-uh," I shook my head knowingly.

He looked at me with a scowl. A sweaty odor from damp armpits clashed with his cologne. He tried to argue with his full mouth, but I cut him off, "She's home-grown, a Scholastic product."

"How the hell do you know that?" he grumbled as he wiped crumbs from his mouth.

"I hired her," I said, pointing to a table in the lounge so we could take a seat.

His jaw dropped. "*You* hired her? How could *you* hire her?" We sat opposite each other.

"I was in Personnel in the New York office when she applied. At that time I screened all editorial and art applicants. If I hadn't referred her, she wouldn't be with Scholastic today. You're right, though. I didn't actually *hire* her. But if I hadn't *referred* her…." I shrugged my shoulders. "She started out as an Editorial Assistant. Just think, Larry. If she hadn't got past me, there might never have been a Scholastic *Babysitters Club*, and you wouldn't be making out million dollar checks for her!"

He shook his head in disbelief. "Are you BS-ing me, Bob?"

"Not at all. That's the God's-honest truth, as surely as I'm sitting here."

"Amazing," he said, shaking his head.

• • • • •

In the early seventies, Carol Rafferty decided to leave Scholastic for what she thought were greener pastures in the mercantile industry. Paul gave me Carol's old title of Personnel Manager of the New York office. In the meantime, our New Jersey office had a small personnel staff headed by a long-time employee named Dolly, an enthusiastic woman, who had started as a fulfillment clerk.

One day, Paul decided that the personnel demands in EC required a manager other than himself because he was too busy with the corporate picture. So he hired another young fellow named Fred, to head up the NJ office.

It took only a couple of months for Carol to become totally disillusioned with her new career, and she asked Paul if she could come back to her old position, which I now occupied. Around the same time, Fred decided to leave the company.

Paul swooped into my office like a torrent from a broken dam, complete with a Shakespearean back-of-the-hand-to-the-forehead, slammed himself up against the wall next to the door and moaned, "Oh my Gawd! Wad am I gonna do?"

I looked up, startled. "What's the matter, Paul?" I tried to be casual, having grown accustomed to his theatrics, and yet, when they happened, I never knew what was behind them, nor where they might lead.

His words tumbled out like coal down a chute. "Fred's leaving and Carol wants to come back to her old job. Gawd! Wad am I gonna do? Wad am I gonna do?"

Even though I knew full-well Paul was manipulating me—he was a master at it—without hesitation I replied, "For God's sake, Paul. What's all the fuss? This is easy: I'll go to New Jersey, and Carol takes her old job back. What's the big deal?"

"You mean it?" I saw in his eyes that he was already congratulating himself for this easy coup.

"Sure!"

"That's settled then!" He slapped the wall in jubilation, and rushed out of the office, unable to contain his glee. Obviously, that's what the performance was meant to achieve. It had to come from me, though. Maybe that's why he liked me—he always felt he could get me to dance to his tunes.

Me? I always saw right through him, so if it suited me, I gave him his victories, no skin off my nose. If I didn't want to do what he wanted, I'd just say no, and walk away.

Since we lived in Englewood at the time, and the New Jersey office was little more than a mile from our garden apartment, it was a no-brainer for me, a win-win all around. I hated the commute into the city, anyway.

That's how I became Personnel Manager of Scholastic's Englewood Cliffs facility.

• • • • •

Enter a whole new cast of characters on a very different stage: the New Jersey office was like landing on another planet after New York City. Those editorial and artistic managers cared very much about their employees, union or no union, plus, they were laid-back folks interested in all manner of artistic and intellectual pursuits, people who loved to chat.

I soon learned that I alone, with one exception, was the advocate for the 200 or so New Jersey middle-aged, clerical women. They were temporary and part-time, a status that denied them health benefits, but they were eligible for Unemployment Insurance in their off-season, the early summer months. But even UI often became a sticky point in salary negotiations. It was all business in New Jersey. No time for dreaming or chatting. No one interested in opera or classical music, or the fine arts in general. This was a fulfillment house, kind of the flip side of publishing.

When I sat at my new desk for the first time in 1971, Clinton "Clint" Smith was the head honcho of the Englewood Cliffs facility as Vice President of Operations. Robbie maintained an office on the first floor near the main entrance. When he visited, once a week or so, he would go around the entire facility and greet each employee by name. Then he would meet with Clint in this first floor office. (Clint's office was on the second floor.)

Clint was a dapper, charming man with a ready smile. He appeared taller than he was, with thinning white hair, combed over creamy-white skin that would burn unmercifully in the sun. He always dressed impeccably. Every working man in those days wore white shirts and dark business suits, especially executive types. Through the sixties and seventies, vests were *de rigueur*. Bosses accepted shirtsleeves in the office, but they insisted upon jackets for meetings and luncheons. When Clint wore his half-rimmed glasses, he reminded me of a college professor. I think he would have liked that impression.

While I generally had a good relationship with him, he had a way of making me feel inferior. He was the boss. For the most part, the editorial and artistic managers in New York didn't treat me that way. I missed the feeling of equality.

"Bob, I need to discuss the new insurance plan," Clint's voice crackled over the phone. "My office. Fifteen minutes." I can't remember that he ever came to my office.

Paul King used to argue with him just for the sake of arguing. Paul didn't think very highly of Clint. He thought him too pedestrian, narrow-minded. "All he cares about is his damned budget—so he can look good to management," Paul would say. "He doesn't give a damn about his workers."

Indeed, Clint focused intently on his bottom line. Paul and I tried over the years to get more money, better working conditions, benefits, etc. for the working women. But Clint was more interested in *saving* money. I understood his position, but stood up for the ladies nonetheless.

Ironically, Clint would often complain to me about morale problems.

"Well, my friend," I'd rejoin, "you can't have it both ways. What do you expect with what we're paying them? And no benefits?"

The work force was evenly divided between Magazines and Book Clubs, some two hundred part-time employees each. The rub was that Clubs far out-produced Magazines in terms of revenue, and this often became a point of contention. Clint always tried to maneuver me to his position of saving money. However, I had the responsibility of managing salaries across division lines, and that gave me some clout.

The next year, I began a project to upgrade and systematize salaries and job descriptions for the entire Englewood Cliffs facility. To strengthen my position, I convinced corporate headquarters to authorize an independent wage and salary consultant to work with me to do a comprehensive study of the entire operations section, namely, Clint's domain. Several sections did not report to Clint, the largest of which was finance, which kept me at arm's length. They were a realm all to themselves.

The trouble would begin with one or two smaller sections that did not report to Clint because that's where the conflict over wages already was. Clint thought these sections were earning too much money, and he wanted to take control of them. He supported my project because he saw a chance to build his empire and at the same time save money.

I wanted fairness for everyone, regardless of who was in charge.

With the battle lines set, Bob, the consultant, and I began with the premise that we needed to document and evaluate every job in the facility, a staggering job that took nearly seven months to complete. With that information we could then name and classify every job in our study. That took several more months because of disputes over how to define and categorize the jobs we found.

A worker in one department might say, "I'm a Control Clerk," while someone in another department claimed, "I'm a Statistical Clerk, I've always been called that, this is what I do, and this is my salary…" —higher than the first clerk's. Bob and I determined that the two jobs were identical and should get the same pay. What salary? What title? We insisted that both title and salary should be based upon the industry salary survey we had conducted for just this purpose. Sometimes no one was happy with our conclusions. That was our greatest challenge.

Clint didn't want to compare his work force with any other, so we had to convince him that this was the *purpose* of the project. We wanted to standardize jobs in every department in order to come up with fair salaries and appropriate titles for all employees no matter where they worked.

The sections that didn't report to Clint had similar clerical jobs, but they were at higher salary levels than his people, and typically had fancier job titles, thus causing the employees themselves to believe they deserved more money. This had always been a thorn in everyone's side, especially Clint's, and I sympathized with his frustration. He wanted to bring the other departments *down* to his level, rather than *raise* the salary levels of his workers.

He had a point, in a way, in that he employed ten times as many workers than the other sections did, so of course his costs would go up astronomically if we raised his salary levels to theirs. But that was *not* our objective, *per* se, and I tried very hard to show him our true strategy. We looked at the labor market itself to compare work performed versus salaries, and come up with both job descriptions and proposed salary levels that would be equitable in terms of the broader labor market, bringing Scholastic in line with other companies like ours.

Fortunately for Bob and me, we had top management on our side, so we were able to move ahead. Clint grudgingly came along. It took nearly a year to complete the entire project, but through our careful analysis of industry-wide standards, we instituted a more level playing field for all the clerical staff, along with standards and procedures for management. In the end, Clint was happy with what we achieved, and signed off on it with smiles and compliments for our hard work.

I thanked Bob, the consultant, and bade him farewell. "All set," I thought. But was it?

Chapter Twelve

George and I

Spring 1971

"Bob?"

I looked up from my desk to see a head and right shoulder leaning in my doorway, right hand on the door frame. Tinted glasses veiled his eyes, but he smiled, revealing a set of sturdy teeth. Quickly I realized this must be George Milne, the new head of the New Jersey operation I'd heard so much about. I leapt to my feet, swiftly maneuvered around my desk and stepped toward him, my hand extended. "Come in, come in, have a seat," ushering him to one of the two metal chairs in front of my desk. "You must be Mr. Milne."

"George," he responded as he crossed the room in three steps, shook my hand with a beaming smile, and plopped into the proffered seat. I slid the other chair around to face him. Dressed in a grey suit, white shirt and caramel-blonde tie, George had the style and charisma of a Jack Kennedy. Built like a linebacker, he looked a bit out of place in a stylish business suit. Well over six feet tall, quick in his movements, he always had a ready smile and an air of confidence that took your breath away. He tended to throw back his straight brown hair, always a bit tussled, with a flair that reminded me of Jack Wilcox, my charismatic voice teacher at Mansfield State Teachers College.

Robbie had brought him on board to save a sinking ship—Scholastic was in financial and operational trouble. Sales were down, the marketing people in New York were screaming at the computer geeks in New Jersey—

like sibling rivals who couldn't care less about helping each other. Promotion labels, the lifeblood of Scholastic's two major divisions, magazine and book clubs, were not being produced on time or correctly. I had no idea about the mechanics of what was happening, but as Personnel Manager of the Englewood Cliffs facility in New Jersey, I knew something was radically wrong.

Milne, now the corporate vice president in charge of all the manufacturing facilities *and* finance, became the most powerful person in the company next to Robbie. Clint didn't like it one bit. He no longer reported to Robbie, but to George, a come-down for him in his eyes. Clint retained his title of divisional vice president, but it soured in his mouth. He was no longer the head honcho in New Jersey.

I was by then New Jersey's Personnel Manager. As I took my seat opposite George, a thought flashed across my mind: In the two or three years I had worked in New Jersey, Clint never once set foot in my office. Here was Clint's new boss—on his first day, early in the morning, come to visit me. I almost said so, but checked myself. No point in bad-mouthing Clint—*that'll come back to haunt you, Robert.*

"I hear you did a super job with a wage and salary review," he said, beaming. "Good work, Bob."

I blushed. How could he know that already? "Thank you, sir."

"Call me George. May I see a copy of your report?"

"Certainly." I rose and started around my desk to the file drawer. As I pulled it out I said, "I only have this one copy—it's quite voluminous. Clint and Paul both have copies."

"I'll have it back on your desk tomorrow morning."

Wow—I didn't expect that. It took over a year to prepare; it would take me that long to read it again. I handed it to him.

He rose as he accepted it. "I'd like to meet with you—just to talk. Can you be in my office at nine o'clock tomorrow morning?"

I blinked. I wasn't used to being asked. Clint always ordered me to be in his office at such-and-such a time. "Or course. I look forward to it. I assume your office is Robbie's old office, is that correct?"

"You got it." He turned and was out of the room in two strides. At the door he turned just long enough to say, "Great to meet you, Bob. You and I are gonna get along just fine. See y' tomorrow." With a flash of his generous smile, he was gone.

A new wind had just blown through my office, and was about to blow through all of Englewood Cliffs. No one saw it coming, including me. The first hint was this visit.

George was the beginning of the greatest and most productive period in my corporate career. He asked the most amazing questions; he had an uncanny ability to cut right to the heart of things. I guess I'll never fully understand why he took a shine to me as he did. In style we were total opposites: he cut to the chase in five words or less, while I have to think about every question, analyze it from every angle. We couldn't have been more different, yet he helped me to focus on what was important, to become more incisive. He never criticized me, (amazingly, that's the truth); rather, he guided me. It was the beginning of a beautiful relationship.

I never had a boss like him before or since.

George rarely called me on the phone; when he needed me he came to my office. Of course, Clint's office was on the second floor, and Clint rarely came to the first floor. George would walk into my office, or if he heard voices inside, he'd stick his head in, survey in an instant what was going on, and say something like, "Excuse me, Bob, when you get a chance, c'mon over." If no one was in my office, he'd walk in with a big smile, "Bob, how'ya doin' today?"

He knew all too well how to use his height and imposing frame. Sometimes, if he wanted to demonstrate his power during a conversation, George would come around my desk and tower over me as I sat in my chair—to make his point. Yes, it was intimidating, even scary at first, yet he was the most supportive boss I ever had. He was always in my corner.

In staff meetings he said very little until everyone else spoke. He never carried papers or a brief case. If he wanted to take notes on anything, he had 3 x 5 cards in his shirt pocket for that purpose. He'd slip one out, write a few words on it, and put it right back. Then, suddenly, when there was a lull in the conversation, he would point to a manager and quietly say, "Good. You're in charge of this project. I want to see a plan on my desk tomorrow morning." Immediately, he'd get up and leave, everyone looking at one another, mouths agape.

"*He* called the meeting. That's *it*?" people would grumble. One by one the rest of us would pick up our papers, charts, notes—whatever—and leave.

I smiled to myself.

• • • • •

One summer—it probably was the summer of 1971—he invited Joan and me on his yacht for a pleasant summer outing. The day was a scorcher with little breeze. Our clothes stuck to us, I complained about the heat—until we got on the water. The ocean breeze made all the difference.

George resided in Englewood, not far from where we lived on Palisades Avenue. We had been guests in his house on several occasions. (He was the only Scholastic executive with whom Joan and I enjoyed social contact.) He kept his yacht on the Long Island Sound, near Greenwich, Connecticut.

We drove there right after church.

On that yachting afternoon, once aboard, we sailed into the sound. Also on board, unknown to us, was a young man of great promise, George had told us, by the name of Richard Cryer, to whom George introduced us, along with his wife, Libby. George's wife and a couple of Milne kids completed the company. Watching the kids scamper around the boat like old hands delighted us. It was the only time in my life I sailed on a yacht in the Long Island Sound.

It was indeed a delightful afternoon, even though on the way home, Joan and I talked about how nervous we both were, moving in such exalted company. What amazed us was how they treated us as equals. We certainly didn't feel the part.

For the first time in my life, a boss took me under his wing and encouraged me, not only for my work, but he urged me to sing as well. Amazing! Every other boss before or since saw my singing as a conflict with my corporate career.

"Your singing is *you*, Bob. I want you to be all you can be," George said with a big smile while clapping me on the back. "Go for it!"

He would call me into his office to discuss not only personnel matters, but strategic corporate operational matters as well. Heady stuff for me. For the first and only time in my life, here was little ole me, a confidant and advisor to the number two man in a multi-million dollar international corporation. Whew!

Small wonder Paul resented my association with George.

• • • • •

One day in 1971 or early 1972, George appeared at my door.

"Bob," he began, "are you aware of the tension between the New York people and the New Jersey operational folk?" He remained standing near the door, I didn't get up. I could never tell whether he meant to stay, or if he'd suddenly turn and leave.

"I've heard rumblings about it, George, but I haven't been able to put my finger on it."

"Bob, there's a dangerous breakdown in communication between the marketing people in New York and the operations staff out here."

"Really? That I didn't know." I pointed to a seat and he took it. "Is there anything I can do?" I was flattered that he talked with me about this high level corporate stuff. I failed to see how I could help from where I sat. I had no clout to bring these people together.

"I'm not sure just yet. But if we don't do something soon, it could bring the entire company down."

"Good Lord!" I didn't know what else to say.

George slapped his knees and rose. As he started toward the door, he turned and said, "We'll need to discuss this some more tomorrow. Stop by and see me, first thing." With that, he was gone. I slowly shook my head in bewilderment.

Like Rev. Beam, George must have seen something in me I didn't know I had.

What we discussed the next day was that our direct marketing campaigns—we called them *promotions*—were going out late. The company's revenue depended upon their timely arrival into the hands of buying teachers and administrators. This failure threatened company revenue. Tens of millions of dollars were at stake. Robbie and all the big brass held George's feet to the fire about it. In fact, he was hired to solve this very problem, unknown to me at the time.

He said to me, "Bob, when I call my people together to solve this mess, all they do is complain and point fingers at each other. This has to stop. How do you think we should solve the communications problem with the New York Office?"

"George, isn't that a little out of my depth? Paul should be the one to handle that. It's a corporate problem, not a New Jersey problem."

"I need a Coordinator—someone who can communicate between these two groups. This person has to speak the language of both sides of the river. They refuse, or simply cannot speak each other's languages. The computer people speak *computerese* and the marketing people speak *marketingese*," he said. "It's like Chinese and Hungarian. We must find a bridge for them."

Again, the *we*. It was daunting, but I listened and thought about it.

These private meetings went on almost daily for several weeks. I knew George was grooming me for something, but I couldn't figure out what. He had me read books on the changing culture of the business world, books like Douglas McGregor's 1960 book, *Theory X and Theory Y*, and Laurence Peter's and Raymond Hull's 1968 book, *The Peter Principle*. I was very affected, not just by these books, but also by George's focus on me. He also told me that my future was not in *staff* management, but in *line* management. "*Staff* advises people. *Line* is where the action is. That's where your career track lies. Your future is there—in line management. There's nowhere to go in Personnel. Think about it."

I thought about it, but still could not fathom how solving this problem would get me out of Personnel. For all his quirkiness, Paul was a much better negotiator than I. So I said to George on one occasion, "Why not Paul?"

"Because you're a better people person than Paul. He aggravates people. Including me. Who do you think could handle this job?" George said.

This subject dominated our conversation for quite some time. Little by little he shifted the emphasis of the conversation from talking about improving communications to finding a Coordinator who can communicate. I said, "I'll contact my agencies and begin a search right away."

George shook his head. "That's not what I want."

I was puzzled. But George didn't say anything further on that occasion.

Then one day I said, "George, I think *I'm* a pretty good communicator. Is this something I could do?"

"What do *you* think?"

Wow! I blew a soft whistle through my lips. *Holy smokes. George really trusts me. He believes in me. Nobody ever believed in me before. This will be a big undertaking.*

I leaned back in my chair. "Yes, I think I could do it."

"Do you *want* to do it?"

"Yes! Yes, I do. I see it as an opportunity to get into line management, as you suggested."

With a slap of his hand on his desk, he rose and smiled. "Well then, let's do it!"

I rose as well. "Ah, what'll I—or we—tell Paul?"

He was already heading for the door. "Leave that to me."

I followed him out.

Looking back on it later, the light finally dawned on me what George was angling for all along. *Mercy, am I slow on the uptake!* He wanted me to take the position all along, but I needed to ask for the job rather than his offering it to me. He was testing my eagerness to do it.

At that point, Paul and I were not getting on very well, anyway. He had not been in charge of, or even consulted about, the salary survey I had completed the year prior, which irked him. I spent far too much time with George, and didn't go into the city to see Paul often enough. In other words, he was losing control of me, and, from his perspective, the entire New Jersey facility. I knew that George was a much more powerful player in the company than Paul was, and I knew very well to whom to hitch my star.

Somehow George finessed Paul into asking for a meeting in George's New Jersey office to discuss me. No doubt his plan was to intimidate Paul by meeting in his office, the one that used to belong to Robbie. On his turf, George held all the cards.

Even though I knew George had carefully planned the whole thing, I was still very nervous about it. Paul had his own way of dealing with situations, and it was hard to predict what he might do or say. After all, I still reported to Paul and he had the power to fire me.

I remember that meeting as if it had happened last week. There was a large, round conference table in the middle of George's New Jersey office, with a large picture window overlooking Route 9W and the woods this side of the Palisades Interstate State parkway and the Hudson River. Robbie's prestige was ever present.

When I arrived, Paul was already there talking to George—about me. That was clear because Paul didn't stop talking when I entered the room. George was at his desk and Paul was seated at the conference table. It actually made a rather silly picture. One man sitting behind a large desk with nothing on it but a computer. The other seated facing him on the other side of a large, round conference table, also with nothing on it, and not another soul in the room.

As I entered, George looked over at me, smiled, got up from his desk, and pointed to the table. "C'mon in, Bob, have a seat." We took up positions around the table so that you could draw an imaginary equilateral triangle from one to the other.

Paul immediately launched into a litany of complaints about me. He grumbled about my not having consulted him about the salary project. He fumed that I did not come to the New York office as much as he desired. "I have work for him to do," he said. "He reports to me, damn it, not you. I expect him to keep me better informed about his activities, and what's going on over here in New Jersey. He's my eyes and ears over here, after all…." And on and on he went.

Through this tirade, George just looked at him with a slight smile. He waited for him to run out of steam, and then asked Paul, "So what do you want to do? Fire him?"

Whoa, George! That's me you're talking about—as if I weren't here! My Lord, George, how can you give him such an opportunity? I thought you were on my *side?*

Paul thought about it for a moment and said, "No, I don't think he should be fired, but…" and continued with his argument.

I don't remember much of this exchange because now I felt as if I were on the chopping block. Throughout this exchange, all I could think was, *Is this a set-up? They're going to fire me.* George's eyes never left Paul's face, and at the first opportunity, he began peppering him with questions, such as, "Why *weren't* you involved with the salary review?" and "What have you done to help Bob grow as a manager?" and other such probing questions.

Suddenly the wind shifted. Paul sat there stupefied, unprepared for such an inquisition, and I could see his face getting redder and redder, until he lost his temper. All of a sudden, his fist pounded the table as he leapt to his feet, he shouted, "All right!" and pointing a finger at George, yelled, "Then *you* take him!"

"Good! Done!" George said with a smile, as routinely as if coffee and rolls had just arrived. He slapped the table decisively with one hand, rose with both hands on the table, while his eyes held Paul's, and said, "Good, Paul, prepare the paper work. I'll see you Monday." (This was a Friday.) In one sweeping motion, George's frame and body language ended the meeting. He smiled at Paul as he crossed back to his desk and sat down at his computer—was it a Cheshire cat grin?

Paul also had risen, but slowly, and stood there with his mouth open so wide his chin almost touched his chest, his bulging eyes glaring at George. I watched Paul's contorted face as he slowly realized he had just been bested at his own manipulation game. Without another word or a glance at either one of us, he stomped away angrily. I thought I saw smoke trailing behind him as he slammed the door.

I got up and looked at George, hardly able to suppress a smile. George's face was glued to his screen. I turned towards the door, glancing back at George who didn't look up, and I went back to my office, also without a word. I had wanted to say, "Thank you, George. How in the world did you *do* that?" But it didn't seem to matter now. It was *fait accompli*.

· · · · ·

On Monday morning I noticed George's brief note on top of the pile on my desk about creating the Promotion Coordinator position. It seemed strange. As Personnel Manager, I had to create a new position—for myself. Sooner than I could fathom it, I would no longer *be* the P.M.

Then, I noticed the requisition I'd just had typed. Slowly, I picked it up… and stared at it. A feeling of excitement clashed with foreboding. *What's your problem, Robert? This is the best thing that's ever happened to you. Dad, shut up. Get with* my *program!*

The following week I began reporting directly to George. While it felt oh so good to be reporting to the number two man in the company, in fact, nothing really changed in my daily routine, except that Paul was now virtually out of my life. Oh, I still had a dotted-line relationship to him, as they called it, so that I had to confer with him on any large, corporate personnel matters, but I don't recall that happening. Day-to-day matters continued much the same as in the past. My staff of two handled most of the recruiting and interviewing. I would handle supervisory level activities, but more and more, my job became that of a peacemaker between cranky managers who would complain about other managers, or their staff, or the New York office people with whom they had to work. This began to occupy most of my time.

For reasons that I didn't know at the time, George and I gradually saw less and less of each other. My duties refereeing the various squabbling departments kept me quite busy, so I didn't notice the change. But it was in the wind.

• • • • •

One day as I sat in my office drinking my morning coffee and preparing for the day's activities, out of nowhere came the thought, *What happened to my spiritual life?* It caught me unaware, and I rolled my chair around to look out the window, trying to divorce myself for a moment from the desk and all its work. I needed to think.

Was God still calling me to the ministry? Truth be told, I rarely thought about it anymore. Between Scholastic, my singing, and my family life, God seemed to be squeezed out of the picture....

Joan and I each had section leader choir jobs on Sunday mornings, and we sang at the Hebrew Tabernacle Synagogue every Friday night and Saturday morning. That seemed to be the extent of our nod to God.

My opera career was beginning to pick up somewhat, and my major focus was to make the best of the few opportunities that came my way.

Harry Ireland, as our insurance agent, continued to visit us, and our friendship with him and his wife, Cecelia, grew. We followed the growth of their two children, Harry Jr. and Ruthann, as well. At every opportunity, Harry would inquire about our spiritual lives, and we would try to convince him that all was well.

On one such occasion, he said, "Bob, how are things with you and the Lord?"

"Fine," I said.

"Fine? Has anything changed?"

"Not really, but singing under Rob Davis keeps us on our toes—focused on the Lord, I mean."

"Who's Rob Davis?"

"You remember my talking about him. No? Well, he's our choir director at First Pres. He's a committed Christian, and prays before every rehearsal and service."

"But do *you* pray, and are you in God's Word regularly?"

I knew that whatever I would say, it would not be enough for Harry. At least I had enough integrity not to lie to him. He was a Fundamentalist, and if you didn't belong to a weekly Bible study and prayer group, your walk with the Lord was suspect. When these conversations came up, I would adroitly change the subject, usually with a question about an insurance policy, or about his family.

As the years wore on, Joan and I became involved in a small Bible study group at First Presbyterian. We also taught Sunday school there. I was on a number of committees as well.

We also began classes in Lamaze in preparation for our first child. This was a very exciting time for both of us. The thought of being parents filled us both with a mixture of pride and anxiety. *This is what marriage is all about*, I thought to myself.

Joan seemed to take her pregnancy in stride as if she'd had a dozen babies. But underneath, I could see her concerns both for a healthy baby and for herself. Giving birth for the first time was undoubtedly a very scary prospect for a woman.

I wanted to be there for her. However, at the time, I was in rehearsal for my debut roles with both the Middlesex Opera Company in Offenbach's *The Tales of Hoffmann* the following spring 1974, and with the Amato Opera Company as Fenton in Verdi's *Falstaff*, which was to take place on February 23, 1974. I was very excited about both projects, being my entry into two opera groups. I wanted to do my best so they would ask me back. Yes, these were small companies, but I knew I had to build an opera portfolio, and these would be my first significant opera companies.

So, I was away from the house more than a husband should have been at a time like this. Joan was not happy about this state of affairs, nor was I, wanting to be in two places at once. We both felt the pressure.

In the wee hours of January 16, 1974, Joan and I rushed to the Englewood Hospital as Joan's time had come. Our Lamaze training certainly came into play. I was very nervous, but once the baby started to crown, we both forgot all else and concentrated on the job at hand. Praise the Lord, it was an easy birth. Rob was born at 11:00 that morning. A prouder Papa you couldn't imagine. Joan came through with flying colors. She sat up soon after the birth and nursed him. We couldn't have been happier. My camera's shutter wouldn't stop. I think Rob was the most photographed baby ever born....

Yes, proud Papa. Wherever I went I showed Rob's pictures to anyone who asked about our new baby. Whether in rehearsals, church, or even in the middle of the day in my office, I smiled at the thought.

One afternoon, after showing the pictures to a colleague in the office, I set aside the papers I had been working on and swung my chair around to look out my window as I thought of Billie Bigelow's, "Soliloquy," from Rogers and Hammerstein's, *Carousel*, in which he broods about raising his son—who turns out to be a daughter. My thoughts, too, went to raising a son. Unlike Billie, I didn't want Rob to grow up to be a tough guy. *Rob will have to go to church....*

Wait a minute. *Some example you'll be. Your singing....* Harry was right: my singing really did come before anything else. *Even God?*

Lord, what can I do to balance my life? Do you want me to sing opera? I believe that if I were to become a famous opera singer, I could do wonders for you, Lord.

"You think so?" I thought I heard God's voice speaking.

Yeah, right.
  Promotions Coordinator, yes. Opera singer, maybe.
  Pastor? I don't think so....

Chapter Thirteen

Scholastic for Sure

Promotions Coordinator?

What's that? Nothing in my background prepared me for a job like this. Why would George entrust this enormous responsibility to me?

As I thought about it, I realized it seemed a bit like learning how to sing. First you have to grasp the language, then the technique of making a good vocal sound. Data Processing and the New York marketing folks each had their own lingo, kind of like English and Italian—oceans apart. Then, there were many steps involved to produce the final labels, which were the address stickers you used to see on every piece of advertising mail you'd get in your mailbox.[23]

To begin my training, George assigned me to Gerry Feinberg, Manager of Programming, who immediately felt like a soul mate. Gerry was thin, a bit taller than I, even with his slight stoop. He had a thick head of salt-and-pepper hair combed over to hide his encroaching baldness. "I hate the idea of getting old," he would say. He dressed more casually than was the norm for Scholastic in the seventies. He wore colored or patterned shirts, not always matching ties, and sports jackets. Gerry was quite a handsome guy, with sparkling blue eyes, a shy, ready smile, and a firm handshake.

---

[23] This was the seventies. Today addresses are electronically applied.

Even though our backgrounds were very different, we found common ground in music, art, philosophy, politics, and religion, not to mention the job. We saw things the same way, so we could talk about them freely. When I told him I sang in a synagogue, he exclaimed, "Really? I'm not a very religious Jew, a secular Jew in fact, so I rarely go to synagogue."

We were standing outside his office in the programming area. The room was filled with cubicles where programmers plied their profession. It was a noisy place, vibrant with men and women, some studiously working, while others clustered around a single desk, loudly solving a systems problem of some sort. Air conditioning cooled the place. Gerry motioned me to follow him into his office where it was quieter. It was stuffy, had a hint of cigarette smoke, though there was no ash tray and no sign that Gerry smoked. *Strange*, I thought.

"I'm there every Friday night and Saturday morning—plus all the holidays," I replied, a bit smugly.

"You gotta be kidding…" he said with a tinge of disbelief, as he plopped into his chair, which appeared quite large for so small an office. He motioned for me to sit in a chair on the other side of his desk.

"No…well, of course, I'm paid to be there." I sat down, smiling at my little disclaimer.

"The only time I set foot in a synagogue is for weddings, funerals, or bar mitzvahs." He chuckled at his own irreverence.

"Actually, I really enjoy it," I continued. "Ever since I dated a Jewish girl in high school, I have been fascinated by Judaism. We Christians stand on your shoulders, you know."

"No wonder we feel weighed down." Gerry brought his fingers tip-to-tip. "Should I move to Israel?" He leaned back into his chair, grinning, and spread his hands to emphasize his question.

I laughed. "You know what I mean. Jesus was a Jew, never a Christian."

"No, I don't know, and with all due respect, I really don't care," he said, still smiling. "Religion, well, I have my own way of communing with God."

"How's that?"

"I love nature, I love people, and I love to have a good time."

"That's your religion? Sounds a bit hedonistic to me," I said, laying a finger across my lips, thoughtfully.

"Well, as I said, I believe in God, but I don't worship him—not the way you do, anyway."

And so our conversations would ramble. I had many Jewish friends, some from the world of music, and some from the synagogues where Joan and I sang.

Gerry once said, "You know more about Judaism than I do."

"Yep," I replied. We both laughed. He felt my deep love for the Jewish faith and culture. Could this have been keeping me from becoming a pastor?

One day around Christmas Gerry came into my office with a wrapped present. Gerry did not celebrate Christmas. The office acknowledged Christmas and Hanukah with a tree. He handed it to me. "I wanted you to have this."

"What is it?" I asked as I opened it. It was flat—I knew it was an LP record. The question was, of what? When I opened it, it said "The Carpenters." I thought it was a joke.

Gerry noticed my discomfiture, and said quickly, "They're a singing group called, 'The Carpenters.' They're really terrific. I know you'll love them."

"Gerry, thank you. I don't know what to say…" I was deeply moved by his gesture. I didn't want to prejudge the music, but I was skeptical. I kept these feelings to myself.

He smiled and said, "Let me know what you think of them."

"Sure thing."

When I listened to it at home that evening, I immediately heard what he was raving about. Both Joan and I became instant fans. Their music, melodic, harmonious, and Karen Carpenter's voice, smooth as velvet, to die for. Her brother Richard, a superb pianist, composer, arranger, and background singer.

I still have the LP record Gerry gave me, and we have added a few ourselves.

Joan and I became friends with Gerry and his wife, Kathy. We saw each other socially and enjoyed some good times together.

At work, Gerry and I used to have lunch while he drove me around the local neighborhoods, listening to music, and talking. Gerry loved to "go see things," as he put it.

"Have you seen the house up on Buckingham Road? No? Oh, you gotta see this one!" And we would pile in his car and go look at it. On our lunch hour, of course.

I noticed that Gerry's windows were always cloudy. When I hopped into the passenger seat, I not only noticed a well-used ash tray, but the stench of stale smoke curled my nose. In the summertime, I could open the window, but in winter, Gerry had the decency to leave his cigarettes in his pocket. He respected my singing throat. Actually, I never realized he had the habit until the first time I got in his car. He never lit up in the office. I think he understood how others felt.

• • • • •

Initially, Gerry put me with the computer operations staff. They handled the marketing mailings at that time. I needed to learn about the workings of the mainframe IBM computer and to meet the folks that made it all happen. The major part of Scholastic's business depended upon this operation.

The Computer Room Supervisor, Al, taught me how to use the key-punch machines for quick turnaround jobs, and we worked out procedures for me to submit them to the Computer Room. Most employees were not permitted in the CR, but I was. At that time keypunching was essential to the operation. With the volume of work I had to do, I got to know the key-punch operators by name.

Scholastic, at the time, published thirty magazine titles and five book clubs, each with its own marketing staff in New York, and it was my job to keep them happy and ensure that the process worked—a daunting task.

George Milne officially presented me in front of the programming staff with the newly created title of Promotions Coordinator. Two of the programmers had already been doing the work now assigned to me. One was now freed up to "proper" programming. The other continued to do the very complex book club labels.

As time went on, I sat down with Gerry to try to systematize the helter-skelter procedures. I spent months designing flow charts and program forms, writing both business and computer procedures, along with instructional memos to all the people involved. The range of programs, procedures, and job streams involved would have sent many in my position scurrying for the door. However, I loved it. New requirements constantly came across my desk from the marketing departments in New York. I had to write separate plans for each request for keypunch, programming, and the Computer Room.

• • • • •

After several years of reporting to Gerry, George called me into his office one day. Now that I didn't report to him, this was quite unusual—it meant going over Gerry's head. I assumed he told Gerry, but wondered why he called me in like this. It made me feel uncomfortable.

George greeted me heartily and motioned me to a seat at the large, round conference table. He sat down opposite me. No longer accustomed to his office in my cramped cubicle next to Gerry's office, I felt like waving to George across this spacious table.

"How's it going?" he asked in his grandest manner.

"Very well, thank you. Gerry and I get along just fine, and he's a great teacher and boss. Thank you for assigning me to him," I said with a smile.

George returned the smile. "Good, Bob, glad to hear it. Now I have to break your bubble, so to speak."

I looked at him apprehensively, wondering what he meant, another assignment, perhaps?

"Do you remember Dick Cryer, the guy you met on my boat last summer—or was it the summer before? I don't remember." He squeezed his lower lip between his thumb and forefinger.

"Sure, I remember Dick," I said brightly. "Libby was there, too. And Joan. Yes, that was an afternoon I'll never forget."

George brightened and leaned back in his chair. "Well," he began, "I'm bringing Dick onboard here to take over the entire systems department, including programming, the operational department and keypunch. The works." His face beamed.

"Wow!" I said, before I could stop myself. I sat forward in my chair.

George went on, "Dick's a statistical analyst by profession, and a keen analytical thinker. I think he'll bring an important—and missing—methodology to the entire systems operation. He'll help straighten out our problems with New York, and I want you to report directly to him. Gerry will also report to him." George's face became grave, his eyes bearing down on me, gauging my reaction.

Well, it certainly stopped me in my tracks. I sat back in my chair, trying to assess what it all meant. I didn't reply immediately. George also sat back, continuing to eye me carefully.

Not to report to you, anymore, eh? What happened? I really had no way to assess what this meant, either to the company, or to me. But I was uncomfortable about Gerry, not just about not reporting to him anymore, but also that Gerry was being pushed down the managerial pecking order.

I didn't know what questions to ask. He didn't *ask* me; he had presented it as a done deal—was this it? As it turned out, it was. I began reporting to Dick immediately, and I no longer enjoyed any direct dealings with George.

•　•　•　•　•

Dick Cryer turned out to be an exacting boss. As George said, he was hired to bring order out of chaos, which he did—with paper and procedures. Everyone had to write everything they did on forms, many of which Dick himself designed. He and I together designed forms for me to use to order keypunch work, and for the computer processes that created the promotional labels. Ordering programming for special jobs was no longer a personal interchange between programmers and me. Everything was now systematized, and we had to follow specific protocols now on paper. Even the mailroom staff had forms for shipping the labels.

Over the next months, Dick decided I needed a staff to help with the work I did. "Too much for one person," he insisted. He placed me in charge of both the production of the mailing labels and the group of ten women who updated the school information on the computer files. He also gave me the title of Manager.

Meanwhile, Dick dubbed my department, Promotional Systems Services Department (PSSD). No one knew what the acronym meant, and occasionally someone would ask. Whether or not they cared what the acronym stood for (some pronounced it "PSST"), everywhere I went in the company, I had to explain what PSSD was and what we did. It became a joke, really, and the "PSSD" moniker stuck with me for the rest of my Scholastic years.

Later, I too was bumped down the managerial ranks when Dick brought in a Swede by the name of Jan Wahlin to be my boss. Jan was a computer whiz, and brought to Scholastic a cutting-edge, technical know-how that we needed to compete in the marketing industry. Jan helped organize and direct my work flow so that it took some of the pressure off me. He also ran interference for me with the New York marketers.

I remained a manager until I retired.

. . . . .

From the sixties into the nineties, I sang every Friday night and Saturday morning in the Hebrew Tabernacle Synagogue in Upper Manhattan, and in church on Sunday mornings. For about ten years—from the mid-1970s to the mid-1980s—Joan and I were the soloists at First Presbyterian Church in Ridgewood, New Jersey. This was an upscale church that could afford to pay section leaders in its choir, which was otherwise volunteer. This was our first contact with Rob Davis, who became the choir director shortly after we came aboard. Joan and I also became Sunday school teachers. I was on a number of committees, and for a time became a trustee, helping to manage the church's money.

. . . . .

In the meantime, our son Rob had grown from an insomniac toddler to an active, rambunctious preschooler. Before age two, he spoke in full sentences and demonstrated unusual musical, literary, and artistic talent.

"Well," friends would quip, "how could he miss, between the two of you?"

He made up songs—music and words, and wandered around the house singing stories that flooded his imagination. One song was about the railroad that passed near our house. He sang, "Railroad track, clickety-clack!" parading around the house with his engineer hat on his head and toy train in hand.

Soon, every pencil in the house found its way into his fingers to draw every manner of beast and traveling machine. Songs and stories flowed from his restless mind at an astonishing rate. Cleaning up a room after he'd been in it for a while became a challenge for us working folks. We loved him dearly despite the parental vicissitudes. (Still do!)

He always delighted his grandparents, the Bishops, Joan's mom and dad, who lived not far away. They took care of him every weekend when we sang in synagogue on Friday evenings and Saturday mornings because their house was on our way into the city. He looked forward to "sleeping over" at Grandma's so much, it became the chief pleasure in his young life.

Rob was a cheerful kid, but he was also given to temper tantrums that concerned us. By the time he was a toddler, we had him evaluated by a therapist, Dr. Susan Rothstein, who lived just down the street from us in Englewood. She recognized his many talents and abilities, and encouraged him. She was also an educator, and we went to a mommy-and-toddler program where she taught us to interact with him in positive ways. He loved her, and so did we.

We became friends with her and her husband, and occasionally exchanged visits with them. Rob was in heaven when she was around. We all looked forward to those evenings.

• • • • •

Since my 1978 spiritual awakening in the car on the way to work (see Prologue), I tried on and off to follow a Christian way of life. However, my desire to sing opera focused all my attention on voice lessons, coaching, learning roles and other repertoire, and performing. While there was nothing inherently wrong with singing—after all, the angels and the apostles sing—for me, singing was totally self-absorbing, and the Christian way of life is not about self; it's about serving others.

Don't singers sing for others? Without listeners, what's the point in singing at all?

But I wanted to be a big star, travel the world, and have people shout, "Bravo!"

Is that a proper Christian desire?

This painful conflict dogged me throughout my life.

Working as the Promotions Coordinator by day, and advancing my operatic career by night and weekends, filled all my time. All my bosses at Scholastic (except George Milne) saw my singing as a conflict of interest.

. . . . .

A couple of years later, one day at the dentist's office, four-year-old Rob proudly announced to the nurse, Miss Banta, that he was going to have a new baby brother soon, pointing to his mother's belly.

"What if it's a sister?" asked Miss Banta.

"I don't want a sister. It's got to be a brother," Rob replied with his typical grit. "If it's a sister, we'll give her to Grandma."

When Joan told me she was pregnant with our second child, I jumped for joy, both figuratively and literally. I couldn't have been happier. In a very special way, God had blessed Randy's conception. It occurred on a well-remembered night when we came home after singing a performance of Vivaldi's, *Gloria*. We were so inspired, we couldn't wait to make mad, passionate love. This piece became very special to us. (Surprise, surprise?)

On September 3, 1979, Randy was born. Unlike with Rob's birth, Joan suffered a number of difficulties. When Rob was born, she sang right up to the day he arrived. Randy seemed to rest on her diaphragm, and she had to stop singing several months before his birth. This cost her valued opportunities to sing in church and synagogue, as well as an opera performance or two. To make matters worse, she had a kidney infection that made the birth itself risky. She was quite sick for several weeks before Randy made his long-awaited appearance.

In this day and age, we shouldn't be having these concerns, I thought. *Surely the doctors can see to it that she has a safe birth—can't they?* Suddenly, I felt as though we were living in the past when every birth created angst for the parents. Our family and friends were also concerned. Everyone, believer or no, prayed for her and a healthy baby.

God smiled on us all the day Randy was born. He was robust, and announced his arrival in ringing, screaming tones. Joan pulled through the birth all right, but it left her quite weak. It took over a month for her to regain her strength. We decided two children were enough.

. . . . .

As both boys grew, the contrast between them fascinated and bedeviled us. Rob had a very short fuse, while Randy smiled through everything. Both of them showed ample evidence of language and musical gifts. Rob loved and protected his new brother from all comers, and went out of his way to keep his little brother safe. Despite their differences, or perhaps, because of them, they got along swimmingly, able to share toys and food.

I can still see Randy sitting in his highchair ready to eat. For reasons that escaped everyone, as soon as we put him in his seat, his eyes would get heavy. Joan would talk to him to keep him awake as she placed his food before him. Invariably, his eyes would droop. The next thing we knew, we saw the top of his head, his face smack-dab in the middle of his plate, fast asleep. We were concerned that he didn't eat, yet no matter what time it was, or however Joan changed his schedule or made special preparations to prevent his going to sleep in his food, this little scenario went on for months. Then, suddenly, it stopped. That behavior has mystified us—and the doctors—to this day. But Randy was healthy nevertheless.

·　·　·　·　·

The piano in our Bergenfield home was on the second floor, as we couldn't decide on a place for it downstairs. We put it in the small front room along with rows of shelves I had constructed, using long boards supported by bricks and decorative patio cement blocks. These shelves housed our extensive collection of opera scores and other music.

The boys used to love to crawl under the piano to play or sleep. When I came up to practice, they skedaddled, usually leaving behind a trail of toy pieces they dropped on the way out. My voice was "too loud" for them in this relatively confined space.

But Oreo, our dog, came up whenever I sang, and curled up under the piano and slept. As soon as I finished practicing, he'd get up ahead of me to lead me downstairs. I smiled.

·　·　·　·　·

In the fall of 1982, on a Scholastic visit to the New York office, I happened to get on the elevator with Dick Robinson, now President, CEO, and

Chairman of the Board of Scholastic, after Robbie, his father, had passed away in February.

"Hi, Bob! How are things in New Jersey?" said Dick.

"Hi, Dick," I replied. It never ceased to amaze me how he, like his father, remembered everyone's name and where they worked. Dick's deep blue eyes burrowed into mine. He was my height, so there was no escaping his gaze. I could see in his eyes that he was aware of my problems "over there in New Jersey," as he put it. He knew we were in crisis mode because the promotions were not getting out on time. He also knew it was my responsibility.

I gulped, and looked down. *Should I tell him the truth?* I knew my answer had to be *yes*, but before I unloaded my concerns, the long chain of command which separated us streaked through my mind. People in my position were not supposed to talk to top brass, even if invited. Lower executives are always looking over their shoulders, making sure that only the information *they* wanted going upward was what was *actually* going up. They were terrified of being blindsided. Nor did I want Dick Cryer pounding my head into the ground.

Cautiously, I began, "Do you really want to know?"

Dick Robinson nodded earnestly, "Yes, I do."

Of course top executives are concerned about information being filtered through their immediate subordinates. I suddenly became the horse's mouth. Knowing I'd never get another chance like this one, I took the plunge. "What we need, Dick, is a database that has the school address information, the teacher name, and order data all in one place so that everyone is looking at the same information. That's not happening right now because of the three or four systems that replicate the data. In fact, we *can't* do it with the multiple systems we have because they can't communicate with each other."

"What do you mean?"

I hastened to explain, in technical detail, how the data resides on each file, but they are not updated in the same way at the same time, so that numbers on sales reports, differ from updating reports on other systems. "We need a marketing database so that information resides in one place, not in three or four systems." This was very expensive technology at that time. "If we had such a database system, all the interdepartmental feuding, fighting, and fussing that often ends up on your desk would go away, I promise you," I said confidently.

I was pleasantly surprised that he understood all the technical jargon I threw at him. He smiled understandingly, perhaps impressed with my grasp of the details, realizing that it meant a major corporate investment. I also was very gratified that he understood that the marketing department required a much higher priority in the present corporate scheme of things. Finance and Operations currently had top priority on the computer, a source of enormous frustration for me. I didn't mention my frustration, but I'm sure he heard it in my voice.

As the door opened for his floor, he gave me a tight-lipped smile and said, "Thank you, Bob," and his face beamed like an inventor with a new idea as he stepped off the elevator.

Remaining on the elevator to go to a higher floor, I was pleased with what I said, yet terrified of potential repercussions. *Oh, Lord! Me and my big mouth! Is this going to come back on my head? Well, what's done is done. Maybe something good will come of it.*

And something terrific *did* come of it. Although I never received any credit or recognition, I believe this conversation led to the development of a corporate database along the lines I outlined to Dick Robinson. It took nearly five years to complete. I worked closely with the systems people in designing it, and later became a point person with the outside vendor who installed it, a company with which we had long ties.

•   •   •   •   •

George Milne would have been proud of me.

In the mid-eighties, George Milne, Dick Cryer, and Gerry Feinberg, all left the company, leaving me feeling like an abandoned orphan.

What will become of me? Can I realistically have a career at Scholastic without George's backing? Can I ever advance beyond the managerial level? Is this what I really want for my life?

Questions like these tormented me. In truth, my strongest desire was to make my living by singing, but the necessary break stayed a step ahead of me, always just beyond my grasp. The distant call to the ministry echoed weakly in my psyche.

•   •   •   •   •

During the building of the new marketing system, Dick Spaulding, Executive Vice President of the corporation, became my new boss. Reporting to the number two man in the company again raised my hopes of someday becoming an executive myself. In 1985, Mr. Spaulding urged me to take a Direct Marketing course at New York University, which I did.

By this time, we had our first database and all the marketing groups had come under Spaulding's direction. He realized we needed to get up to speed with "target" marketing, the buzz word at the time, by reorganizing the department I had managed for many years.

After a year or so of reporting to him, Dick brought in a long-time Scholastic sales and marketing manager, Tom Noone, to form a group known as Marketing Information Management, which he would head. PSSD was absorbed into this group, with Tom becoming my new boss. Since he had the title of director, my hopes of advancing to the executive level in the company once again went bye-bye.

Now I was pretty much stuck in my Promotions Coordinator position, manager or not. I had sought the position Tom got, but Spaulding had refused, saying I was far too important in my present post. "Who can do what you do?" he explained to me one day on the phone. "There's no one to replace you. You have to stay put, Bob."

I think he thought he was patting me on the back, but I didn't see it that way. To my way of thinking, he had just cut off any opportunity for me to advance.

After several years as the Promotions Coordinator in New Jersey, Tom moved me to the New York headquarters and put me in a cubicle just outside his office. *Was this to keep an eye on me?* On paper, the staff in New Jersey still reported to me, but in reality, I had become a computer technician—*hack* was the word I used—devoted to writing programs to produce promotional labels. My glory days of being involved in the top corporate decisions and hobnobbing with top executives had become a distant nothingness.

•   •   •   •   •

One day Tom took me to lunch at a posh restaurant in downtown Manhattan, which was his custom for my annual review. No matter what I did or failed to do, I typically received a three percent increase in salary over the years.

Tom, taller than I by several inches, wore glasses that gave him a professorial air. He had been a teacher, but abandoned that career in favor of selling books to schools for Scholastic. Always dressed nattily, I don't doubt that he was quite successful, because he had a keen, analytical mind, and understood the school market as well as anyone in the industry. He spoke and wrote very articulately, and had a mischievous sense of humor. We enjoyed a close working relationship, and loved to talk about all manner of subjects.

As I sat down at our table in the restaurant, I noticed a familiar figure across the room.

"Isn't that the Executive Vice President of the Book Division over there?" I pointed toward a corner table where he was seated alone.

"Yep, that's the one," Tom replied. "He dines here every day when he's in town."

I chuckled, knowing that this new EVP was in charge of the Book Division. Remembering how Scholastic had lured him from another major publisher, I said, "Well, he can afford to eat here. By the way, thank you for bringing me to this fine restaurant. If it were not for you and Scholastic, I'd never get to dine in a place like this." I chuckled.

With a wry smile, Tom nodded and leaned over the table conspiratorially. "He doesn't have to spend any of his own money. Scholastic pays for his meals."

"What?" I was aghast. "With his salary and bonus, he gets over a quarter of a million a year, doesn't he?" I had read the annual report and was astonished that he earned more than Dick Robinson when they hired him. They accommodated that embarrassing situation by setting his salary slightly under Dick's, but with an annual, guaranteed bonus to make up the difference.

Tom shrugged in affirmation of my comment. "Not only that, but he gets a company car, an apartment here in New York, and the executive health plan. He doesn't pay a penny for anything."

At the time, in the mid-eighties, I was making about $75,000 a year. I said angrily, "I make a fraction of what he makes, I have to buy my own lunches, buy and maintain my own car, pay for bus and subway to get to work, plus, I have a $600 deductible on my family insurance."

I was quite livid, but knew I had to keep a lid on it. A little more calmly, I said, "Is his apartment the corporate one down the street?"

"No. He has his own."

"His own? Do you mean they pay for his New York apartment as well? How does he rate that?"

Tom nodded, but was nonplussed. "He lives in somewhere in New England, big house. He commutes home every weekend." Noticing my outraged expression, he continued, "Bob, that's just the way it is. Nothing you or I can do about it, except strive to get to his level. Then we'll have those perks as well."

At that moment, I was furious at all the perks and money this executive received. I had nothing against him personally. But I was disturbed at Tom's comments about striving to get to his level. I thought, *That's why executives strive for more and more. No matter how much they make, they're always looking at those who make more than they do, and push themselves to get to that level.* Then I paused, *Really, Robert, this is corporate America, Wall Street World.*

Then I thought about the time this Executive Vice President asked me to sing at a book club party at a New York restaurant. *How did he know I sang opera?* I didn't even know he knew who I was, but, as it happened, he was quite an opera fan. Someone must have told him about me. That night, the moment he saw me, he asked me to sing. At first I demurred, but then I noticed the background music in the restaurant was Pavarotti singing arias—very unusual for a restaurant, in my experience, but was probably why he held the party there. So, I approached him. "If you can, get the manager to back up the CD to '*Recondita Amonita*,' I'll sing along with Luciano."

The EVP beamed. "Really?"

I nodded, and he sent someone off to find the manager.

Soon, I heard the intro music, and I shouted over the din of the party, "This is it!"

The EVP instantly shushed everyone and motioned for them to sit down and listen. I sang quite well that night as I recall. He was most impressed with my singing, and never forgot me.

• • • • •

Someone asked me why I hated this particular executive so much. I said, "No, no, I have nothing against him. In fact, I like and admire him for his achievements, not to mention that he's a great guy, and always treats me well." Although I did not work directly under his supervision, I worked for him in an advisory role.

No, my anger was—and is—not directed at any individual, but at our corporate, Wall Street system, which has created a gap of biblical proportions between the one percent very rich and the rest of us, because they control ninety-eight percent of the country's wealth. What's wrong with this picture?

My EVP friend illustrates this systemic, societal problem in a microcosmic way.

The conversation I had with Tom that day got me to thinking about how unjust our society is. Even with what many people would consider a posh job—mine—I always felt like a have-not, certainly in comparison with the corporate executives of the world, especially those who make millions and even billions. Don't the rest of us work just as hard as they do? Why then should they make ten times, and a hundred times what we make?

Many people think of us as a Christian nation, yet our economic system is anything but "Christian." Actually, our economy today looks very much like the biblical economy, and it also looks like our economy a hundred years ago with the Asters, Carnegies, and Vanderbilts. Just like the billionaires today, the millionaires at that time also controlled everything, made the big bucks, and had all the perks. Why can't we have a more level playing field?

Socially minded people have been raving about this discrepancy since ancient biblical times. Capitalists say that anyone can become rich if they really want to, but is that true? More to the point, is such an economic system fair?

All through the Bible God sent prophet after prophet to decry this system. Why does it persist? Why do so many Christians support this unbiblical travesty? And where are the prophets today, like Bernie Sanders,[24] who cry alone in the wilderness?

---

[24] US Senator, a primary candidate for President in 2016. At this writing, "Bernie" has succeeded in changing the political debate to precisely what I'm talking about in this section. Baruch ata Adonai! He lost the Democratic Primary to Hillary Clinton.

My anger may be linked to my own unfulfilled dreams in opera. It's really the same in the field of sports and entertainment. Top stars have it all. The rest of us scrape and go through hell to make a living at our crafts. Seems to be a systemic problem for capitalism. It's demeaning, unfair, and most certainly **unchristian**. How and why is it that the Christian Right supports such an unbiblical plight?

(In my mind's eye, I see Charlie Chaplin as the little tramp picking up a penny from the street. *Sometimes I feel like him.*)

·　·　·　·　·

Over the next several years, I often thought about this, and started watching the corporate field as it began to change. Most of the executives at Scholastic in the mid-eighties made six figures. Over the next two decades, executive salaries soared, but mine did not.

By the 1990s executives in large corporations were making millions, while I was still getting my three percent increase. In 2000 and beyond, the millions became billions, and if I had remained at Scholastic, I would probably still be getting my three percent. I should say that by that time I would have been in six figures, a tidy sum. Three percent becomes more significant. But low six figures still is a *long* way from millions—or *billions*.

This money gap got me to thinking that perhaps I could make a difference as a pastor.

·　·　·　·　·

After many years working as a secretary, Joan had long since become weary of it and yearned for a more fulfilling line of work.

"I have a college degree for heaven's sake," she said. "Why not put it to good use?"

Her passion was to become a psychotherapist. After unsuccessfully pursuing various avenues of counseling education, Joan went to our pastor, the Rev. Dr. Willis A. Jones, at the Wyckoff Reformed Church for guidance. He suggested that she attend seminary. "That way," he said, "you can probably get some of the counseling training you want. Of course, the seminary focuses on preparing for the pastorate, but there are some counseling opportunities available in the church."

"Well," said Joan, "I really want to be a therapist, but maybe being a pastor...?"

By 1990, both of us were still employed in our corporate jobs, but we had pretty much decided to become pastors largely from kicking around the issue of the terrible financial inequity that has virtually ruined our country. Joan felt the call to the pastorate; I felt called to study theology, but I longed to do something about the unfair economy. We looked into the educational requirements and discovered through Dr. Jones that we could most likely qualify at the Reformed Church's seminary, the New Brunswick Theological Seminary (NBTS) in central New Jersey. We sent letters of inquiry and received the necessary applications, to which we responded. In addition, we had to apply to the overseeing church body, known as the Classis, to begin the long oversight process leading to ordination. The seminary would award the necessary master's degree for ordination, but the church was responsible for ordinations.

In July of 1991, Joan began courses at NBTS. One evening, a week after she began, she came home very excited, and began telling me about the courses, and how great her instructors were.

"You'll be so dogone smart I won't be able to talk to you anymore," I replied.

"Bob, why don't you come along? Wouldn't it be fun if we went to seminary together?"

"Hmm," I said. "Yeah, that would be fun. Then I could study Hebrew as I've always wanted to."

Another idea came to me. How about going on after seminary to the Jewish Theological Seminary in New York for in-depth Hebrew study? Studying the Hebrew Bible and Jewish history suddenly became a real option for me, and put a new spring in my step. At that point, I was still ambivalent about becoming a pastor.

I really wanted to become a college professor, and I viewed seminary as a first step toward a Ph.D. I didn't tell anyone at Scholastic that summer I had entered seminary. It seemed unwise.

Meanwhile, at Scholastic, nothing in my background had prepared me for the technology I was now required to learn. All my mainframe computer expertise of the past twenty years went zap, out the window. Wake up to the age of desktop computers, Robert. All the rules had changed while I wasn't looking. No more keypunch cards, no more working with computer room operators—you were now your own computer expert. It's all in onscreen tutorials.

What did I know of Boolean logic and algebraic expressions? The last time I had anything to do with algebra was forty years ago—my freshman year at Lock Haven State. But I needed that understanding to write the programs to produce the labels—wait a minute, no more *labels*. Now the addresses were sent over the wires to the fulfillment houses out west. Adrift without a paddle, that's me.

I'd go home at night and Joan would say to me, "What's the matter, Bob?"

"Oh, I don't have a clue what I'm doing with this new technology. I used to be the expert in all this stuff. Now I feel like a dodo standing outside and looking in wondering what in the heck is going on." I stopped to look at her. She put her arms around me. I cried.

This difficulty made me fear for my job. Fortunately, my twenty-five years with Scholastic protected me against the ole pink slip. Scholastic always had venerated its long-term employees, and bosses had to follow a carefully documented process to fire anybody.

After nearly two years in the New York office, no one at Scholastic knew I was attending seminary several nights a week. In the second year of seminary the pressure at work got to me, I had to take a semester off to preserve my job—and my sanity.

Without the distraction of my academic studies, I learned the new system (called Analytics) to Tom's satisfaction, and I became rather proficient at it. That helped things go more smoothly, and I thought I could bring Tom into my confidence. Doing so relieved an emotional tension between us, but in some ways my relationship with him was never the same after that. I sensed he wanted a young career person in my place to whom he could assign the more technical aspects of marketing that he currently did himself, so he could concentrate on other things.

The staff I had left behind in New Jersey reported to me on paper, as did the staff in Missouri, but in reality, since Tom had taken over my budget, *he* was their boss. He controlled their salaries, so I was essentially sidelined as far as being a manager was concerned. I had become a programming marketing technician—a lowly technician.

· · · · ·

That was a sad way to end my thirty-year career with Scholastic, truly a downer for me. Yet my Scholastic experience shaped me in many ways. I saw the evolution and inner workings of a large corporation over the course of thirty years. I watched Scholastic grow from a $25 million company to a more than $2 billion one.

Bottom line for me is, I truly enjoyed my job, despite its sad ending. Working for Scholastic was a privilege, and I shall always remember it fondly. The good people I met, even the cranky ones, the travel, the great parties, the work challenges, and the rewards all have blessed me mightily. Thank you, Lord, for those thirty marvelous years.

The reason I survived them, and more than fifteen bosses, I believe, was that building a *personal* empire never interested me. Rather, I always worked for the good of the company and treated my people as though they truly mattered. I believe God smiled on that, despite the fact that I ran—like Jonah—from his call all these years.

But then, Lord, I went to seminary, didn't I?

· · · · ·

The captain came to Jonah and said, "What are you doing sound asleep? Get up, call on your god! Perhaps the god will spare us a thought so that we do not perish."

The sailors said to one another, "Come, let us cast lots, so that we may know on whose account this calamity has come upon us." So they cast lots, and the lot fell on Jonah. Then they said to him, "Tell us why this calamity has come upon us. What is your occupation? Where do you come from? What is your country? And of what people are you?"

Jonah replied, "I am a Hebrew. I worship the Lord, the God of Heaven, who made the sea and the dry land."

Then the men were even more afraid, and said to him, "What is this you have done!" For the men knew that he was fleeing from the presence of the Lord, because he had told them so.... "Please, O Lord, we pray, do not let us perish on account of this man's life. Do not make us guilty of innocent blood; for you, O Lord, have done as it pleased you...."

(At one point, Jonah reluctantly agreed to go to Nineveh, but he was extremely angry with God.)

And God said, should I not be concerned about Nineveh, that great city...?

• • • • •

At this point, one might have expected that my Jonah-like odyssey had reached its goal. Jonah had finally relented, and angrily agreed to go to Nineveh. He was not happy about it, but he went. After he got there, the city immediately repented. Jonah was furious. He didn't want them to repent—he wanted God to destroy them. But God let them live. Jonah became angry with God, and asked Him to "take my life from me."

The Lord asked, "Is it right for you to be angry because I saved the city?"

And again, Jonah ran away to build a booth that protected him from the noonday heat. He waited and watched to see what would become of the city.

God sent a bush to keep Jonah cool. Jonah was happy, but God sent a worm to destroy the bush, and Jonah was furious again, and again, he asked God if he might die.

God said, "You are concerned about the bush, for which you did not labor. So should I not be concerned about this evil city of more than a hun-

215

dred and twenty thousand persons who don't know their right from their left, and also many animals?"

That enigmatic question ends the story.

Jonah had reached his destination of Nineveh, but why was he there?

Did he do what God asked him to do?

Am I doing what God asked of me? Does our country know its right from its left?

Are we the animals?

• • • • •

In the spring of 1997, Joan and I earned our Master of Divinity degrees. But we had no *call* to Nineveh. First, we needed to be ordained. We also needed to hold on to our jobs at Scholastic and Datascope, otherwise, who would pay the bills?

• • • • •

"We thought you already had a call. You've been talking about that through the entire book."

"We had calls from God, but not from a church congregation."

"So?"

"Have you ever heard of a Classis?"

"What's that?"

"Read on, my dears, read on."

• • • • •

216

Chapter Fourteen

What's a Classis?

Ecclesiastically speaking, Christ has three *offices*: prophet, priest, and king. As prophet, He proclaims God's truth. As priest, He intercedes with God on behalf of the people. As king, He rules the universe. The RCA attributes the first two offices also to pastors. Only Christ Himself can be King.

• • • • •

My road to ordination had more rocks, holes, and detours than a climb up the peaks of Patagonia. Indeed, my story was beginning to sound like a rip-off of Jonah's. One stumbling block was whether I should attend seminary at all. Would it get me to where God wanted me to be? Should I sing, teach, or preach? Or had it been staring me in the face all along?

From the decision to enter seminary, I liked the idea of going back to college at the graduate level. My dream to study Hebrew, and eventually go on for a doctorate in Hebraic studies was alive and well. I'd preferred a school like the Jewish Theological Seminary in New York City, and often imagined myself as a college professor—if I couldn't support my family through singing.

By 1991, the idea of becoming a pastor had been a distant memory. My supposed journey to the pastorate reminded me of this Escher painting, with steps

going nowhere, or into a blank wall, or that you couldn't tell which way they were going—something like my life.

Note however, that pursuing Hebrew studies would have guided me *away* from pulpit ministry. Early in my career, the only reason I aimed toward a graduate degree was that an advisor had told me I needed that professional standing to be taken seriously in Christian-Jewish relations. Having a "Reverend" in front of my name would help; a "Reverend Doctor" would be even better.

The current block to that dream was that the NBTS offered only one year of Hebrew, a course to help students in biblical study, a required course. Many students thought it wasn't even necessary because of the many translations and guides that are available nowadays.

After taking the standard Hebrew course at seminary, I took another elective in reading the language. Soon after those studies, I called the Jewish Theological Seminary (JTS) to plan my future. Professor Rabbi Burton L. Visotzky picked up the phone—he was a key commentator and organizer of Bill Moyer's 1996 PBS television series called, *GENESIS: A Living Conversation.*

"Jewish Theological Seminary." A baritone voice I recalled from the television series answered the phone.

"May I speak to someone about graduate studies?"

"Certainly. This is Professor Visotzky. How may I help you?"

"Oh, well...." I suddenly became flustered, talking to a television person-ality. "Uh, I'm studying to be a Christian pastor, and my passion is the Hebrew Bible. I'd love to continue my seminary studies by studying Hebrew from a Jewish perspective." I chuckled nervously. "I like to think of it as studying at the feet of the rabbis."

"Well, you've come to the right place. What do you have in mind?"

"I thought I'd study the Talmudic writings."

"Why on earth would you want to do that?" his voice rose, tinged with sarcasm.

"Ah...as I understand it, the Talmud is the Jewish interpretation of the Bible."

"No, my friend, you understand it incorrectly. The Talmud consists of the rabbis arguing among themselves. There are a dozen or more very large vol-umes, depending on the editions. I doubt you'd learn much about the Hebrew Bible. What you want is the Midrash. And, by the way, I teach Midrash, and I'd *love* to have a Christian student in my class."

Wow, that would be great! I thought. I almost said, "What's the Midrash?" but I caught myself in time, "Ah..., the Midrash...." as if I knew what it was.

"Of course. The Midrash interprets the Bible. The Talmud interprets the Midrash."

"Oh, I see. You're right, I didn't understand it correctly. Well then, thank you for steering me toward the Midrash."

"Have you studied Hebrew?" he continued as if processing a potential student.

"Oh yes, I've had more than a year of it: one class and two semesters of private study."

"A *year*?" he said, aghast. I could almost see him shaking his head. "You know—or you *should* know—that to study the Midrash, you'll need at least the equivalent of a bachelor's degree in Hebrew," his tone became professorial. "In any case, you'd need to be fluent in it. To study the Midrash here, you must first pass a Hebrew fluency test, *and* demonstrate a thorough knowledge of the Hebrew Bible—in Hebrew, of course." He paused as if expecting me to answer, but quickly continued, speaking almost as a lawyer, "It makes sense, does it not, that to study the interpretation of something, you must know the language and the subject in order to study its meaning?"

A pause while my heart dropped.

"Oh...yes, I see what you mean." I knew immediately that one year of Hebrew simply wouldn't cut it. *Oh, drat—another dream out the window.* "Well, thank you very much, Professor Visotzky. By the way, I saw you on the *Genesis* series on PBS. Quite fascinating. I was particularly intrigued by your remarks on evil. You said that if God created everything, then he must have created evil as well."

"Of course!" he responded energetically. "You Christians got yourselves into an impossible juggernaut with your notion of the Trinity and the sinlessness of your Christ. Just doesn't make any sense—well, to me, anyway."

Tempting as it was, I decided against engaging him—it would be like a conversation with Dr. Eckstein all over again. After that, he told me of his latest book, on Exodus. I went right out and bought it.

• • • • •

Sadly, "studying the Hebrew Bible at the feet of the rabbis" was clearly out of my reach. First, the tuition cost at JTS was far beyond our means. Secondly, there was no way I could make up the Hebrew language deficit.

• • • • •

I had begun singing at the Hebrew Tabernacle in 1968. Cantor Ehrenberg was one of the kindest men I had ever met. He became a father figure to me in the absence of my own father, who had died in 1966. Joan and I saw the Cantor every weekend of the year, Friday nights and Saturday mornings, and daily during Jewish holidays. In commemoration of him, I want to share two special stories.

The first story occurred not long after my epiphany of Christ in 1978, described in the Prologue. Shortly after that Christ encounter, I tried to tell Cantor Ehrenberg why I believed Christ was truly the Son of God. I was extremely nervous, thinking that if I were to offend him, he might fire me. Feeling called by the Holy Spirit to do this, I soldiered on. I don't remember exactly what I said to him, but I was prepared to argue from the Hebrew Scriptures about appearances of Christ in the "Old Testament" (Hebrew Bible), called "theophanies."[25]

---

[25] "Appearance of God," literally. Christians believe these appearances were of the pre-Incarnate Christ.

I spoke to him before a service one Friday evening. Joan and I usually arrived early, as a result of leaving plenty of time to drop off the children at her
parents' house, the unpredictability of traffic, and the difficulty of parking in
Manhattan. I spoke to him in the hallway, trying to be casual about it. He listened patiently, smiling indulgently at my efforts. His response has remained
with me ever since:

"You know, Robert, we all worship the same God. There's more that binds
us than separates us."

That stopped me in my tracks—I couldn't think of anything to say.

He smiled, thanked me, and walked towards his office on the other side
of the synagogue.

His words have blessed me all these years. I have often quoted them when talking with Jewish friends and acquaintances. Occasionally, I quote him in a sermon
or Bible class. Perhaps most precious to me is quoting them during a discussion
that seems to be getting out of hand, and tempers are raised. The good cantor's
words always have a calming effect on others, just as they've always had on me.

The second tale came when Cantor Ehrenberg retired from Hebrew Tabernacle in the mid-eighties. I was surprised and deeply honored when he asked
me to replace him as Cantor. Naturally, I'd have to convert, and I gave it serious thought. If I had accepted, I couldn't become a pastor. Joan was opposed
for social reasons: she felt we could never fit in to the temple community. She's
an introvert, so that would have made her life miserable. It's indeed a very different culture, but I felt I could cope with it, although I knew there would always be some who would oppose me.

Nevertheless, I decided against conversion for theological reasons. Christmas
is not only my favorite holiday, but fundamental to my Christian understanding. I
believe that Jesus, who is the Christ, was (and is) the Incarnate Son of God. To become a Jew, I'd have to renounce that. Christmas also has strong family ties as well,
both in my family and Joan's. While every rabbi to whom I've spoken refuted the
Incarnation, the Resurrection (Easter) doesn't have as forceful a theological objec-
tion for Jews, because there are instances of resurrection in the Hebrew Bible.[26]

However, when Rabbi Lehman heard of the Cantor's idea, he quickly
trounced it. I think at first he thought it was a joke—what a preposterous

[26] See Genesis 5:24, 2 Kings 2:11 and Ezekiel 37, for examples.

suggestion! But when he realized the Cantor was serious, I can imagine his face turning red with rage and shooting his internal thermometer up to boiling. The good rabbi was not a fan of Christianity, and he would have opposed me from the get-go. He was always courteous and friendly to us, but when I spoke to him about Christ, he became quite angry. I backed off very quickly because I didn't want to lose my job. Also, antagonizing someone doesn't usually lead to their hearing what one has to say.

All of this had a direct bearing on my struggle to become a pastor. As early as the mid-seventies, I had become involved in the Christian-Jewish Dialogue, which grew out of Vatican II and Nostra Aetate (1965).[27] At first, I corresponded with local principals involved in the conversation. Later, I attended meetings, lectures, and larger symposia, such as the one in January of 2003 at Temple Emanu-El in New York City on the subject of the "Challenge of Evil to Our Faith Traditions." Speakers representing the three monotheist religions debated the issues, with a Moderator to keep things moving. I wrote a detailed paper on it that I sent to friends and former seminary teachers.

The Classis of Passaic Valley[28] nearly refused my application to be taken under care. In the Reformed Church in America (RCA)—and in most mainline denominations—a candidate must jump through many hoops to become a pastor. Established pastors and denominational leaders encourage and welcome candidates, and often bend over backward to help those that they feel could be good pastors. However, the ancient, written rules governing the ordination process are stringent and must be adhered to.

Every year at the national church assembly, efforts to change the rules and procedures are introduced. Some pass; most don't. Change is difficult. The oversight, or "care" process, dates back to the Protestant Reformation of the sixteenth century, but follows much of what came before, going back to the first century church.

---

[27] For more information, simply Google, Nostra Aetate.

[28] "Classis" = regional ruling body of churches. "Classis," singular; "Classes," plural, pronounced "Clas-SEEZ."

The local congregation initiates the first step: in our case, the Wyckoff Reformed Church (WRC) in Wyckoff, New Jersey. Joan and I were welcomed eagerly as candidates because everyone knew our work in the church.

"We know you guys will make great pastors, but we'll sure miss your beautiful voices," folks would say. We were choir soloists, thus quite visible every Sunday, plus, we were involved in many church activities and served individually on several boards. No one questioned our faith.

With WRC's endorsement we applied to our local Classis for approval. "Classes" are bodies of church folks, pastors and elders, who rule geographically assigned groups of churches. To be taken under care for seminary studies, the entire Classis must approve it with a majority vote. Dissenting voices are always given serious consideration, however. Depending upon their reason(s), their objections could carry the day.

Since the Classis meets typically three times a year, the process usually drags out for months. They scrutinized our backgrounds for "fitness for ministry." A Pastoral Care Committee does the grunt work, and their recommendation is generally approved.

For us, things went smoothly enough. Our advisors assured us that we would be approved, barring some unforeseen circumstance. It would take something quite drastic for them not to. With that hope we began seminary classes in the fall of 1991. Because our Classis was being reorganized, we had permission to begin seminary classes before being approved.

It wasn't until the Classis meeting in the spring of 1992, towards the end of our first year in seminary, that we received an email asking us to address the Passaic Valley Classis. This came just a day or two before the meeting itself. I felt a rock in my stomach; the thought of standing before this august church body seemed like being on trial for my life.

Joan and I wondered why they informed us at the last minute, with no word about what we should say, or even how we should dress. Some people wore their Sunday best to classis meetings, some dressed casually. We didn't have time to prepare anything, even if we knew what to speak about. We decided to show up in our Sunday best to be on the safe side. I assumed Joan had already prepared her remarks because she knew God had called her to the pastorate. Since I was uncertain about becoming a pulpit minister, I had no idea what to say. I dashed a few scenarios through my head, but nothing specific.

Oh Lord! What can I say about my reason for going to seminary?

When we arrived at the meeting, all the candidates were herded into a side room. We waited. And waited. Finally someone came in, and we all pounced on him at once, "What should we say?"

"Just tell them why you want to become a pastor."

"Why didn't anyone tell us that in advance so we could prepare something? That's all we need to tell them? No biblical references? No theologians to cite? Nothing like that? Will they ask us questions?"

"Nope. Questioning candidates comes much later in the process after you've taken all the prescribed courses. For now, just tell them why you want to preach, teach, and be a pastor. You'll be received with smiles and appreciation, I'm sure."

"Oh." The group was relieved. We looked at each other and shrugged our shoulders.

"Okay. Who wants to go first?"

I began to feel guiltier and guiltier about being in this process. Still unsure that God was calling me to the pastorate, I worried whether or not seminary was right for me. Sweat began to ruin my shirt. That made me angry, so I sweated all the more, making me even more uncomfortable and grouchy. The others, sure of themselves, relaxed because they already knew why they wanted to be pastors. Not me. My mind raced.

Should I ask Joan what to say? No, that wouldn't be right. She's probably already figured out something for herself, and I can't expect her to help me. Oh, Lord, what do I do?

When my time came, I walked out in front of the assembly as though I were going to sing a concert. In an instant of forgetfulness, I even looked around for a piano and thought, *Where's my accompanist?* My mind jumped back to reality. *This is not a concert, stupid. Get with the program!*

My face beaming, I began, "Good afternoon, good folks of the Passaic Classis. I'm Bob Mitchell from the Wyckoff Reformed Church in Wyckoff."

I paused, taking in the smiles, not having a clue what to say next. I mentally berated myself for saying "Wyckoff" twice. *They all know that, dummy.* I continued, "They told me to tell you why I want to be a pastor...." I paused. "Well, uh, you see, I've been involved in the Christian-Jewish dialogue for the past twenty years. I have much to say on this subject, but they tell me that I won't be taken seriously unless I *am* a pastor, that is, someone with credentials to speak authoritatively about Christianity."

Some eyebrows raised. Others mouthed to each other, "What's he talking about?"

"You may not think this is a sound reason for becoming a pastor, but I invite you this afternoon to take a look at Romans, Chapter 11 beginning in the eleventh or so verse, where Paul speaks about the Jews and how we've been grafted into their tree...etc." By this time, some people began to look at one another, wondering where in the world I was going with this speech.

From there, I launched into a long discourse on how Paul argued that we are, through Christ, inheritors of all the covenants and promises of God, and I concluded with verse 26, which states that *all Jews will be saved.*

"Therefore," I announced, "we should *not* proselytize the Jews."

You could have heard a feather bounce off the floor. The assembly stared at me in astonishment, anger, bewilderment, some with expressions of disdain, others turning stormy with rage, and still others refusing to look at me at all.

Before anyone could speak or throw something at me, I said, "Thank you for your attentive listening. I wish you all a good afternoon," and beat a hasty, but dignified retreat, as if leaving the stage after a successful performance. I waved with a big smile as I departed. But there was no applause, just stony silence from some, and murmurs from most.

Every candidate sat in the back room, waiting. It seemed very quiet out in the auditorium, but soon we could hear some voices raised in anger, not quite able to make out what they were saying. I looked down so as to avoid eye contact. *Are they talking about me? Oh God, I hope not.*

Eventually someone came into our room and invited all candidates *but me* to come out on the dais. I sat there alone and afraid. I could hear voices, then applause.

They're getting applause. Oh God, what's to become of me?

They were being received and approved for study, and then asked to wait back in the room where I was. After a short while, some started to grumble because they couldn't go home. No one knew why. *Was it because of me, Lord? I'm sorry....*

Joan sought me out. "What in the world did you say out there?" she asked, as she sat next to me.

"Oh, just that we shouldn't proselytize the Jews. I was trying to convince them that I needed to be a pastor in order to be an effective voice in the Jewish–Christian dialogue."

"What?" she said angrily, a little too loud. She glared at me. "Why in the world did you go there?" She shook her hands at me in frustration, sat down next to me, and leaned in, her face close to my ear. "That's not what they wanted to hear. They wanted to hear how you're called to serve as a pastor." Before I could respond, she turned away from me and rose. She paused, turned back to me, leaned in, and hissed, "Bob, for heaven's sake, what were you thinking?" She then turned on her heel and crossed the room, presumably to sit elsewhere.

I hung my head, the room seemed to get hotter and hotter. I looked up at her imploringly, shrugged, my palms out. "That's what the Lord laid on my heart." She stopped to listen, but didn't turn around. "What can I tell you? It just came out of my mouth." She turned, retraced her steps and stood in front of me. "I didn't know what to say, so I just went with the brain flow. You know how ambivalent I am about being a parish minister...." I spoke softly so only she could hear. "Right now, the Christian-Jewish dialogue means more to me than serving a church. Geez, what a mess!"

Joan shook her head in dismay, looked away, and said, "I don't know, Bob." She waved her hands in frustration, then abruptly moved off to sit in another chair, keeping her distance.

My heart sank even further at her disapproval. Others in the room had their ears cocked in my direction, trying to hear what we were saying while trying to be inconspicuous about it. Of course they were dying to know why I had been excluded.

Silence as if listening for God to speak. Whiffs of mingling perfumes began to permeate the heat-shrouded room. We all fell silent and waited. And waited some more. Not long after that, someone came into the room and dismissed all the other candidates with congratulations, but asked me to remain.

Joan had to stay because we had come in one car. Well, I guess she could have gone out to the car, or asked someone to drive her home, but she didn't. Soon a small delegation of pastors formed before me. Joan came over and sat next to me.

"Well, Bob," began a pastor friend from Wyckoff Reformed Church, Rev. Everett "Rett" Zabriske, who was the Clerk of Passaic Valley Classis. "It was a struggle, but we got them to agree to take you under care if you would agree to be mentored by a senior pastor." Rett had a slim, medium build, fair hair and complexion, always dressed in slacks and a sports jacket, a very bright man, scholarly in fact, with an outwardly friendly manner. His blue eyes smiled down at me.

"Mentored? For what?" I asked, a bit too defensively.

"Bob, you really can't think you didn't ruffle a lot of feathers with that little speech of yours."

I shrugged my shoulders.

"Really, Bob! Don't you know this Classis? There are many very conservative pastors out there who were furious that you said we shouldn't proselytize Jews, not to mention lecturing them about the Bible. You told us all the wrong things about yourself. I could go on…."

"No, Rett, I *don't* know the Classis that well," I said, fighting to suppress an anger that had flashed up in me. "Never had the opportunity…nobody told me or advised me what to say…we were just thrown out there to the wolves…."

Rett held up his hand like a traffic cop, nodding his head sympathetically. "It's okay, Bob. We're sorry for not preparing you better. We need to get ourselves better organized as far as candidates for ministry are concerned. I really am sorry about that, and embarrassed, because it was my responsibility. But the important thing is that we got them to take you under care."

"Okay. So what's all this mentoring business about, and who's to be my mentor?"

"Do you know Fred?" he said, gesturing to another man standing nearby. I shook my head.

227

"This is Rev. Frederick Herwaldt, and he has been assigned to mentor you." Turning to him, he said, "Fred?"

Fred was heavy-set with a bit of a paunch, affable, with a generous smile, dressed in a brown suit. His grin certainly seemed friendly enough as he sauntered over to me. He extended his hand as I rose to meet him. His hand felt like a warm glove in my clammy one. He seemed perfectly relaxed.

"Bob, it's really nice to meet you."

I smiled back. "Thanks for standing up for me, Fred."

"Okay Bob, let's you and me talk a bit." He pointed the way to a room off to the side.

The upshot of our conversation was that Fred was to mentor me in the book of Romans for six months. That was the condition of my being taken under care. He seemed eager to get started on this project. A good sign, I thought.

I looked at him, wondering if he might not agree or listen to my understanding of Romans. I had strong views on the matter. *What if he…?*

"Don't worry," he smiled. "I'm not such a bad guy. They tell me you're a bright fellow who knows his Bible very well, so I think we can have some wonderful conversations about scripture, spiritual things, and just getting to know each other."

I smiled with relief.

As it turned out, we did have a wonderful time together. During one session with Fred, I remember taking him to lunch at the very high-class Il Villagio Ristorante in Carlstadt, just north of Scholastic's offices in Lyndhurst where I worked. I hadn't yet been transferred to the New York office.

Fred was struck with wonder when we walked in. "Bob, I'm not sure I can afford this place," he whispered.

"Don't worry, Fred. Scholastic's paying for it." I motioned for a waiter.

"What?"

As we walked to our table, I said, "I don't usually do this sort of thing. My boss has taken me here a number of times. And I, as a manager, have an expense account, but, I so rarely use it, I don't think anyone'll question it. I'll report you as a client. It's all right."

"But that's cheating, isn't it?" He sat down on the chair the waiter offered him.

The waiter came around to help me as well. Looking at Fred across the table, I said, "Yes, but I think God will look the other way. It's for Him after all."

"I hope you're right." He smiled broadly.

"We'll all get our papers corrected in Heaven," I said as I unfolded my napkin.

He laughed, as he tucked his napkin into his shirt.

We had a good time over those six months. Fred must have given the Classis a good report because I was eventually taken under care unconditionally.

* * * * *

Several years later, Fred left the RCA for the Roman Catholic Church, a surprise to us all. Fred seemed to be Evangelical in his theology, so we wondered where this decision came from. Later, we discovered he had passed away rather suddenly of cancer. We had lost touch with him, but the news shocked us. He was a good, kind man.

* * * * *

In preparation for seminary, we had to gather transcripts from all the colleges we attended to send to the New Brunswick Theological Seminary to prove we were qualified to study on a graduate level. We also had to write papers and appear before various church and academic boards to demonstrate that we were seminary and pastoral material.

In September of 1991, Joan and I began our studies. At this point, I still had not given up singing opera, or my career at Scholastic. In November, I sang what turned out to be my last role, Don Jose in *Carmen*, after realizing that I could not carry such a heavy load.

I was still not sure I wanted parish ministry, preferring a career as an academician of some sort. But I knew not to say anything about that to anyone, especially church boards. So I told them what they wanted to hear. Yes, I felt guilty about it, but if that was what it took to pass through seminary, well… what can I say? Somehow, I knew that God was in all this. Surely He didn't like my dissembling the truth, but I felt He had a plan for me. I just didn't know what it was.

I only hoped my story wouldn't end like Jonah's: up in the air.

Chapter Fifteen

Seminary at Last!

When Joan told our teenage son, Rob, that she planned to go to seminary to become a pastor, he said, "I can't imagine you preaching a sermon, Mom." Rob, bright, talented in music, accomplished on the violin, loved to draw and write, having composed a number of pieces, written plays and stories, always had keen insights about many things, including his parents.

"Why not? You of all people have heard enough sermons from me."

"Yeah, but you have to say something of substance from the pulpit."

Uh-huh. Rob also has a sharp sense of humor.

Randy, a preteen, was proud of us for having the courage to make this major life change, especially at our age. He had his own busy life with his guitar and debate team at school. He also studied the violin. A top student, he seemed to excel in whatever he undertook. His bright disposition was a model to us all.

By means of a family confab, we all agreed that Rob was old enough to be responsible for those evenings we had to travel to New Brunswick for classes. The ground rules were simple: do your homework and any necessary chores, *then* practice your guitar, violin, or watch television, and go to bed at a reasonable hour. As far as we knew, things went smoothly at home when we were out.

"I hope I never have to eat another sandwich in the car—*ever!*"

That was Joan's summation of our seminary experience. The hundred-mile travel back and forth itself caused us both considerable stress. Couple the trips with the rigors of classes and constant home study of Bible, church history, theology, not to mention a host of other subjects, our first semester was daunting.

Holding our full-time jobs all through seminary was no picnic while also trying to raise our two boys. On the nights we had classes, Joan would drive from her job in Montvale, near the New York State border, down to the Meadowlands in New Jersey where I worked, right across from Giants Stadium. I'd wait for her in an agreed-upon spot in the vast parking area. Often Joan's first words as she got out of her car were, "You're driving tonight, right?"

"No, I thought you were," I said, walking around my car to hers, parked next to me.

"Not again! Bob, I'm tired…" she groaned, leaning against her front door.

"So am I," I broke in, a bit peeved. "Okay. I'll drive down. Will you drive home?"

With a scowl on her face, she opened the passenger door of my car and got in.

"Did you lock it?" I asked, as I got back into my car.

She reached into her handbag for the key, shaking her head wearily.

And so it went. We negotiated who'd drive, and then leave the other car in the Meadowlands lot. As soon as we got on the New Jersey Turnpike, we'd unwrap the sandwiches to eat on the way down to New Brunswick. There was no time to stop.

After classes, we'd come back to the Meadowlands to pick up the other car. Typically, we'd get home well after midnight.

Getting up the next morning felt like climbing up a sheer cliff without a rope. I had nightmares of scratching my way up steep, rocky precipices.

This brutal schedule challenged us for the six years it took to graduate from seminary. By that time I too developed a distaste for sandwiches while driving—always messy, and sometimes dangerously distracting. We couldn't rest on weekends either. Friday nights and Saturday mornings we sang in synagogue, and again in church on Sunday mornings. Sunday afternoons, we took the kids to eat at the Bishop's. That usually took up the rest of the day, sometimes into the evening hours. I don't remember how I got my studying done.

· · · · ·

Someone once asked me, "Does seminary change your outlook on faith?"

Oh yes, most certainly. Seminary, at least a theological seminary like the New Brunswick Theological Seminary, provides a varied perspective about what faith itself means. From Bible to history, from **eis**egesis to **ex**-egesis (two forms of interpretation), from languages to hermeneutics (what does this mean to the person in the pew?), from philosophy to theology, from myth to spirituality, seminary provides a trip you never imagined. Did it change me? Did it change the way I look at faith? As my old friend Hickey used to say in his inimitable drawl, "Oh yeah, you bet."

· · · · ·

Every seminarian was assigned an advisor. I had the good fortune to have as mine, the Rev. Dr. John Coakley, Th.D., who taught church history. If you were to see John walking across the campus, you'd know right away he was a college professor. Tall, with slightly stooped shoulders, he walked with a determined gait, but his blue eyes seemed not to be looking where he was going. Handsome, unruly brown hair, bearded and bespectacled, he nevertheless always had a hint of a smile that reflected the charming and caring man within. His knowledge of church history is encyclopedic, and he has penned articles, papers, and books on this and other related subjects.

He also has a delightful sense of humor. In one class he was explaining a concept in terms that made him stop. Apologetically he said, "This explanation is a bit Mickey Mouse...." He paused again with his hand to his chin. "Actually, I rather like Mickey Mouse."

We all roared with laughter.

In one of our first mentoring meetings, I explained to him about my interest in Jewish history, and how I hoped to be able to be a player in the Christian-Jewish dialogue.

"Is that your reason for coming to seminary?" he asked.

"Yes, sir," I replied.

His reply stopped me short. "That doesn't sound like a call to Word and Sacrament to me."

I was speechless. "But I thought...." *I don't know* what *I thought.* At last I muttered, "Does this mean I'll get kicked out of seminary?"

"No, you can continue your studies, but I don't see how you could be ordained as a pastor."

I went away from his office realizing for the first time that I really didn't understand the seminary process, nor the ecclesiastical, that is, *church* procedures, for becoming a pastor. I thought I could become an "academic" pastor, that is, have all the qualifications, rights, and privileges of a minister without having to serve a church. Apparently, I was mistaken. I knew about earning college degrees—this *ordination* thing escaped me. I didn't know what questions to ask, nor could I formulate a way to ask the ones I had. The key issue for me was that you couldn't receive the title of *Reverend* without being ordained.

I guess the only thing for me to do is stick with it until I can figure this stuff out and make sense of it for my life.

So be it. Back to the books.

The first classes in church history challenged both Joan and me, because we were not accustomed to the volume of work required, both reading and writing papers. The old saying, "Hit the ground running," certainly became a reality for us.

In that fall semester of 1991, rehearsals for *Carmen* were in full swing with the performance coming up in November. Although I did not intend it, that performance became my last[29] because I couldn't handle singing opera, my job at Scholastic, and seminary all at the same time. Need I mention commuting to jobs, coaching sessions, and rehearsals in the city? Although I had intended to continue singing opera that last performance clinched the deal. It wiped me out so much that I had to call in sick the next Monday.

•　•　•　•　•

---

[29] See Tales of a Tenacious Tenor, Chapter 15, p. 148, for a detailed account of this performance and its aftermath.

In January of 1992, Joan and I took Oral Communication 1, basic public speaking. We wrote short speeches and practiced them in front of one another. The professor videotaped us so that we could see ourselves in action. Very helpful, even if sometimes embarrassing.

That spring came New Testament Introduction, a rigorous examination of the Greek Bible, as we were taught to call it.

One of the outstanding lessons I learned was that each writer of the "books" of the Bible had not only his/her own voice, but his/her own theology. At first, ideas like these were difficult to grasp. Many Christians have been influenced by the Harmony of the Gospels, meaning that the books of the Bible never "contradict" one another, thus forcing them to accept *either this* idea *or* that one. What I learned was to think both—*and* in place of *either-or*. It's all true, contradictory or not.

In one memorable class, Dr. Johnson had just expounded this notion. Matthew, for example, seemed to be concerned with showing how Jesus stood squarely in Hebraic tradition. Some scholars call Matthew, "the New Torah." Mark, on the other hand, seemed more interested in Jesus' Passion (Suffering), considering he spent nearly half his Gospel on that subject. Dr. Johnson also spoke about how slow the Disciples were to understand Jesus. She quipped, "The Disciples jist didn't git it; they were as dumm as a box o' rocks."

Then she brought up Paul, another case altogether. He had two theologies, she said, "justification by faith" and his "theology of the cross." She mentioned Jesus' theology, if one could say he had one, which she called, "the kingdom of God."

One elderly, well-dressed gentleman in the back of the lecture hall got to his feet and intoned, "My Gawd is not a Gawd of Con-*fu*-shun. Which of these two pro-po-*si*-tions am I to be-*lieve*?"

Without skipping a beat, she leaned on her lecture podium, looked up at him with a beatific smile, and crooned right back at him, "You are to believe all of it; it's *all* true."

Struck dumb, the gentleman slowly sank back into his seat.

Let's talk Hebrew!

During the summer of 1992, I took a course called Biblical Hebrew, required for ordination in the RCA. The first challenge was to master the Hebrew alphabet with characters called *radicals*. Verbs are parsed, not conjugated. Parsing Hebrew verbs became the most challenging enterprise for us students, as it was so totally unlike western-style verb conjugation.

Joan and I were already acquainted with Hebrew characters and sounds from singing in the synagogue. We also followed the service in the prayer book, which has both English and Hebrew. Joan sailed ahead of me in this, as she has an unfailing memory and gift for languages.

Most students hated Hebrew because it was so difficult and they had no background for it. They took it because it was required. Truth be told, I had the same difficulty parsing verbs. Towards the end of the summer, Joan bought us all t-shirts emblazoned with the words:

THIS TOO SHALL PARSE!

Joan and I still have ours.

In the fall of 1992, we took a course called Hebrew Exegesis, of which I remember very little. The following spring, I took a Hebrew reading course taught by a tall, charismatic professor with movie star looks, named Dr. Richard Blake, who always rushed into class at the last minute with stories—like this one:

"Malachi didn't exist, you know," he announced proudly one afternoon as he dumped his books on his desk in front of the class.

Stunned silence.

"It's simple. The word is not a proper name in Hebrew. The English '-i' on the end is a pronominal suffix meaning 'my.' You all know what a pronominal suffix is, right?" He scanned the class, but went right on, "The rest of the word is *Malach*, and you all know what that means, right?" He smiled menacingly at us. "RIGHT?"

"Yes," I said quickly, "it means 'angel' or 'messenger.'"

"Good, Bob." Sweeping the rest of the class with his eyes, he asked, "Does *that* sound like someone's name?"

Some heads bobbed, some shook, but all eyes froze on him. I held my tongue this time.

"Come on, guys! It means, 'My Messenger.' Since when is that a name? There could be a lot of biblical characters called 'messengers.' How many of these beings did God send in the course of the Hebrew Bible? Can you count 'em? Actually, we have no idea who this person was, or who wrote this book. That's the long and short of it."

Someone was brave enough to ask, "But there are people today—well, certainly since Elizabethan times—named Malachi. How do you know this wasn't a name at *that* time?"

Whirling around toward the questioner, he said, "Good question. But it really makes no sense in the context of this small book, with which I've spent a considerable amount of time. The name isn't used anywhere else in scripture, so I doubt this was someone's name. The fact that some English folks made it into a name only demonstrates their ignorance of Hebrew. I did my doctorate on Malachi, and believe me, I checked this out upside down and sideways, and I concluded in my thesis that this was *not* the name of the person who wrote this short book.

"By the way, for reasons I've never understood, most English translations divide it into four chapters. But in the Hebrew Bible, there are only three.

"Anyway, since I was awarded my doctorate, I think I'm right about all this."

Later, I looked up Malachi in the *Harper's Bible Dictionary*, which confirmed his position: "The Septuagint [Greek version of the Old Testament] as well as other versions do not take the title as a personal name and most scholars regard the author as anonymous."[30] So, either Dr. Blake could have saved himself a lot of toil and years of study if he had checked Harper's to start with, or he's in very good company.

A year or so later, I took an independent study course in Hebrew at Rutgers University. I had to get special permission from NBTS to do so, but it suited my schedule to a tee. I arranged for my lessons on my lunch hour at Scholastic, my Meadowlands office being only fifteen minutes away from my teacher's office in uptown Newark.

My professor was a wiry, energetic little man by the name of Dr. Robert Stieglitz, who looked more like a medical doctor than a professor of Hebrew. He certainly had a wonderful bedside manner. When we first met, I asked him if he was a rabbi.

---

[30] Harper's Bible Dictionary, Harper & Row, San Francisco, 1985, p. 597.

"No, no," he chuckled. "I'm an archeologist." He ushered me into his small, narrow office, pulled out a chair for me, and, with a big smile, invited me to sit down at a rather large, wooden table. He grabbed a chair and sat next to me. From the arrangements of papers and books, I could see this was his operating desk.

"Really?" I said. "How interesting! I've never met an archeologist before." We turned toward each other and smiled.

He was equally fascinated by my being a Christian, and a seminarian at that.

"Haven't had many Christians studying Hebrew," he said. "Mostly undergraduate Jews."

"Well," I replied, "that doesn't surprise me for a secular university. Few Christian students I imagine, other than those studying for the ministry, would have much reason to study Hebrew, unless they wanted to be a diplomat or foreign correspondent or teacher or something."

"Yes, you're probably right. Interesting, eh, wot?"

"Indeed," I said, laying my books and notebooks on the table.

We hit it off from the start. He enjoyed picking my brains about Christianity as much as I did his about things Hebraic.

"Where do you want to start?" he asked, pointing to my Hebrew Bible.

"We already looked at Genesis, and my last professor had us studying Isaiah."

"*Isaiah?* Was he crazy? Isaiah is the most difficult Hebrew in the Bible. No, no, no! We can't start with that. By the way, have you studied Modern Hebrew?" He looked at me quizzically.

"No, I haven't."

"Well, you see, Modern Hebrew is basically biblical Hebrew, but the scholars had the good sense to get rid of all those crazy verb constructions that probably drove you nuts, right?"

"Yes," I laughed.

"Yeah, they got rid of the hipel, hopal and hitpael forms, which drove *everyone* crazy."

"But they're in the Bible, so we have to know what they mean, do we not?" I asked.

"Yes, but that's why you should study Modern Hebrew *first*—just to learn the language. Then if you want, with that basis under your belt, it's much easier to delve into those complex forms later."

"That makes a lot of sense. I'd love to study Modern Hebrew, but I have to learn the biblical stuff, and I doubt we can do all this in two semesters, can we?"

"No, you're right about the time. I think we should start with a book that has simple Hebrew. I suggest First Samuel," he said.

"Sounds good to me."

And so we began. I was amazed at his knowledge of the language. He would have me read and translate. Often he stopped on a word and would say something like, "You know, this word has a Persian origin," and he'd explain the context and how it got into the Bible, and why it was important to understand the Persian influence on the language and context of the passage. I sat there, enthralled. More often than Persian words, he'd stop on Aramaic words, which is a kind of colloquial or dialect of Hebrew. Hebrew lectionaries generally have separate Aramaic sections.

One morning I greeted him in German, "Guten Morgen, Herr Professor."

He answered in such fluent German that it surprised me, and I had to switch to English. I said, "You're Israeli, aren't you?"

Chuckling, he said, "Goodness, no. I was born in Riga, Latvia. I grew up speaking German."

"Oh, my goodness! My voice teacher of many years, Madame Ryss, was also born and raised in Riga. She too spoke German before she spoke Russian."

"Ja, ich auch," he said, "aber *viel* später." (Yes, me too, but *much* later.) He spoke Russian, as well. He learned Hebrew growing up, he said.

"But you speak Hebrew so fluently."

"I lived in Israel for over twenty years. I became very proficient in the language."

"Ah, no wonder.... Hmm, I always thought you were Israeli," I said, scratching my head.

And so it went. My two semesters with him were a highlight of my seminary experience. He delighted in the fact that I, a Christian, asked so many questions and expressed such an interest in Judaism. Plus, I was an opera singer! When he learned about my job at Scholastic, he quipped, "You're quite the Renaissance man. How do you do all this?"

Towards the end of my time with Dr. Stieglitz, he invited me to come to his excavation in Israel. He told me his specialty was nautical archeology, and he was digging in the harbor of Caesarea. I nearly flipped. Of course I'd love to go. I'd always wanted to travel, and to go to Israel would be a total blast. Dr. Stieglitz referred me to his website, where all the necessary sign-up information was. When I read it, my heart sank. I'd not only have to pay my own way, but I'd have to live in a commune with other students. Married folks were not encouraged because of accommodations, and I'd have to find a place for Joan if she was not part of the team.

I blush to say I hadn't given Joan a thought up to that point. She was not supportive of the idea. "How can we pay for it? You'd be gone all summer—how could you keep your job at Scholastic? Bob, get real!"

Clearly, the price tag and time off from Scholastic was a deal killer. No way.

Joan felt sorry for me, but was quite relieved.

Me? I was very sad indeed. What a lost opportunity.

•   •   •   •   •

One day in the fall semester of 1994, in Hebrew Bible (Old Testament) class, Professor Weis assigned us Genesis 18, the story of the three men who appeared to Abraham by the oaks of Mamre.

"Here's what I want you to do," he began. "To make these stories come alive for our congregations, we must think of them as drama as well as story. After all, what is story but drama? Your assignment is to prepare a diagram or chart of this scene."

A hand shot up. "What do you mean?"

Professor Weis rose from his desk and went to the board. He sketched a large rectangular box, and turned to us. "I suggest you start with the tree." He turned and drew a large stick tree dominating the middle of the box. "The tree is central to the picture you want to create, so you can put it in the middle—or not, as you see fit. You're the stage director in this drama. You decide how you want the scene to look."

He turned back to the box and quickly drew three crosses with circles on top. "These are your three men. You place them wherever you want them."

240

He laid the chalk down and again faced us. "You decide where Abraham and Sarah go in your picture, and then figure out where to set the meal they prepared for the men and so forth—don't forget Sarah, where is she? Remember, you are the stage director of this play. It's up to you to decide how the drama unfolds. Okay? That's your assignment for next time."

I went home and eagerly began to work on this assignment. Without even thinking, I drew a trapezoid, not a rectangular box, on a large sheet of paper. I then sketched in a tree, the three men on one side, and Abraham on the other. Off to the right, I drew a building with Sarah inside, peeking out the door at the scene in center stage.

Center stage, I thought. *What am I doing here?* Suddenly the light came on—I realized that I was doing exactly what I had been doing for the past forty years when I began work on an opera role! It's called "blocking." For each scene, we would prepare a chart of where we were to be on stage, where we were to enter, to leave, and how we were to move around according to the words we sang, what the composer wanted, how the stage director wanted us to do it, etc.

If you were to look at any of my opera scores, you'd find such charts, big and small, all over the pages dictating where I'm to be on stage, usually singing, but sometimes not. It was how I learned my roles. I always had difficulty memorizing the words, and these charts enabled me to learn my lines. Music, text, and stage movement all came together, and it was through this totality that I built my operatic character, and thus, my onstage persona for each role.

I could hardly wait for the next class. When I walked into the room, I went straight to Professor Weis and told him what had happened. He smiled broadly. "Bob, I'm so pleased."

"But Professor, that's not the half of it. Don't you see? God has been preparing me all these years for this. I knew there was a reason why singing was so important to me. God was grooming me for the pulpit all along!"

He felt my joy, but he couldn't fully grasp what all the fuss was about because he knew very little about my singing career, and what it had meant to me.

Later that night on the way home in the car, I began to see the larger picture. As I told Joan about it, haltingly at first, it became clearer and clearer. At last I was able to articulate the connection between my love of singing opera and God's call to the ministry. In this one assignment, God had completed a life-long cycle that He began in my backyard in Lock Haven. It took forty-three years to bring it to fruition.

Now I knew His call was real. I was so excited I wanted to shout it to the whole world, hug everybody in sight, and dance for joy—but I was driving home in the car with Joan.

Thinking back to that starry night in my back yard, begging God to help me sing like Mario Lanza, my entire life flashed through my mind. From Sunday school at Trinity Methodist Church, to the *kaboom!* of those innocent sodium balls, through the endless years of training to sing opera, the long career at Scholastic, and now, seminary.

What a ride, Lord! Thank you!

Suddenly, a warmth calmed my entire body from head to toe. I felt God's presence wrap me in a holy embrace. *Go in peace, my son. Trust me, work for me—I'll never let you down.*

Of course, Joan understood very well what I had discovered. We had sung six operas together, so she had experienced that part of my life with me. When we arrived home, she immediately threw her arms around me and tearfully said in my ear, "Thanks be to God, Bob. I knew He was calling you all along. Now He's sent you a sign to confirm it. I couldn't be happier for you." We cried together.

Would anyone else understand, I wondered? We had lost contact with our opera-singing friends since I had stopped performing in 1991. Our new seminary friends smiled when I told them, but they really didn't have a clue what I was talking about because none of them had any stage experience. Those in the Hebrew Bible class sort of understood, but neither had they performed, so they too couldn't see the connection. Neither my family nor Joan's had backgrounds in the theater to understand the full thrust of this breakthrough. Church friends, too, smiled, but more because of my elation than what they understood. I could see in their eyes they had no idea.

Johnnie got it. He sent me blessing after blessing from his missionary home in France. He had seen me on stage on one or two of his furlough trips here in the United States, and though he was oblivious to the mechanics of stage blocking, he knew what the opera meant to me. It was my life, my passion. He encouraged me to turn that passion into the Lord's work.

Rob and Randy both understood, too. Although neither was into opera, Rob had acted and even written a couple of plays and skits in high school and college. He understood and shared my excitement. Randy, too, had watched and heard me practicing all those years, and understood intuitively what it meant to me. He had become a champion debater in high school, and also performed as a guitarist, not to mention, had lived with us all through my performing years. Both boys said to me the next time we saw one another, "Dad, I'm really happy for you! Now go out there and give 'em hell!"

Well, no matter who understood or who didn't, in the end, God knew, and Joan and I knew. Now my future was clear.

Jonah, you can go back to the Bible now, and stop haunting me.

But that was not the end of God's surprises for me. It was the beginning of preparing a new life, a life of ministry for the Lord. The wait-and-see attitude I had lived with for so long evaporated. I knew now that God wanted me in pulpit ministry, so I set about my seminary work with a freshness and verve that had been missing. There was still a long way to go.

Other courses such as Pastoral Identity, Congregational Dynamics and Development, and Pastoral Care dotted the seminary landscape. In the first, we learned that pastors are different from other folks, largely because of congregational expectations of them. Seems strange to say that, yet such is the reality. In studying the dynamics of congregations, we learned something of the "schizophrenia" of church people, how on one hand they revere their pastors, and on the other, they try to manipulate them, and they are unforgiving when the pastor doesn't behave the way they think he or she should.

The course in Pastoral Care had a twofold thrust: caring for congregants and ourselves. We were urged to look after ourselves as pastors—it's a stress-filled job, and a pastor needs to take care of him or herself. Time off is crucial. Relaxation, self-study, and spiritual nourishment are essential. But few pastors do it as needed. Including me, *malheureusement*.[31]

. . . . .

When Mom died in December of 1993, none of us siblings had lived in Lock Haven for quite some time. Both my sisters lived out west with their husbands and families since they graduated from high school in the mid-1950s. Johnnie was married in 1961, and he and his wife, Bev, packed off to France shortly thereafter, answering God's call to the mission field. They have remained there ever since, returning to the states every six years or so on furlough.

Dad had died in 1966, and while Mom remained alone in the house for several years after that, she eventually became quite lonely. "I think of him every day," she once told me. Eventually, she sold the house and moved to an apartment along the Susquehanna River in lower Lock Haven. The disastrous flood of 1972 almost swept away the small apartment building on Water Street. Because her apartment building was no longer safe—it was condemned and subsequently torn down—Mom felt there was nowhere else she could go but to Martinsville, Indiana, to be near Cissie and her family. For a while, between marriages, my sister Joan lived in an apartment in Martinsville as well. Johnnie was in France; Joan and I still thought of ourselves as newlyweds, living in an apartment in New Jersey. Cissie at least had a house. Mom remained in Indiana until her death at the age of eighty-seven.

We brought her back to Lock Haven to be buried alongside Dad.

With Johnnie living in France, Cissie living in Indiana, and our sister Joan living then in Arizona, we couldn't remember the last time we had all been together. But I can say that this unhappy day was the last time the four of us were ever together again. Both sisters died in 2012.

My wife Joan and I had driven up from New Jersey, where we lived at the time.

At the funeral home, my eldest sister Joan livened things up by approaching the lady who played background music on a small electric organ in a side room. The music was piped into the viewing rooms as a

---

[31] Unfortunately

background comfort for visitors. Joan asked her to accompany the Mitchell quartet in some favorite old hymns that Mom loved. Sister Joan sang soprano, Cissie, alto, Johnnie, tenor, and I reverted to my former baritone to round out the ensemble.

Joan said, "Come on, guys, let's sing Mom's favorite hymns like we used to at Christmas and Easter, remember? Hey, looky here—a Methodist hymnbook! What was Mom's favorite hymn?"

"'Ivory Palaces,'" I said.

"No, no, no. That was Dad's favorite," she said.

"She loved 'Day Is Dying in the West,'" Cissie chimed in.

"Great," said Joan, "let's do it."

Thus began a love fest for Mom that drew what few visitors had come to her funeral into that small room, perhaps a half dozen folks, mostly women none of us knew. They must have been friends of Mom's, or knew Mom and Dad from church. We smiled at them.

Sister Joan seemed to recognize someone and went over and embraced her warmly. After a brief exchange of words, she came back and whispered to us, "Never saw that lady before in my life." We all chuckled as discreetly as we could.

We must have sung for nearly an hour before we looked up to notice that all the guests had gone. Even the organist made her excuses and left. We formed our own little circle with arms around each other and had a good cry.

Johnny Yost, the funeral director and an old family friend, was the only other person in the room by that time. I noticed him standing in a dark corner with tears running down his face, and motioned him into our family circle. He was family, after all, and knew us from the day we moved into our house on Susquehanna Avenue forty-eight years prior, and cried together with us.

"Bye, Mom."

•　•　•　•　•

In the fall semester of 1994, we had begun Practicum courses, such as Reflection Group and Supervised Ministry. There was also an academic course, Historical Ethics.

The reflection groups were a lot of fun, yet quite serious. We had a wonderful, pastoral educator, the late Rev. James Seawood, for our instructor/counselor. We brought in problems to discuss and pray about. Rev. Seawood had an easy manner, delightful stories, and keen insight, all of which he generously shared with us.

Supervised Ministry, a practicum for preachers, provided hands-on, in-the-pulpit experience. First, we learned how to speak in public, and then came courses in sermon preparation and practice delivering sermons. The RCA required a license to preach, which required a review by the Supervised Ministry faculty. The entire process took about three years in all, but I remember supplying pulpits before the end of the three years.

In the meantime, there were other courses to tackle, such as Church History II, Intro to Christian Education, Theology, and Church Administration. We also had to study biblical Greek, RCA Polity (denominational government, practices, and procedures, etc.), and other electives. One of the last courses Joan and I took together was Texts and People, a course co-taught by two professors, featuring critical commentary on various Bible passages. This was an exciting time, covering such subjects as women in the Bible, how they had been blamed for the Fall, and the question of using masculine pronouns to refer to God—given God is above gender. We studied feminist theologians who suggested a new way to think of the Trinity: *God the Creator*, *God the Redeemer*, and *God the Sustainer.* Praise the Lord!

* * * * *

The feminist view of the ancient masculine language changed my way of thinking about God, and the masculine language in the Bible. This understanding opened my mind to observe how the Hebrew language in scripture itself is dominated by masculine words, and I'm convinced it expressed and contributed greatly to male dominance in ancient cultures.

An example that comes to mind is *b'ne Yisrael,* meaning, "Sons of Israel." Most Bible translations today speak of the "*Children* of Israel" to correct this prejudice. But the Hebrew remains *b'ne Yisrael* in most Hebrew Bibles—if not all. *B'ne means "sons."*

I believe masculine language like this helps sustain male-dominant cultures. I also believe that the reason it took more than two thousand years to question this bias was that it was so deeply imbedded in the language that it was taken for granted. It took the twentieth-century feminists to challenge it.

One of their legacies in seminary was that we were required to never write "Him" for God in *any* paper submitted for *any* course. Failure to observe this rule was an automatic failing grade for that paper.

$$\bullet \quad \bullet \quad \bullet \quad \bullet \quad \bullet$$

The final challenge of seminary was Ecumenics & Credo. Ecumenics presented various Christian understandings of the faith, while Credo required us to write a master's thesis on the fundamental theological issues of the faith. We had to write theologies of God, the Son, Holy Spirit, Soteriology (Salvation), the Trinity, the Authority of Scripture, the Fall, the Virgin Birth, and other such weighty issues. This was a daunting, but fun paper to write. My theology professor, Dr. Fries, encouraged me to think outside the box in his class. But Dr. Holland was my teacher for this Credo paper, necessary for graduation, a Master of Divinity degree, and for ordination as a minister of Word and Sacrament in the RCA.

One sunny afternoon, after I had submitted my paper to Dr. Holland, the phone rang.

"Bob, this is Dr. Holland. I'm calling about your Credo paper. Are you sure you want to submit it as is?"

"Yes, sir, at least I think so. But since you're calling me about it—what's wrong?"

"You question the Trinity." He paused.

I jumped in. "Yes, I think it's a questionable theology and should be challenged, logically and biblically," I said with authority, but pleasantly. I didn't want to antagonize him.

"You may very well be right, but I can assure you, you will not be ordained with this paper."

That grabbed my attention. "Really? Why not?"

"Bob, this will raise a storm of controversy. Any Classis reading this paper will refuse to ordain you. Can't you see that?"

"Sir, I didn't know the Classis would read it. I thought it was for the seminary only, that is to say, for the master of divinity degree. Ordination in my mind is a separate, Classis issue."

"Goodness gracious, no! This is your thesis. This is what you believe. The Classis has every right to read it. Plus, it's part of the ordination process. How could it not be? Now, between you and me, you can believe anything you like. But I can assure you it will not pass muster with the Classis, and perhaps even some professors—me included."

You included? Good grief.... "Oh dear! I never thought my paper would have to endure such scrutiny." I sat down to regroup.

"Yes, it will. This is a make-or-break paper for you, my friend. If I were you, I would not submit it—if you want to be ordained."

"Of course I want to be ordained. I'm sorry, sir. I'll rewrite it straightaway," I said with energy and determination.

"Good man. Do it immediately—there's not much time left, okay?

"Yes, sir. I'm on it as soon as we hang up."

And rewrite it I did. It pained me to have to excise my brilliant argument concerning Philippians 2:6—that *equality* is not the same thing as *being* the same. Dr. Fries loved it. But I now wrote what I thought they wanted to hear, and in the end, my paper was accepted.

I received an A- on it. Maybe the minus had to do with all the grief I caused Dr. Holland.

After completing the course called Advanced Preaching, we were given an official "license to preach." Over the summers, there were many vacant pulpits with pastors on vacations. The seminary used this as an opportunity for licensed seminarians to practice.

My first pulpit as a student pastor was the Reformed Church of Cortlandtown in Montrose, New York. I remember it clearly and fondly. The Montrose Church is a historic one with a venerable history dating back to 1729, with Dutch Reformed roots in the Hudson Valley of the early 1600s.

When I arrived, the organist greeted me, and then showed me to the office and the sanctuary. During the service, halfway through the sermon, my voice gave out, and I had to place the mic right next to my lips to finish the service. Very embarrassing, as I prefer not to use a mic—I don't need it with my singing voice.

On the way home, I ruminated about what happened. Why did I get so hoarse? It didn't take long for me to realize that it happened because I had stopped singing. My last opera was in 1991. I continued to sing in church and synagogue, but by the summer of 1995, Joan and I had stopped singing altogether because we planned to preach on Sunday mornings. I had also quit my regular job at Hebrew Tabernacle due to the pressure of studies. I simply didn't sing anymore.

I didn't notice at the time that when I preached, I felt quite at home, very much as ease. I was nervous beforehand, but not during. What was that all about?

As I drove home over the mountains from Montrose, I more and more began to sense something familiar about being up there in the pulpit, which slowly morphed into a vision of being on stage. "That's it!" I shouted. "The *stage*, of course. I didn't perform forty opera roles all those years for nothing. I saw the connection with my blocking experience with Dr. Weis. Yes, indeed. God was preparing me for this day not only through singing, but through acting as well. Praise the Lord!"

Yes, my long opera career had prepared me for this moment. Nothing else gave me such a sense of fulfillment. Is not the pulpit a kind of stage? Harry would have been shocked to hear me say this, I imagine, but now I saw the complete picture: in order to be a good preacher, I had to prepare myself in much the same way as I prepared opera roles. The blocking experience with Dr. Weis came to mind. That's a piece of it. Translating texts as we were trained to do in both opera and in seminary is another piece of the preparation. The singing and acting part contributed to communicating a message to the people.

There's the complete package, exactly the same formula for preaching.

Those who see me in the pulpit—even today—notice I'm different from most preachers. My thespian and singing talents pull the people into the message. They tell me how much they *enjoy* my being there. It's not just the sermons, but also my presence. "You're the best. When are you coming back?" they'd say. Such praise has always humbled me.

"God," I said out loud as I cruised along Route 9, the scenic Hudson River to my right, sheer cliffs on my left, fresh summer air wafting through the car, "you old so-and-so. Thank you, Lord, for the gifts you have given me. I am humbled by them. Did you trick me into this? All those wonderful, glorious years I had onstage, you were preparing me for the pulpit! Your pulpit!" Tears sprung into my eyes.

"Oh, dear Lord, how can I thank you? You kept me out of harm's way by closing the opera doors that would have led to a full-time career. Yes, it devastated me every time I heard those dreaded words at an audition, *Thank you*—which really meant, "Get lost, Bozo. There's nothing here for you." *But You knew all along.*

Joan always said to me, "Bob, if you had ever had a career singing opera, they would have eaten you alive. You could not have taken the pressure, the intrigues, the backstabbing, the snobbery, or the scratching your way to the top. You're too nice a person. To be a successful opera singer, you have to be a self-confident, self-absorbed person who doesn't really care what others think about him. That's not you. That's why I love you so much. I hate to say it, because I know it makes you mad, but I'm glad God kept you out of the opera. I love you, darling."

Thinking on her words as I crossed over the Hudson River on the Tappan Zee Bridge brought me joy. Yes, a tear of regret appeared, because I really wanted to prove to Dad, dead or not, that I could have made it big in opera, that I did what I wanted to do, not what I was forced into by fate. I hated his mantra, "You'll do what you have to do, not what you want to do."

But God had just brought me full circle. I have to do what God wants me to do because I *want* to do it. The trip down route 9W on the Jersey side of the river to Bergenfield seemed sunnier than usual. Now I knew there was no difference. I could use the gifts He gave me to sing and act and speak to further His kingdom. From the pulpit. Finally, I had come home to answer God's call. A new life awaited Joan and me.

In the name of God the Creator, God the Redeemer, and God the Sustainer,
As it was in the beginning is now and ever shall be,
One God forevermore, world without end.
Amen.

The official graduation portrait from NBTS.
Robert P. Mitchell, M.Div.
Joan Mitchell, M.Div.
(No "Reverends" yet.)
The gold crosses were graduation presents to one another.

. . . . .

While continuing to work our full-time jobs, we graduated from NBTS in June of 1997, but ordination would come *after* we received a *call*. (This kind of *call* is a written document, essentially a formal agreement between congregation and pastor.) The *call* comes after the congregation votes to invite you to be their pastor. We had to keep our jobs until we received a *call*, and had a starting date. Only then could I retire from Scholastic, and Joan from Datascope. To set that process in motion, we sent out profiles as in any job search.

I must have sent out one hundred or more profiles to churches we knew were looking for pastors. Those who answered said no. For the next year, Joan and I were limited to pulpit supply—substituting for regular pastors. Good thing we had kept our full time jobs!

In the spring of the following year, NBTS graciously invited churches to come to the seminary to interview candidates. The advantage for congregations was that they could interview many candidates in one day. One such church was the Marbletown Reformed Church of Stone Ridge, New York. They sent six representatives.

We pitched them the idea that we, a married couple, offered more than a single, young graduate could. Moreover, we both were in the business world for many years, raised children, and had life experience beyond that of a young graduate. Also, women could feel more comfortable coming to a woman for counseling, and the two of us could cover more ground in the parish.

They loved our background in music. "You can really raise the level of music in the church," someone said.

"We'll work with the music folks you have, and perhaps together we can 'make a joyful noise unto the Lord,'" we offered.

Stone Ridge, New York seemed much like where I grew up, so it felt like coming home. We had a wonderful chat, and we all agreed that our being their pastors would be a good fit.

The *call* process would take several months to complete. We had yet to appear before the New York Classis, a separate entity from our New Jersey Classis.

In the meantime, they had to draw up the *call* contract stating the purpose, terms, and the expectations of the congregation. It had to be approved by both Classes.

We received the *call* in June of 1998. I retired from Scholastic in July of that year, from which I had medical insurance, plus a generous cash severance that enabled us to buy two new cars, much needed for traveling the New York countryside to visit folks in need.

We were ordained together in September at the Wyckoff Reformed Church in Wyckoff, New Jersey, our home, the "sending" church. (The sending church and sending Classis do the ordaining – at least in our case, they did.) Both our home pastors, along with other friends, participated in the service. Joan and I sang John Rutter's "Benediction" to end the ceremony.

Our installation took place at the Marbletown Reformed Church (MRC) in Stone Ridge, New York, later in October. A pastor friend came up to speak, and Joan and I sang the same benediction at the end of the service.

Thus began our pulpit ministry together, completing the long journey from crib to pulpit. The harmony we felt with the good folks at MRC bolstered our spirits. They made us feel very much at home, and we looked forward to serving them the rest of our days, Lord willing.

Thanks be to you, O Lord.

Two Brief Afterwords

The Silly Limo Story

Mid-1990s while in seminary

My phone rang. It was my Scholastic boss, Tom.

"Bob, I just got a call from Jefferson City. Seems there's a problem between our School File staff and the Club Fulfillment people. I need you to go out there right away and resolve the problem. Okay?"

"Sure, Tom. I'm on it—due out there anyway."

Why didn't they call me? They report to me. I can't miss another class in New Testament. Professor Johnson will have my head. But I can't tell Tom that.

My buddy George lived a few blocks from us in Bergenfield, and for the last couple of years we commuted together to the Meadowlands office. Since he went to JC so often, I loved to travel with him because he knew all the ropes about plane schedules, renting cars, hotels, where to eat, and so forth. I called him and it just happened that he was leaving tomorrow, so I arranged to go with him.

The return trip was a minor problem. He had to stay until Friday, but I had to be back Thursday night for that class at seminary. We left together for Jefferson City, arrived just after lunch. I went straight to my people to work out the problem.

By noontime the next day I had completed my business. In the meantime, I arranged for my own flight back, and hired cars: one to drive to St. Louis airport, and the other, a limo service from Newark to the seminary.

The trip to St. Louis broke some speed records. I bit my nails all the way because I wasn't sure where I was going. The huge airport bewildered me. The car rental place turned out to be halfway across the airport from my flight. I had to run all the way to make it. By the time I arrived, my clothes were sweaty and my glasses steamed. I hated that feeling, concerned how I'd smell that evening in class.

During the trip back, my stomach growled. I agonized whether we'd get to Newark in time to travel the thirty miles to my class. We arrived at Newark on schedule. In the arriving area I found my driver, but there was no time to get something to eat. Rather, he guided me to a very long Lincoln stretch limousine. It gleamed white from bumper to bumper, with a bright red interior. I shook my head, whistled, and said, "Geez, I didn't expect a car this big. I'm all by myself—or is this party time?"

"No, not this time," the driver answered with an embarrassed smile and a shrug. "It's the only hack they had left."

I sat in the back of this dancehall feeling quite lonely.

Speaking to the driver required the car telephone. I called him up and gave him directions to New Brunswick. "Cancel Bergenfield," I said. Equal distance, so my expense report would be the same.

He got me there on time, thank heaven, so I gave him an extra tip. Joan would be at the class, my ride home. I wondered if she had brought a sandwich for me.

As we pulled up to the seminary entrance, with its plate glass façade, a crowd of students quickly gathered by the front door, inside and out. Some had their faces pressed to the glass, staring at the limo incredulously. Outside, one of my friends came running up the steps toward the limo. When he saw me, he shouted, "Bob! It's you!"

I said, "Who'd y' think it was, the President?"

He turned to the others and yelled, "Hey, guys! It's only Bob Mitchell." He turned back to me and said, "No, we thought it must be the Pope."

"Hey, I quipped back, "Maybe I'll *be* the Pope some day!"

Everyone laughed. Thank Heaven, Joan had brought a sandwich for me, bless her.

2. Settling into a New Life

August 1998

When we arrived in Stone Ridge and moved into the parsonage across the street from the church, we were as happy as newlyweds, though by this time we had been married for thirty-six years. We praised God for His great goodness in finding us such a promising new life in His service.

A number of congregants greeted us at the house and helped us move in, set up furniture, arrange the office, and showed us where everything was. We basked in their love and embraces, trusting that God had placed us here together with them, after the many years of our striving to find our way to serve Him together.

The parsonage, built in 1895, was a white Italianate Colonial style with a front porch that spanned the front of the house. The enormous front door opened into a large hallway with a grand staircase. To the right an archway led into a grand sitting room with a converted fireplace. Standing in front of it you could feel the history and almost smell a cozy, warm fire. Our baby grand piano seemed to stretch out its arms in joy for all the space it had now in our new home.

Next to the staircase, a hall went directly into the office in which the six-foot desk Scholastic had given me fit nicely. Our books, some three thousand or more, found homes all over the roomy house.

We climbed to the second floor, where there were three ample bedrooms and a remodeled bathroom.

Our two sons, now grown, who had encouraged us all along the way, joined in our excitement. Rob was married by this time and living in Florida with his new bride. They sent us congratulatory cards and notes. Randy moved with us and enrolled in the local college, the Ulster County Community College. From there he transferred to SUNY New Paltz the following year.

Joan and I settled in for the long haul: we planned to spend the rest of our lives serving God and His people in this peace-filled, bucolic setting.

Thank you, Lord, for everything!